ON TRIAL FOR MURDER

COURTROOM DRAMAS THAT GRIPPED THE WORLD

Written by

Emily G. Thompson

DK | Penguin Random House

DK Penguin Random House

Senior Editor Alastair Dougall
Art Editor Jon Hall
Designer Gary Gilbert
Picture Researcher Ridhima Sikka
Production Editor Marc Staples
Senior Production Controller Mary Slater
Managing Editor Rachel Lawrence
Managing Art Editor Vicky Short
Managing Director Mark Searle

First published in Great Britain in 2024 by
Dorling Kindersley Limited
One Embassy Gardens, 8 Viaduct Gardens,
London SW11 7BW
A Penguin Random House Company
10 9 8 7 6 5 4 3 2 1

001–342602–Jul/2024

A CIP catalogue record for this book is available from the British Library.
ISBN 978-0-2416-9183-0

Set in 10.5/13.5pt Bembo MT Pro
Typeset by Jouve (UK), Milton Keynes
Printed and bound in Great Britain by Clays Ltd, Elcograf S.p.A.

www.dk.com

Contents

Who Wielded the Axe?

The *Fall River Globe* referred to the Lizzie Borden trial as "The Great Criminal Trial" on the 4th of June 1893, and even today, it retains a prominent position in US criminal history and culture. It captured the attention of the national media at the time, even inspiring a well-known children's nursery rhyme. Intriguingly, opinion on whether Lizzie Borden wielded the hatchet that slew her parents remains deeply divided . . .

"Lizzie Borden took an axe

And gave her mother forty whacks

When she saw what she had done

She gave her father forty-one."

Anon

The affluent Borden family lived in a modest, Greek Revival-style home in Fall River, Massachusetts. Their maid, Bridget Sullivan, whom the family nicknamed "Maggie", after a previous maid, was resting in an upstairs bedroom shortly after 11 a.m. on the 4th of August 1892, when she heard 32-year-old Lizzie Borden call out from downstairs: "Come down quickly! Father is dead! Someone entered and killed him!"

Maggie rushed downstairs to find Lizzie's father, Andrew, slumped on the couch, his body bearing ten or eleven hatchet-like wounds. Upstairs in another bedroom, Lizzie's stepmother, Abby, had suffered a similar fate, enduring multiple blows to her face and head, her life extinguished on the bedroom floor. Fall River police officers initiated their enquiries at the Borden residence, questioning both Lizzie and Maggie, the only people other than the victims known to be at home at the time of the murders.

The police promptly grew increasingly suspicious of Lizzie due to her inconsistent accounts of her movements that morning. She initially claimed to have been outside in the yard when she heard groans, scraping noises, or cries for help coming from the house. She later asserted that she had heard nothing because she was in the barn's loft, a claim officers found dubious, as the day was hot and the dust on the loft floor was undisturbed.[1]

Adding to their concerns, Alice Russell, a friend of Lizzie's who lived nearby and had come to stay after the murders, reported seeing Lizzie burning a dress in the kitchen stove a few days after the murders. Alice asserted that Lizzie said the dress had been stained with paint.

With the weight of circumstantial evidence against her growing, Lizzie found herself under arrest on the 11th of August, charged with the murders of Andrew and Abby. Following her arrest, newspapers and women's clubs rallied to her defence, finding it highly implausible that a young woman could commit such heinous crimes. At the time, society still saw women as the weaker sex. The *Fall River Daily Evening News*, in particular, suggested that officers "in their eagerness to detect and punish the guilty" had "perhaps been led to do injustice to the innocent".[2]

On the 12th of May 1893, Lizzie Borden pleaded not guilty, and, after several delays, her trial commenced in New Bedford on the 5th of June.[3] A jury of twelve men was assembled, mostly farmers and tradesmen. In those days women were not permitted to serve on a jury because they were not allowed to vote. The panel of three judges was presided over by Chief Justice Albert Manson. Lizzie's defence team included former Massachusetts Governor George D. Robinson as her lead attorney, with the assistance of Andrew Jennings and Melvin Adams. Prosecuting the case were Hosea Knowlton and William Moody.

Lizzie entered the courtroom just before 9 a.m. and took her designated seat beside her defence team. She wore a blue serge dress, and a hat adorned with blue rosettes and a small blue feather. The courtroom was guarded by two deputy sheriffs, and Lizzie was the sole woman present, save for two female reporters.[4]

In his opening statement, Assistant District Attorney Moody outlined the prosecution's intent to establish Lizzie's guilt beyond a reasonable doubt. He asserted that she had committed the murder of her stepmother first, then, two hours later, killed her father. (The police had concluded that there had been a lengthy delay between the two murders because when the officers arrived, they had noted that Andrew's blood was still fresh, whereas Abby's had already coagulated, indicating that her death preceded his.) Moody emphasized that, at the time of these horrific acts, only four individuals were present in the house: Andrew, Abby, Lizzie, and Maggie.[5] At the time, Emma was visiting friends in Fairhaven, some sixteen miles from Fall River.

A hushed silence enveloped the courtroom as Moody proposed a motive for the murders: "Andrew Jackson Borden, the person named in the second count of the indictment, was at the time of his death, a man of considerable property – somewhere, I believe, between $250,000 and $300,000." He went on to explain that, despite Andrew's affluence (a former carpenter, he ran furniture and undertaking businesses, among other interests) he was known for his frugality, which deeply upset Lizzie, who desired a more luxurious lifestyle. Moody continued, stating, "Mr Borden had seen fit to do some benefaction for a relative of Mrs Borden, and in consequence of that fact the daughters thought that something should be done for them by way of a pecuniary provision as an offset."

Sarah Borden, the mother of Lizzie and her sister Emma, had passed away in 1863 and Moody maintained that Lizzie had a strained relationship with her stepmother Abby that worsened following Andrew's decision to financially support one of her relatives. Notably, when an officer enquired at the crime scene about the last time Lizzie had seen her mother, her response was, "She is not my mother. She is my stepmother. My mother is dead."

DA Moody proceeded to narrate a possible sequence of events leading up to the murders. He recounted that, two nights prior, illness had afflicted both Andrew and Abby. They had experienced persistent vomiting throughout the night; Lizzie also showed signs of illness to a lesser extent, while Maggie was unaffected. The following day, Lizzie allegedly visited a drugstore, requesting ten cents' worth of prussic acid under the pretext of using it to clean a sealskin cape. Despite being denied the poison because she did not have a prescription, the prosecution argued that Lizzie intended to harm Andrew and Abby, speculating that when she couldn't obtain the poison, she had resorted to other, more direct methods.

Moody informed the court that the night before the murders, Lizzie claimed she had locked the front door upon her return home. This door had three security features: a spring latch, a bolt, and a lock operated with a key. That evening, both the cellar door, which was accessible from outside the property, and the house's front door had been securely shut. Later, when Maggie arrived, she found the side door locked. She unlocked it and subsequently secured it again before retiring upstairs to bed. According to the prosecution, this indicated the killer had to have been someone already inside the house.

That night, John Vinnicum Morse, the brother of Sarah Borden, Lizzie and Emma's mother, was staying overnight at the Borden home to talk business with Andrew. The following morning, Maggie was the first to rise. She went down to the cellar to fetch fuel for the stove and then briefly unlocked the side door to retrieve the milk, promptly locking it again. Breakfast was taken by Andrew, Abby, and John, who departed around 7:45 a.m. Afterwards, Andrew left for town, while Abby went upstairs to change the sheets in the room John had slept in.

Moody asserted, "You will be satisfied, gentlemen, that it was not far from half-past nine o'clock, and upon the evidence, you will be satisfied that she never left that room alive." Andrew returned home sometime after 10:30 a.m. after visiting several banks and stores in town. Upon his return, he unlocked the front door, but finding it bolted, he needed Maggie to admit him. At that moment, Maggie heard Lizzie laughing; the laughter came from an upstairs bedroom.[6]

Maggie was cleaning the kitchen windows when Lizzie approached her and remarked that Abby had left to attend to a sick friend after receiving a note. According to the Assistant DA, no such note existed. Maggie then went upstairs, leaving Lizzie alone downstairs with her father. Shortly thereafter, Lizzie alerted Maggie that her father's lifeless body lay in the living room.

Maggie hurriedly made her way to the residence of Dr Seabury W. Bowen, the Borden family's physician, while Lizzie stepped outside for some fresh air. Her neighbour, Adelaide Churchill, saw her, and Lizzie beckoned to her, saying, "Do come over. Someone has killed father." As Dr Bowen pronounced Andrew dead, Maggie and Adelaide went upstairs to check on Abby after Lizzie said she had heard her return home. As they approached the bedroom door, they glimpsed Abby's lifeless body partially concealed beneath the bed.

Assistant DA Moody then drew the jury's attention to Alice Russell's statement in which she claimed to have witnessed Lizzie burning a "paint-stained" dress three days after the murder. Despite an extensive search of the house, officers had found no clothing with paint stains or bloodstains, but they had discovered two hatchets. Additionally, they found a hatchet head in the cellar, and speculated that the killer could have removed the handle because it had blood on it.

Moody observed that no murder weapon was found near the victims' bodies, concluding, "Doubtless you will consider that fact well when you come to consider whether these homicides were the acts of an intruder or stranger fleeing from his crimes with the bloody weapon in his possession through the streets of Fall River at noonday, or the acts of an inmate of the house familiar with its resources for destruction, obliteration, and concealment."

He then drew the court's attention to various inconsistent statements that Lizzie had made as to her whereabouts at the likely time of at least one of the killings, and what she may or may not have heard before allegedly running inside and discovering the dead body of her father. Moody concluded his statement with a dramatic flourish by displaying Andrew and Abby's skulls; they had been removed and defleshed by Dr William A. Dolan. At the sight of them, Lizzie fainted.[7] After Lizzie was revived, approximately ten minutes later, the proceedings resumed with witness testimony.

John Vinnicum Morse recounted that, upon his return to the Borden home at approximately 11:20 a.m. on the morning of the murders, he was informed that "something" had occurred. He also stated that when officers arrived at the scene, they were given unrestricted access to the house for their search.

Following his testimony, a succession of cashiers and treasurers from Union Savings Bank, National Union Bank, and First National Bank, as well as store clerks took the stand. They corroborated that Andrew had visited their premises between 9:30 a.m. and 10:45 a.m. that same morning.

In a composed manner, maid Bridget "Maggie" Sullivan then told how, upon Andrew's return home, she had heard Lizzie upstairs. "As I unlocked it [the front door] I said, 'Oh, pshaw!' and Miss Lizzie laughed . . . Her father was out there on the doorstep. She was upstairs."

According to Maggie, Lizzie said that Abby had left the house after receiving a note from a sick friend. Maggie noted that Lizzie had been dressed in a dark blue dress that morning but couldn't recall if it bore any "light spots or light figures". Maggie also testified that after discovering Andrew's lifeless body, she asked Lizzie where she was when the crime occurred, and Lizzie responded that she had been in the yard when she had heard a groan. During cross-examination, Maggie stated she hadn't witnessed any family conflicts or signs of trouble between Lizzie and her father and stepmother that morning.

By the third day of the trial, half of the spectators in court were women, in stark contrast to the first day.[8] Dr Seabury W. Bowen, who had arrived at the house that morning to pronounce Andrew and Abby dead, also testified regarding Lizzie's attire. He recalled that at some point during his visit, Lizzie had gone to her bedroom and changed from a blue dress into "a pink wrapper, morning dress".

Lizzie's friend and neighbour, Alice Russell, then took the stand and recounted her conversation with Lizzie on the day before the murder. Lizzie had expressed fears that Andrew, Abby, and herself were suffering from poisoning, hence their sickness. According to Alice, Lizzie had stated: "I feel afraid, sometimes, that Father has got an enemy. For he has so much trouble with his men that come to see him." She did not identify which men but mentioned that on one occasion she had encountered a strange man in the house. She also claimed that the barn had twice been broken into.

Alice testified that, three days after the murder, she saw Lizzie burning a dress in the kitchen stove. Lizzie claimed the dress had paint on it. Alice mentioned that she left the kitchen briefly and, on her return, saw Lizzie tearing part of the dress. Alice had remarked to Lizzie: "I wouldn't let anybody see me do that," to which Lizzie did not respond.

The focus then shifted to the note Lizzie alleged Abby had received from a sick friend. Dr Bowen had been unable to locate it. Alice testified that when she asked about the note, Lizzie hesitated before stating that she didn't know where it was. Dr Bowen remarked, "I have looked in the wastebasket" – to which Lizzie replied, "Yes, she [Abby] must have put it in the fire."

Assistant City Marshal of Fall River John Fleet then told the jury that when he interviewed Lizzie at her home, she said that nobody else was in the house at the time of the murders other than herself and Maggie. However, she said that, earlier that morning, she had heard a man who "spoke like an Englishman" speaking with her father at the front door, possibly about a business dealing.

Alice was in the room during this interview and pushed Lizzie to tell Fleet what she had earlier told her. Lizzie then stated, "About two weeks ago, a man came to the house, to the front door, and had some talk with Father, and talked as though he was angry." Later, while searching the cellar, Fleet came across a box "on a shelf or a jog of a chimney". Inside was the head of a hatchet, alongside some other tools.

Officer Philip Harrington told the jury that when he interviewed Lizzie, she said she was in the barn loft and hadn't heard a thing, contradicting her earlier comments to others. Officer William Medley testified that Lizzie told him the same thing. He said he examined the loft and found a layer of dust, indicating that nothing had been disturbed and nobody had been up there for some time. He added, "Well, I know it was hot [in the loft], that is all, very hot."

Next to testify was Officer Michael Mullaly, who said that Lizzie informed him that nothing had been stolen from the house. She also mentioned that her father had valuable possessions including a silver watch and chain, a pocketbook containing money, and a gold ring, all of which were still on his person. Officer Mullaly then asked Lizzie whether there was a hatchet in the house, and she led him to the cellar and showed him two hatchets. He also confirmed that no bloodstains had been found inside or outside the house, other than on Andrew and Abby and around their bodies.

When Dr William A. Dolan was called to testify for the prosecution, he confirmed finding the items mentioned on Andrew's body. He also examined the two hatchets discovered in the cellar and found two unidentified hairs on one of them as well as marks that appeared to be blood or rust. However, on further analysis, Dolan determined that the marks were not blood. Moody asked him whether the wounds found on Andrew could have been "inflicted with a hatchet by a woman of ordinary strength". He responded: "Yes sir." He further said that the wounds on both Andrew and Abby could have been caused by either of the hatchets.

Physician and chemist Edward S. Wood testified that when he examined Andrew and Abby's stomach contents, he found no prussic acid. He also inspected Andrew and Abby's clothing and the hatchets found in the cellar. He also identified a white under-skirt belonging to Lizzie with a small blood spot consistent with human blood but, under cross-examination by defence attorney Melvin Adams, acknowledged it could be menstrual blood. Wood also admitted that he didn't believe the hatchets had been washed to "remove any traces of blood" stating, "It would cling in those angles there and couldn't be thoroughly removed. The coagula would cling."

Testimony then focused on the single hatchet head found in the family's cellar. According to physician Frank W. Draper, who examined Andrew and Abby's bodies at the mortuary, this could have caused the injuries to the Bordens. In a grim display, he lifted up Andrew and Abby's skulls and demonstrated how the hatchet head "fits in the wounds". Under cross-examination by defence attorney Adams, he said that the weapon and the killer should have been "spattered with blood", but no blood was discovered on any of the potential weapons, and confirmed Wood's earlier testimony that there wasn't a significant amount of blood on Lizzie's clothing.

Eli Bence, a pharmacy clerk, was next called as a prosecution witness. He was expected to testify that a woman resembling Lizzie attempted to buy prussic acid the day before the murders. However, the defence objected that his evidence was irrelevant to the case, because no prussic acid was found in Andrew or Abby's stomachs. The judges agreed and excluded Bence's testimony.

Defence attorney Andrew Jennings' opening statement empha-sized that the prosecution's case relied entirely on circumstantial evidence. He pointed out the absence of eyewitnesses, a murder weapon, and bloodstained clothing, and contended that the indi-vidual attempting to buy prussic acid, as mentioned in the prosecution's opening statements, was not Lizzie.

Jennings portrayed Lizzie as an honourable person who attended church and volunteered for charities. He described the murders as

11

brutal and insinuated that a woman could not have committed such an act, suggesting an "insane person or a fiend" as an alternative. He reminded the jury that the prosecution bore the burden of proof, needing to establish Lizzie's guilt beyond a reasonable doubt.

Martha Chagnon, a neighbour living behind the Bordens, was called as the first defence witness. She reported hearing pounding noises around 11 p.m. the night before the murders; she suggested it was someone hitting the Bordens' fence. Charles Gifford, whose father lived near the Borden house, recounted seeing a man on a neighbouring house's side steps around the same time. He was asleep with a straw hat covering his face. Gifford touched his arm, causing the hat to fall off. He struck a match, illuminating the man's face, but couldn't identify him. Another neighbour Mark P. Chase mentioned seeing a horse hitched to an open buggy near the Borden house at about 11 o'clock on the morning of the murders. He said there was a man in the wagon. Chase then went back inside his house (it is not known for how long); when he came back outside, the buggy and the stranger had disappeared.

Dr Benjamin J. Handy, a physician, testified that as he walked past the Borden home at 9 a.m. on the morning of the murders, he observed a young man of medium height and "of very pale complexion, with his eyes fixed on the sidewalk". He said that when he walked past the same place sometime after 10:30 a.m., he saw the man again. "He was paler than common, and acting strangely," he recalled. To Dr Handy, it looked as though he was "agitated or weak, staggering or confused". The man was wearing a light suit, collar, and necktie, and was unknown to Dr Handy.

Next to testify was Delia S. Manley, who recounted passing by the Borden home around 9:45 a.m. on the morning of the murders. Like Dr Handy, she had also observed a stranger outside the Borden residence, leaning on the gatepost. Following Manley's testimony, the defence called Hyman Lubinsky, an ice-cream seller who drove past the Borden home shortly after 11 a.m. that morning. Lubinsky had seen a lady emerging from the barn but couldn't identify her. He noted, however, that it wasn't Maggie, to whom he had previously delivered ice cream a couple of weeks earlier.

Thomas Barlow, a local man, was the next defence witness. He explained that after the murders, he was walking past the Borden house when he saw officers outside. He wished to investigate further but wasn't allowed in. He said he then visited the barn loft "to see if anybody was in there" and contradicted what Officer Medley had previously stated, telling the jury that the temperature was cool in the barn.

Joseph Lemay, who lived about four miles from the Borden home, testified that on the 16th of August, he was travelling in the woods on his farm when he heard a man exclaim "poor Mrs Borden" three times. He followed the man's voice and found him sitting on a rock behind a wall. He spoke to the man who responded by grabbing a hatchet that was lying nearby and shaking it threateningly. The man then leapt up, vaulted over the wall, and vanished from sight. Lemay noted that the man's shirt bore dark spots of what could have been blood.

Lizzie's sister, Emma, then testified regarding the dress Lizzie claimed was stained with paint. She explained that the house had been painted shortly before the date of the murders, and the dress had acquired paint stains. Emma noticed the dress hanging on a clothes press when officers were searching the house. She asked when Lizzie intended to "destroy that old dress", emphasizing that it not only had paint stains but was also "soiled" and severely faded. Three days after the murders, Emma saw Lizzie burning the dress in the kitchen stove. She also told the court that relations between Lizzie and Abby were "cordial". Dressmaker Mary A. Raymond corroborated Emma's statement, telling the jury that she had been shown the paint-stained dress.

After a 12-day-long trial, including just two days for the

defence, the proceedings drew to a close. Defence attorney George D. Robinson's concluding statements emphasized that there was no direct evidence linking Lizzie to the murders, and there was no discernible motive. He confidently pointed out the absence of any incriminating bloodstains, declaring, "Not a spot from her hair to her feet, on dress or person anywhere. Think of it!"

When Hosea Knowlton delivered his closing arguments for the prosecution, he implored the all-male jury to make their decision based on certain prevailing attitudes towards women. He stated, "If they lack in strength and coarseness and vigour, they make up for it in cunning, in dispatch, in celerity, in ferocity. If their loves are stronger and more enduring than those of men, on the other hand, their hates are more undying, more unyielding, more persistent."

Following a court recess, Lizzie was granted an opportunity to address the proceedings. She rose to her feet and softly uttered, "I am innocent. I leave it all to my counsel."[9]

The jury retired to consider its verdict. After deliberating for a mere one hour and six minutes, they re-entered the court. Lizzie Borden was declared not guilty of the murders of Andrew and Abby Borden.

In the aftermath, Lizzie and Emma relocated to a more modern home in the select enclave of Fall River known as The Hill. Since Abby's death had preceded that of Andrew, the entire estate passed into the sisters' possession.[10] Despite her exoneration, Lizzie continued to live under a cloud of suspicion, with many Fall River residents convinced that she had escaped justice. She confided to a friend, "When the truth comes out about this murder, I want to be living here so I can walk downtown and meet those of my old friends who have been cutting me all these years."[11]

Lizzie Borden passed away from pneumonia on the 1st of June 1927. She reportedly had a net worth of over $250,000, equating to more than $4 million today.[12]

Over the years, many theories have been advanced about the case and the list of suspects, both feasible and far-fetched, is a long one. Some have speculated that Lizzie and Emma – whose evidence helped exonerate her sister – were conspirators in the murders. Assuming Lizzie was innocent, another theory suggests that Bridget/Maggie was the killer because she was allegedly being mistreated by Andrew and Abby. Yet another is that William Borden, Andrew's illegitimate son, killed Andrew and Abby after trying to extort money from them; it is conceivable that he was the man with the hatchet seen by Joseph Lemay. Perhaps the murders were committed or arranged by an enemy of Andrew Borden, or even by Dr Bowen himself, who is alleged to have been on bad terms with Andrew and Abby. Despite numerous sleuths seeking to crack the case, it remains one of the most intractable in US criminal history.

Lizzie's story has inspired several books; a ballet (*Fall River Legend*, 1948); an opera (*Lizzie Borden*, 1968); a play (*Blood Relations*, 1980); and more than one TV drama (*The Legend of Lizzie Borden,* 1975, starring Elizabeth Montgomery of *Bewitched* fame, and *Lizzie Borden Took an Ax,* 2014, which became a series (*The Lizzie Borden Chronicles,* 2015). The house where the murders took place has been transformed into a museum and a bed and breakfast, where guests are invited "for a hauntingly fun time".

---

[1] *Mount Vernon Argus*, 10 August 1892 – "Miss Borden's Ordeal"

[2] *Fall River Daily Evening News*, 10 August 1892 – "The Borden Tragedy"

[3] *Fall River Daily Evening News*, 8 May 1893 – "I Am Not Guilty"

[4] *The Boston Globe*, 6 June 1893 – "Selecting the Jury for the Trial of Lizzie Borden"

[5] *Trial of Lizzie Borden Edited with a History of the Case* by Edmund Pearson (https://www.lizzieandrewborden.com/wp-content/uploads/2011/12/TrialLBPearson.pdf)

[6] *The Waterbury Democrat*, 6 June 1893 – "Lizzie Borden Faints in Court"
[7] *Chicago Tribune*, 7 June 1893 – "Her Trying Ordeal"
[8] *Boston Evening Transcript*, 7 June 1893 – "Line of Defence, Inkling of it's Character Given"
[9] *The Boston Globe*, 20 June 1893 – "I Am Innocent, Said Lizzie Borden to the Jury Who Are to Judge Her"
[10] *The New York Times*, 26 July 1992 – "Lizzie Borden Took an Ax"
[11] *Hartford Courant*, 6 June 1927 – "Lizzie Borden Ambition"
[12] Last Will and Testament of Lizzie Andrew Borden (https://lizzieandrewborden.com/wp-content/uploads/2011/12/Lizzies-last-will.pdf)

"A Species of Insanity"

The Thaw-White murder case possessed all the captivating elements to entice public attention. The prominence of both perpetrator and victim, their considerable wealth, the involvement of a young and alluring woman, and the very public nature of the murder itself combined to create a sensational spectacle. Sometimes dubbed the "Trial of the Century", the case captivated audiences far beyond the borders of the United States.

———————

"It is that species of insanity that inspires of every American to believe his home is sacred. It is that species of insanity that persuades an American that whoever violates the sanctity of his home or the purity of his wife or daughter has forfeited the protection of the laws of this state or any other state."

Attorney Delphin Michael Delmas

———————

Harry Kendall Thaw was the youngest millionaire in Pittsburgh, the heir to a multi-million-dollar fortune as the son of the coal and railroad baron, William Thaw Sr, who had died in 1889. Thaw had become smitten by Evelyn Nesbit, a popular artists' and photographic model, chorus girl, and actress. He had sat through at least forty performances of a Broadway show titled *The Wild Rose* just to see her on stage as Vashti, the Romani girl.

A charismatic and prominent figure in New York society, White was famous for shaping the city's skyline, including the design of Madison Square Garden. His wife and son lived on Long Island, over fifty miles from Manhattan, and his liking for girls young enough to be his daughters was an open secret. White had an opulent apartment at West 24th Street where he conducted his liaisons. In 1903, Thaw persuaded Evelyn to take a luxurious European vacation, during which he beat, sexually assaulted her, and forced her to confess her past high-profile affair with the famous architect Stanford "Stanny" White (she had also had a passionate romance with the famous actor John Barrymore).

The beautiful Evelyn, 15 or 16 at the time, had attracted the 46-year-old White's attention in 1901. Thaw confided to a friend, "He became acquainted with Evelyn, took her out to after-the-theater suppers and out in his automobile. You can guess the rest." Thaw, mentally unstable, self-indulgent, addicted to various drugs, and a violent womanizer himself was consumed with jealousy. In addition to viewing White as a love rival, Thaw had a deep-seated grudge against the older man, accusing him of obstructing his access to New York's social elite.

Despite her experience of Thaw's violent jealousy, Evelyn needed the financial and reputational security of marriage. She and Thaw were married in 1904, a wedding that newspapers referred to as a "society sensation".[1]

On the evening of the 25th of June 1906, accompanied by two friends, Truxton Beale and Thomas McCaleb, Thaw and Evelyn went to see the revue *Mam'zelle Champagne*, which was playing at Manhattan's Madison Square Garden's Rooftop Theater. As the show drew to a close around 11 p.m., Thaw spotted 53-year-old Stanford White in the audience.

During the first verse of the finale, "I Could Love a Million Girls", Thaw abruptly rose from his seat. He made his way to where White was sitting with three companions at a table, produced a pistol from the breast pocket of his coat, and fired three shots. One bullet struck the corner of White's left eye, the second penetrated his brain above the right eye, while the third lodged in his right shoulder.

White was killed instantly, and it took witnesses several moments to realize that the shooting was not part of the show. Fireman Paul Brudi swiftly intervened, wresting the gun from Thaw's grasp and handing him over to policeman Anthony Debes. "Is he dead?" Thaw enquired. "Yes," replied the officer. Thaw remarked, "Well, I'm glad that I made a good job of it."[2]

News of the murder spread rapidly across the nation. Thaw was transported to the Manhattan House of Detention (nicknamed The Tombs). The following day, he faced a first-degree murder charge in Jefferson Market Court.

Thaw was ordered to stand trial for White's murder, and in January 1907, jury selection commenced. After scrutinizing two hundred potential jurors, twelve men were chosen. For the first time in American history, the jury was to be sequestered owing to the overwhelming public interest in the case. According to former judge John Palmieri, "Never before had a murder trial seen such meticulous jury selection."[3]

District Attorney William T. Jerome's initial strategy was to have Thaw declared legally insane and committed to a mental asylum. Thaw's defence attorney, Lewis Delafield, concurred with the prosecution's approach, believing it the only means of sparing Thaw from facing the electric chair in New York's Sing Sing prison. Thaw, however, adamantly asserted his sanity. He argued instead that the killing of White was "justified"[4]. He promptly fired Delafield and replaced him with John B. Gleason. As a result, DA Jerome's prosecution tactics changed: he was now determined to prove that Thaw's actions had been premeditated and motivated by jealousy pure and simple.

The trial commenced at the New York Criminal Court on the 4th of February. That morning, onlookers thronged around the building, with police stationed at each entrance.[5] *The Buffalo Times* drew a parallel with the 1872 trial of New York businessman Edward Stiles Stokes, who had shot and killed his partner and rival in love James Fisk and served just four years in prison for manslaughter. Now, once again, a millionaire was standing before a jury on a murder charge "for the sake of a woman".[6]

Justice Fitzgerald presided over the case. Thaw had assembled an impressive legal team, including Delphin Michael Delmas, renowned as one of the most resourceful and assertive lawyers in the nation, having never suffered a defeat.[7] Thaw's mother had footed the bill for his defence, which was rumoured to cost around $1 million. That morning, Thaw was escorted into the courtroom and took his place alongside his defence attorneys.[8]

Assistant DA Francis Patrick Garvan began his opening statements at 10:45 a.m. He spoke for only ten minutes, telling the jury that it was the prosecution's argument that Thaw had killed White in cold blood. He concluded, "The murder was criminal, cruel, malicious, and the state will prove these facts."[9] Testimony then got underway with Lawrence White, Stanford White's son. He simply told the court that, before his father went to Madison Square Garden, they had dined together at Café Martin. As Lawrence spoke, Thaw's gaze rarely left the table in front of him.

Robert Paxton, an engineer, subsequently testified regarding the layout of the roof garden where the murder took place. The prosecution then summoned Meyer Cohen, an eyewitness to the murder. Garvan asked Cohen to demonstrate how Thaw had approached White. Leaving the witness stand, Cohen imitated the deliberate, unhurried manner in which Thaw had advanced towards White's table. Cohen testified, "He stepped aside and walked around and approached White from the rear. Thaw fired three shots and then held the revolver above his head by the barrel."[10]

The next witness was Henry S. Plaese, the superintendent of the publishing company holding the rights to *Mam'zelle Champagne*. Plaese informed the courtroom that he had observed Thaw on the night of the murder at the rear of the roof garden. He recounted that Thaw had remained there for a period of six or seven minutes, attentively surveying his surroundings. Subsequently, Plaese recounted how he witnessed Thaw advancing towards White and shooting him.

Fireman Paul Brudi then described how he had disarmed Thaw following the fatal shots. He stated that after he took away the weapon, Thaw uttered, "He ruined my wife." Evelyn was now standing by her husband's side, and as recounted by Brudi, she remarked to him, "Look at the fix you are in." However, Brudi did not catch Thaw's response. Another eyewitness, William Paxon, however, heard Thaw reply, "Well, dearie, I have probably saved your life."[11]

The arresting officer, Patrolman Anthony Debes, identified the pistol used by Thaw, along with the bullets and empty shells, all of which were entered as evidence. Debes said he asked Thaw if he had shot White and Thaw replied, "I did." Debes then enquired about the motive, to which Thaw replied, "because he ruined my wife" or "life" – Debes couldn't definitively say which word Thaw had used.

The state presented several more witnesses, including the coroner's physician, Dr Timothy Lehane, who provided a detailed description of the three gunshot wounds sustained by White. The prosecution also called Dr Sylvester Pechneer, who had examined White shortly after he fell and declared him dead. Dr Pechneer affirmed that White's death must have been instantaneous.

At 12:45 a.m. the state concluded its case, prompting Justice Fitzgerald to call for a recess until 2 p.m. John B. Gleason then presented the defence's argument, asserting that Thaw's actions were driven by a "mental unsoundness proceeding from a disease so that he did not know what he was doing". Gleason also contended that Thaw had acted in self-defence without any malice when he fatally shot White.[12]

Addressing the jury, Gleason stated, "We will show you this man's temperament, in which the seeds of insanity were implanted, liable to spring up at any time." He emphasized that the defence would illustrate how Thaw "had what doctors call the psychopathic temperament" and that he had suffered from "a disease of the brain" which culminated in the shooting of Stanford White. Furthermore, Gleason argued that his "insanity" was hereditary, a burden he had been "tainted" with from birth, thus absolving him of responsibility for the murder.[13]

Gleason recounted how Thaw and Evelyn had met in 1901: "He loved her with as honourable a love as anyone in this room has loved a woman whom he would choose as his wife." In 1903, Thaw took Evelyn to London where he proposed for the first time, but Evelyn refused. The defence attorney continued, "Gentlemen, the circumstances of the refusal – the reasons she gave – you will learn from her own lips. Suffice it to say that those reasons were connected with an occurrence in the life of that girl with reference to Stanford White."

The first witness presented by the defence was Dr C. C. Wiley, the Thaw family's physician, who also had affiliations with the Dixmont Insane Asylum. Gleason posed a hypothetical question regarding Thaw's mental state. He asked Dr Wiley if he could provide insight into the sanity of an individual who could shoot someone during a crowded theatre performance. Dr Wiley responded: "I can", but before he could elaborate, DA Jerome interjected, stating, "You must not state a belief, that is not evidence. You must give an opinion." In response, Dr Wiley clarified, "My opinion is that the man who committed the act described was suffering from insanity." He went on to explain that Thaw's post-shooting remark about saving his wife's life was indicative of an insane delusion.

Dr Wiley's testimony then shifted to the topic of hereditary insanity. He said that in hereditary insanity, the common blood that flows through a family may follow the same hereditary influence. However, Dr Wiley admitted that he was not "acquainted" with this form of mental illness. DA Jerome questioned whether Dr Wiley considered himself an expert. He replied, "I feel I have had experience", but was interrupted by the DA who said, "That is not the point. Are you an expert?" Dr Wiley replied that he thought he was competent.

Dr Wiley contended that while, in his opinion, Thaw was insane, he knew that shooting White was wrong. He began to elaborate but was interrupted by Gleason, who thought his response wasn't beneficial to Thaw's defence. When asked again if Thaw knew what he was doing was wrong, Dr Wiley declared, "No."[14]

During Dr Wiley's testimony, Thaw appeared visibly nervous, frequently biting his nails when his state of mind was discussed. Thaw's defence team attempted to introduce testimony suggesting a history of insanity in the Thaw family through Albert Lee Thaw, who mentioned that his father and Thaw's father were first cousins. He disclosed that his father had died in an asylum. DA Jerome objected, arguing that the relationship was too distant to be relevant. He asserted, "And the law is not satisfied that a man is insane merely because he dies in an asylum or a retreat for persons suffering from mental disorders."

The defence subsequently called Benjamin Bowman, the doorman at the Madison Square Garden Theater who was familiar with both White and Thaw. Bowman recounted an incident from Christmas Eve, 1903. After the show, White approached him enquiring about Evelyn's whereabouts. Bowman informed him that she had left with Thaw, prompting White to angrily accuse him of being a "goddamn liar". Bowman suggested White check for himself, and White returned a while later, brandishing a revolver and vowing, "I'll find and kill that son of a bitch before daylight." Bowman clarified that White was referring to Thaw.

A couple of days later, Bowman informed Thaw about the threat. He recalled, "His face was black with anger." Bowman asserted that he had not been compensated for his testimony and had received no promises in exchange.

Martin Green, an eyewitness to the shooting, next took the stand. He was asked to describe Thaw's demeanour following the shooting and reported that Thaw appeared with bulging eyes. Once Green stepped down, Dr John Franklin Bingaman was summoned. He said that he had known Thaw for over thirty years and was one of the family's physicians. He testified that he had treated Thaw for "children's diseases and St Vitus' dance". He also said that Thaw's personality could be described as exhibiting "a neurotic temperament".[15]

After Thaw was returned to his cell at the end of the day's proceedings, he was described as being in a "frenzy"– furious with Gleason for pursuing an insanity defence. Delphin Michael Delmas took over the legal team. Delmas was determined to change the defence's tactics and also the jury's attitude to Thaw. He had an ace up his sleeve: the testimony of Thaw's wife, Evelyn.

Evelyn shocked the court by tearfully stating that Stanford White had drugged and raped her when she was 16 years old. In response to this revelation, a man in the courtroom exclaimed, "I wish I could have killed him myself!"[16] She explained that she first met White in September 1901 while she was in the chorus of a show titled *Floradora*. White wined and dined her, sent her a hat and a boa, and invited her to a surprise party. He then collected her in a carriage and brought her to Madison Square Garden and his luxurious apartment which, among many other treasures, contained a red velvet swing that Evelyn delighted in. White then escorted her back to her mother's residence.

Sometime later, Evelyn visited White's studio on East 22nd Street. White directed her to the dressing room, where he asked her to don a kimono and took several photographs of her. Afterwards, he sent her back to her mother. The next night, White dispatched a carriage to bring Evelyn to his apartment. He gave her a glass of champagne and insisted she drink it all.

Evelyn continued, "I don't know whether it was a minute after or two minutes after, but a pounding began in my ears." The room began to spin, and Evelyn lost consciousness. When she came round, she discovered all her clothing had vanished and she was in bed in White's mirrored bedroom. "I started to scream. Mr White was there and got up and put on one of his kimonos." He told her not to scream, adding, "It is all over, it is all over." (Despite this incident, Evelyn and White's affair continued for some time afterwards.)

Evelyn recounted that she felt compelled to tell Thaw of this occurrence when he asked her to marry him in 1903 and described his reaction. "He would get up and walk up and down the room a minute and then come sit down and say, 'Oh God! Oh God!' and bite his nails like that and keep sobbing." She said that he didn't "think anything less" of her, and still wanted to marry her. "I refused to marry Harry at first because I loved him – it was because of my reputation. I loved him more than all else – more than my own life. I did not want to ruin his career, to estrange him from his family, and blast his future."[17]

Evelyn's dramatic testimony – whether wholly truthful, or well-rehearsed with Delmas – resulted in a shift in public opinion. This was clear the next morning as the jury walked from their hotel to the court building. They passed a streetcleaner, Thomas Palmer, who shouted, "Now, boys, go to it, get together and acquit Thaw."[18] Evelyn returned to the witness box that morning, pale and trembling. She told the jury that after her marriage to Thaw, White tried to steal her away, telling her that Thaw was "a morphine fiend" and "a very bad man".[19]

After Evelyn's lengthy testimony, the jury were taken through documents collected by Anthony Comstock, head of the Society for the Prevention of Crime. Comstock couldn't testify in person because he was ill with pneumonia. Around a year before the shooting, Thaw had hired Comstock to gather evidence that White was "preying upon the chastity of young girls".[20]

Comstock's documents read in part: "I know that Stanford White was a human monster. I know that much of what Mrs Harry Thaw has stated as a witness is true. I know that Stanford White's den was as she has described it. I know that White made a business of ruining young girls." According to Comstock, his investigation showed that White had preyed on another 15-year-old girl. He said that two or three weeks before the shooting, he saw Thaw, who frantically told him, "You must keep on! You must stop this man!"

The defence team had supporting evidence for Comstock's claims that White had targeted other young girls. After his death, detectives conducted a search of his apartment. They discovered two locked drawers concealed in the walls. Forcing them open, they discovered six articles of clothing, each labelled with the name of a young woman and a date. Among these items was clothing bearing the name Evelyn Nesbit.

Evelyn was summoned back to the witness box, and DA Jerome presented a stack of receipts indicating payments made to her and her mother by Stanford White. She acknowledged that she and her mother moved to a plush apartment in the Audubon hotel for a couple of months in 1902, with White covering the rent. He also paid to have her teeth fixed to help her career and for her brother Howard to attend military school. Jerome insinuated that Thaw had coerced Evelyn into fabricating the story of White drugging and raping her. He proposed that it was in fact Thaw who had been abusive towards Evelyn, but she refuted this suggestion.

The defence team also called Dr Charles R. Wagner, a psychiatrist who bolstered their temporary insanity argument. He asserted that Thaw had acted out of "a sudden impulse" and "had no idea of killing White up to the very time he shot him". Dr Wagner said that Thaw told him, "I knew he [White] was a foul creature, destroying all mothers and daughters in America, but I wanted to bring him to trial." Dr Britton D. Evans also testified about Thaw's frame of mind. His view was that Thaw had a predisposition to mental unsoundness that was hereditary.

In his closing argument, Delmas portrayed Thaw as having been overcome by a sudden passionate impulse, "a brainstorm", and cleverly insinuated to the all-male jury that Thaw had acted as many a man in his situation might have done, casting him as a defender of American womanhood: "And if Thaw is insane, it is with a species of insanity known from the Canadian border to the Gulf. If you expert gentlemen ask me to give it a name, I suggest that you label it *Dementia americana*. It is that species of insanity that inspires of every American to believe his home is sacred. It is that species of insanity that persuades an American that whoever violates the sanctity of his home or the purity of his wife or daughter has forfeited the protection of the laws of this state or any other state."

The jury retired to consider its verdict. Many of the jurors had been moved by Evelyn's testimony, which portrayed a young and innocent girl victimized by Stanford White, with her husband cast as her saviour. Nevertheless, the jury subsequently reported to Judge Fitzgerald that the members were deadlocked. Seven jurors thought Thaw guilty of first-degree murder, while the other five maintained he was not guilty by reason of insanity. Judge Fitzgerald adjourned the court and ordered a retrial.

The second trial commenced on the 6th of January 1908, with Jerome continuing as prosecutor. However, Thaw had assembled a new defence team, including Martin W. Littleton, Daniel O'Reilly, and Russell Peabody. Judge Victor J. Dowling replaced Judge Fitzgerald. A significant portion of the testimony mirrored that of the first trial, with the defence maintaining that Thaw had experienced a bout of temporary insanity at the time of the shooting. Ultimately, after 25 hours of deliberation, on the 1st of February, the jury rendered a verdict of not guilty by reason of insanity.

Thaw was committed to the state hospital for the criminally insane in Matteawan, New York, "until discharged by due course of law".[21] His two controversial murder trials etched the case into the annals of crime, elevating the insanity defence to unprecedented prominence, especially with Delmas' "*Dementia americana*" argument during the initial trial. Harry Kendall Thaw spent the remainder of his life shuttling between insane asylums and courtrooms. In August 1913, he escaped from Matteawan and sought refuge in Canada, though he was quickly apprehended and returned to New York. Some suspected his mother's involvement in the escape plot.

Evelyn, who had received financial support from Thaw's family throughout the two trials, initiated divorce proceedings in 1915 when this assistance ceased. Some believed that this financial support had served as an incentive for her testimony in Thaw's favour. Despite the divorce, they maintained communication through letters. Thaw experienced a brief release in 1915 but found himself arrested in 1916 on charges of kidnapping, whipping, and beating a 19-year-old named Frederick Gump. Thaw had persuaded Gump to leave Long Beach and stay with him in New York.[22]

Thaw remained confined to Kirkbride Asylum in Philadelphia until his release in April 1924. Upon regaining his freedom, he authored a book titled *The Traitor*, wherein he detailed the reasons behind his shooting of Stanford White while vindicating Evelyn, who had moved to Hollywood with her son and appeared in several silent pictures. In 1940, Thaw acquired the former Lippincott mansion on Spruce Street, Philadelphia. To celebrate this acquisition, he threw a party, extending invitations to "ladies over 16 and gentlemen over 18".[23]

On the 22nd of February 1947, aged 76, Thaw passed away. In his will, he bequeathed $10,000 to his former wife, Evelyn, and allocated $40,000 to Ethel May Moody, Miss Philadelphia 1929, a woman whom he had encountered only once.[24] Evelyn capitalized on her notoriety in various ways for the rest of her life, penning two memoirs, *The Story of My Life* (1914) and *Prodigal Days* (1934). After a turbulent life involving a further marriage and divorce, love affairs, a suicide attempt, alcohol and morphine addiction, work as a burlesque artist, and teaching sculpture classes, she died in 1967, aged 82.

The Thaw-White murder was dramatized in the 1955 Hollywood movie *The Girl in the Red Velvet Swing*, which told the story from Evelyn's point of view and cast Stanford White in a surprisingly sympathetic light, only vaguely hinting at his more nefarious proclivities. It starred Joan Collins as Evelyn, Ray Milland as Stanford White, and Farley Granger as Harry Thaw.

---

[1] *Piqua Leader-Dispatch*, 26 June 1906 – "Last Act of Misspent Lives"
[2] *The Cincinnati Post*, 26 June 1906 – "Famous Architect Dies in Building He Had Planned"

[3] *The Journal*, 6 February 1907 – "Ex-Judge's View"

[4] *The Buffalo Enquirer*, 19 January 1907 – "Thaw Wins His Way at Last"

[5] *The Nebrasksa Daily Press*, 24 January 1907 – "Thaw Trial Begun"

[6] *The Buffalo Times*, 27 January 1907 – "Misspent Life of Harry K. Thaw"

[7] *The Davis News*, 3 January 1907 – "Legal Giant to Defend Thaw"

[8] *Hartford Courant*, 21 January 1907 – "Thaw Murder Trial This Week"

[9] *Pittston Gazette*, 4 February 1907 – "Testimony Opens"

[10] *The Dayton Herald*, 4 February 1907 – "No Changes in Thaw Jury"

[11] *Sioux City Journal*, 5 February 1907 – "Begin Thaw Defense"

[12] *Press and Sun-Bulletin*, 4 February 1907 – "Hereditary Insanity Is Thaw's Plea"

[13] *The San Francisco Examiner*, 5 February 1907 – "To Drag Thaw Skeletons to Light to Save Son"

[14] *The Baltimore Sun*, 6 February 1907 – "Doctor on the Grill"

[15] *Chicago Tribune*, 6 February 1907 – "Next Witness Gets Off Easily"

[16] *The Brooklyn Daily Eagle*, 7 February 1907 – "Evelyn Nesbit Tells Her Pitiful Story to the Jury"

[17] *The Great Harry Thaw Case* by Benjamin H. Atwell

[18] *The Piqua Daily Call*, 7 February 1907 – "Evelyn Thaw Exposes Shame to Save Husband"

[19] *The Nation Star*, 8 February 1907 – "Seeks Evelyn When Married"

[20] *The Philadelphia Inquirer*, 10 February 1907 – "Comstock Says Evelyn Thaw's Story Is True"

[21] *The Indiana Democrat*, 5 February 1908 – "Thaw Sent to Asylum"

[22] *Columbia Missourian*, 9 January 1917 – "Thaw in Limelight Again"

[23] The Philadelphia Inquirer, 23 February 1947 – "Harry K. Thaw Dies in Florida Home at 76"

[24] *The Philadelphia Inquirer*, 30 March 1947 – "Thaw Leaves $40,000 to Miss Phila. of 1929; Ex-Wife Gets $10,000"

Brighton Trunk Murderer

In 1934, the popular English seaside resort of Brighton, East Sussex, known as "The Queen of Watering Places", was shaken by a horrifying discovery: the dead bodies of two women crammed into separate trunks in two different locations. The second woman was identified as Violet Saunders, leading to the arrest of her criminal boyfriend, Toni Mancini. What initially seemed an open-and-shut case swiftly evolved into a trial that, decades later, brought shocking revelations.

"It is not necessary to establish motive. The concealment of the body is the outstanding feature of the case. Is not such conduct contrary to human instincts and human nature, unless there is for such conduct the overwhelming reason of guilt?"

Prosecutor J.C. Cassels

On the 17th of June 1934, the dismembered torso of an unidentified pregnant woman was found in a trunk abandoned at
Brighton railway station's left-luggage office. Sussex Police sought
the assistance of London's Metropolitan Police, leading to a door-
to-door search on the 16th of July. The decomposed body of another
woman, a scarf knotted around her neck, was discovered in a trunk
at a flat at 52 Kemp Street, Brighton.[1] Newspapers dubbed the killings the "Brighton Trunk Murders" and the city "The Queen of
Slaughtering Places".

The flat where the second body was found had been leased by a
26-year-old man known as Toni Mancini, a waiter with various
aliases and an extensive criminal history involving theft and
loitering with intent. Mancini had been living with his 42-year-
old girlfriend, Violet Saunders, a dancer and sex worker who used
the stage name Violette Kaye, since September 1933. Violet had
been married as a teenager, but since then had "lived her own life".
One of her brothers said, "We heard little of Violet. She was always
roaming and sometimes we would not know for six months or so
where to find her."[2]

Reports indicated that Mancini and Saunders' relationship was
marked by frequent conflicts and disagreements. It was no secret
that Mancini lived on Violet's money. Following a particularly
heated dispute at the Skylark Café on Brighton's seafront on the

10th of May, 1934, during which Violet accused Mancini of a romantic relationship with a young waitress named Elizabeth Attrill, Violet mysteriously disappeared. Her concerned friends reported her disappearance to police.

Following the discovery of the first body at Brighton railway station, detectives questioned Mancini at Brighton police station, suspecting that the deceased woman may have been Violet. However, after Mancini provided a description of Violet, it became clear that the woman was not her – this victim was younger, only about 25. According to Mancini, Violet had left him a note saying she had left with a man "who could afford to keep her".

After the interview, Mancini vanished, but the body in his flat was soon identified as Violet Saunders by her mother.[3] The renowned pathologist Sir Bernard Spilsbury, instrumental in the 1910 conviction of wife murderer Doctor Crippen and the 1915 "Brides in the Bath" murderer George Joseph Smith among others, determined she had died from a fatal blow to the back of her head.[4] Police across the country searched for Mancini, who they described as obviously "cross-eyed" with a pronounced lisp. He was tracked down near Blackheath, Southeast London, on the 17th of July and charged with Violet's murder. He told the judge, "All I can say, sir, is that I am not guilty."[5]

The trial of Mancini at Lewes Assizes, East Sussex was scheduled for the 10th of December 1934. His defence team included Norman Birkett, John Flowers, and Eric Neve, while the prosecution was led by J.C. Cassels, supported by future Lord Chancellor Quintin Hogg. Mr Justice Branson presided over the case. The jury was comprised entirely of men. Outside the courtroom, a lengthy line formed as inquisitive spectators vied for a seat. Mancini was escorted into the courtroom and described as having a "dejected appearance" as he "sank" into his chair in a "listless manner".[6]

The prosecution's opening statements got underway with Cassels telling the jury that Violet and Mancini came to Brighton in the autumn of 1933. They rented a flat on Park Crescent on the 15th of March 1934, and Mancini began introducing Violet as his "wife". The prosecutor described how Mancini started working as a handyman and waiter at the Skylark Café on the 5th of May. He said that between 2:30 and 3 p.m. on the 10th of May, Violet was seen at the café where Mancini worked, and a woman overheard them arguing about Mancini's love affairs. The prosecutor said, "He [Mancini] certainly is the last person, so far as the prosecution is concerned, who ever saw Violet Saunders alive."

During that time, Violet's sister, Olive Watts, had been preparing for a holiday scheduled to begin on the 14th of May. Prior to this, she had arranged to meet Violet at Park Crescent. However, on the 11th of May, Olive received a telegram, supposedly sent by Violet, that read: "Going abroad. Good job. Sail Sunday. Will write – Vi." Addressing the jury, Cassels observed, "One question which might arise in the course of this case for you to consider would be who sent that telegram? The Post Office officials who received it cannot say." He pointed out that the telegram was composed in printed capital letters, akin to the style on the menu cards at the Skylark Café.

Cassels said that, from this moment on, Mancini went to great lengths to explain Violet's disappearance. On the 11th or 12th of May, he went to a dancehall with Elizabeth Attrill, the young Skylark Café waitress Violet accused him of having an affair with. Cassels stated, "Mancini told her that Violet had gone away to Paris. He took her to the flat, to the basement of 44 Park Crescent. They were alone there, and Mancini got her a green costume and a fawn hat, both of which had been brought from a credit draper by Mancini on the 17th of April." Cassels said that Violet had been seen wearing this outfit before her death.[7]

About this time, Mancini bought a black trunk – the same trunk that Violet's body was discovered inside two months later. On the 14th of May, Mancini moved from Park Crescent to 52 Kemp Street and used a handcart to move the trunk. He told friends and acquaintances that Violet had left for France with her uncle. He told another woman, Joyce Golding, that he had left Violet because she was constantly "nagging him".

The prosecution then called their first witness, Mrs Phyllis Josephine Summers, a friend of Violet's for fifteen years. Summers recounted how, in June, Mancini had informed her that Violet had gone to Paris. Sometime later, she encountered Mancini at the Skylark Café, where he handed her a shopping basket along with a knife, a fork, some spoons, and a table centrepiece. These items were introduced as evidence and identified as belonging to Violet. During cross-examination by defence attorney Birkett, Summers said that Mancini and Violet always seemed to be on the "most friendly and affectionate terms".

Another witness, Martin Melvyn Charteris, who stayed with the couple in their Park Crescent flat for two weeks in March 1934, said they presented themselves as a married couple. Charteris recounted that on the 19th of June, he encountered Mancini in Brighton and asked about his wife. Mancini replied that she had left for Paris with a bookmaker. During cross-examination, Charteris said that Violet was "very jealous" of Mancini.

Elizabeth Attrill, who characterized Mancini as a "casual boyfriend", was asked about her last encounter with Violet – during lunchtime at the Skylark Café on the 10th of May. She recalled that the couple argued. Attrill recounted that the following day, she went dancing with Mancini at Sherry's dancehall, where he told her that Violet had left for Paris. Attrill confirmed that either that evening or the next, she accompanied Mancini back to his flat at Park Crescent and noticed bloodstains on one of his shirts. She remembered saying, "Look at the blood on your shirt, Toni!" He claimed the bloodstains were caused by a shaving cut.[8]

The prosecution then called Joyce Golding, a waitress who had worked with Mancini at the café. When Mancini said he had left

Violet, she asked whether he missed her. His response was a firm "no" and she further remarked, "They had been quarrelling, and now there would be no more following him in the streets and calling him names." When cross-examined by Birkett, Golding stood her ground, affirming the truth of her testimony in the face of his suggestion that her account was "quite false".

Witness testimony then revolved around statements made by Mancini following Violet's disappearance. Frederick Samuel Coftrey, asserted that Mancini confided that he had given Violet "the biggest hiding" she had ever had in her life. Coftrey recalled Mancini adding, "I bashed her from pillar to post." Another witness, George Boxall, asserted that Mancini had bragged to him: "Why knock women about with your hands? You only hurt yourself. Hit them with a hammer and slosh her out the same as I did."[9]

Home Office analyst Dr Roche Lynch reported that he had found human blood on two shirts, a pair of blue striped trousers and a pair of flannel trousers that belonged to Mancini. He also discovered the head of a hammer in the Kemp Street flat and said it appeared to have been burned. Dr Lynch had examined Violet's body and noted a minute trace of morphine in her organs. Asked by Birkett if it was enough to cause death, he responded, "I am not prepared to answer that question."

During the trial's third day, a tearful Doris Irene Saville – another girlfriend of Mancini's – recounted going on a trip with Mancini to Lee Green, Southeast London, during which he asked her to keep a secret. "He said, 'It is about a murder. If I happen to be caught, you are to dictate this story to the police.'" Mancini allegedly instructed her to state that she met him on the Brighton seafront at the end of May and they proceeded to "have tea with a woman at Park Crescent". This woman, presumably Violet, was supposed to have informed them that she was expecting three men to visit her. Mancini instructed Saville that she should tell the police that they left the three men alone with Violet, and upon their return, they found her dead.

This wasn't the only explanation Mancini gave to account for Violet's body being discovered in his flat. Chief Inspector Donaldson testified that during an interview at Lewisham Police Station on the 17th of July following Mancini's arrest, Mancini claimed that, after completing his first week at the Skylark Café, he collected his wages and returned to the flat he shared with Violet and knocked on the front door. Receiving no response, he entered through a window. He told the Chief Inspector, "I went into the bedroom, and she was lying on the bed with a handkerchief tied round her neck. There was blood all over the sheets and everywhere."[10] Mancini added that he was afraid he would be held responsible as he couldn't prove his innocence. "I decided to take it [Violet's body] with me, so for that purpose I bought a trunk. She was a prostitute. There were men always coming to the house all night. I do not know who killed her, as God is my judge."

In a surprising turn, Sir Bernard Spilsbury presented a section of Violet's skull to the court, highlighting the precise location of the fracture. He suggested that the injury had occurred mere minutes before her death, the blow matching the description of the hammerhead provided by Dr Lynch. He further testified that most likely the smaller end of the hammer was used. Birkett proposed the possibility of the injury resulting from a fall down the stairs that led to their front door, but Spilsbury refuted this. He also asserted that had she survived for any duration following the injury, she would have succumbed to brain haemorrhaging.[11]

Following the conclusion of the fifteen-and-a-half-hour-long prosecution case, Mr Norman Birkett addressed the jury for the defence. He emphasized the prosecution's responsibility to establish, beyond all reasonable doubt, the defendant's guilt. Birkett further asserted, "And the submission I make on behalf of this defendant here now is, with all the evidence for the Crown before you, they have failed in that duty." He stressed that mere suspicion and doubt were insufficient grounds for conviction.

Birkett said that the prosecution's main argument rested on the assertion that Violet was murdered with the hammerhead discovered in Mancini's apartment. He highlighted an inconsistency in Sir Spilsbury's testimony when the pathologist claimed that Violet was killed with the smaller end of the hammerhead. In his previous statement, during the inquest, he had suggested the larger end caused the fatal injuries.

Birkett posed the question: "What do you think of that? That hammerhead, you know, which has been introduced into this case – that is a matter which does not want Sir Bernard Spilsbury or medical experts; it is a matter for men such as you are." He also suggested that the bloodstained clothing could have come into Mancini's possession following Violet's death.

He referenced testimony about Mancini allegedly admitting to others he gave Violet a "hiding" but noted that there was no evidence of any bruising on Violet's body. He then continued, stating, "A fact which has never been disputed is the concealment of the body and the lies to explain it." He highlighted that it wouldn't be the first time in history that a man, overwhelmed by his emotions, took a "wrong step".

Birkett then drew attention to the morphine found in Violet's body. He proposed that she could have consumed a fatal dose and then fallen down the stairs or hit her head on a stone ledge outside their front door. Another theory, he suggested, was that somebody else killed Violet. "She was a prostitute. She was visited by men. Blackmail of a husband or a father is not, unfortunately, too rare."[12]

The courtroom fell silent as Birkett announced, "I now call the prisoner," and Toni Mancini took the witness stand. He maintained that he wasn't responsible for Violet's death and that he had never acted violently towards her. He stuck to his initial statement, given to Chief Inspector Donaldson, that he had returned home to find her dead. He had put her body in the closet because he couldn't bear the sight of her lying there. He said he eventually placed her body in the trunk he had purchased and told the jury, "I decided that the only course was to keep it a secret until I could, if possible, find out what [sic] had killed her."[13]

Cassels asked him why he didn't think to call for assistance. His response was, "Because I was afraid, as is proven now, sir, that I should be blamed for it." He said that, because of his criminal record, the police would not have given him a "square deal". He denied that he had pressed or crushed Violet's body into the trunk but admitted that he had sent the telegram to Violet's sister to give the impression she was still alive. He claimed that testimony that he had boasted about giving Violet a "hiding" was fabricated and that he had never seen the hammerhead found in his flat until it was presented in court.

Mancini said that he and Violet had moved around a lot and that she "seemed to be in fear all the time". She used three different names in Brighton and was the one to consistently pay their rent during his unemployment. He recalled, "Some evenings when I got home, she would come in and say, 'Pack up all the clothes. We've got to go.'" Mancini portrayed Violet as someone who often drank to excess, and he speculated that she may have been addicted to drugs. He mentioned a small bottle in her drawer that she would take into another room, closing the door behind her; however, he remained uncertain about its contents. He claimed that he had never purchased morphine and had never administered any to Violet.[14]

Closing arguments were then presented. For the defence, Birkett poured scorn on the testimonies of Sir Bernard Spilsbury and Dr Lynch and denounced the entire prosecution case as "riddled with doubt". He said that alternative theories must be considered, including the possibility that Violet fell down the stairs and hit her head. He reminded the jury that it wasn't his job to prove such a theory. Birkett concluded, "There was also the other theory – that somebody else killed this woman."[15]

In his closing argument, Cassels made clear the case for the prosecution: "Was not the outstanding feature . . . the concealment of the body from all eyes that fatal evening of Thursday, the 10th of May – concealed in a trunk specifically bought for the purpose?" He reminded the jury that Mancini did not call for help and promptly began covering up the crime by telling people Violet had gone to Paris or that they had broken up. He said to the jury: "It is not necessary to establish motive. The concealment of the body is the outstanding feature of the case. Is not such conduct contrary to human instincts and human nature, unless there is for such conduct the overwhelming reason of guilt?"

Following the judge's summing-up, the jury withdrew. After just two hours and fifteen minutes, they returned. The Clerk of Assize directed the foreman to announce the verdict. The words "Not Guilty" reverberated through the room, prompting gasps from onlookers. Mancini rose from his seat, visibly overwhelmed with emotion. Mr Justice Brandon addressed him, stating, "You are discharged." Mancini bowed his head and descended the steps of the dock before being escorted into an adjacent room with his mother.[16]

The trial and verdict left numerous questions unanswered. However, Norman Birkett's victorious defence boosted his career. He was much sought-after for various high-profile cases, culminating in his appointment as a High Court judge in 1941. He later served as the alternate British judge at the Nuremberg trials of Nazi war criminals in 1945.

It was not until 1976 that Mancini finally shed light on the lingering mysteries surrounding the murder of Violet Saunders.

Shortly before his death, in a conversation with a reporter from the *News of the World* tabloid, Mancini confessed to Violet's murder. He recalled a heated altercation, during which she grabbed the coal-breaking hammer and attacked him. Mancini asserted that he managed to disarm her, but in the ensuing struggle for the hammer, he inadvertently hurled it, resulting in a fatal blow to her head. Despite his confession, the law of double jeopardy – whereby a suspect, once acquitted, could not be tried for the same crime twice – prevented him from being charged a second time. (This law still applies, though in April 2005 it was changed and allowed to be overruled in exceptional circumstances.)

The victim of the first Trunk Murder was never identified and her murderer never found. It is possible that she was the tragic victim of a backstreet abortionist. The bigamist and murderer George Shotton has also been linked to the crime. The widespread publicity surrounding the Brighton Trunk Murders, with its exposé of Brighton's seamy side, helped to inspire the atmosphere of Graham Greene's famous 1938 novel *Brighton Rock*, filmed in 1948 and 2010, while the first Trunk Murder influenced author George Orwell's 1939 novel *Coming Up for Air*.

------

[1] *Leicester Evening Mail*, 16 July 1934 – "Brighton Trunk Crime No. 2"

[2] *Evening Express*, 16 July 1934 – "New Trunk Murder Mystery"

[3] *Manchester Evening News*, 17 July 1934 – "Mancini Charged With 'Trunk Crime 2'"

[4] *Evening Standard*, 15 August 1934 – "Sir B. Spilsbury on How Violette Kaye Died"

[5] *Evening Post*, 3 August 1934 – "Brighton Murder Charge"

[6] *Coventry Evening Telegraph*, 11 December 1934 – "Brighton Trunk Mystery"

[7] *Evening Standard*, 10 December 1934 – "Toni Mancini Says 'Not Guilty'"

[8] *Evening Post*, 11 December 1934 – "Waitress Cross-Examined in Mancini Trial"

[9] *Evening Sentinel*, 11 December 1934 – "Trial of Waiter on Charge of Murder"

[10] *Coventry Evening Telegraph*, 12 December 1934 – "Girl's Remarkable Story in Brighton Trunk Murder Case"

[11] *Evening Standard*, 13 December 1934 – "Mr. Birkett and Sir Bernard Spilsbury"

[12] *Evening Standard*, 13 December 1934 – "Mr Birkett Outlines Mancini's Defence"

[13] *Evening Standard*, 13 December 1934 – "Toni Mancini Cross-Examined"

[14] *Manchester Evening News*, 13 December 1934 – "Mancini Tells His Story in Witness Box"

[15] *Manchester Evening News*, 13 December 1934 – "Suggestion Dancer Was Blackmailed"

[16] *Hull Daily Mail*, 14 December 1934 – "Toni Mancini Acquitted of Trunk Crime"

Crime of Passion

On Easter Sunday, the 10th of April 1955, after a tumultuous, two-year-long relationship, 28-year-old Ruth Ellis shot dead 25-year-old David Blakely, outside The Magdala public house in Hampstead, Northwest London. Her trial captured public attention, not only because she was a woman, but also for the complex emotions and societal issues it raised. As the last woman to be hanged in the UK, the case marked a significant moment in the country's legal history, sparking debates about the nature of justice, the treatment of women in abusive relationships, and British law's attitude to what was widely perceived as a "crime of passion".

"Ruth Ellis's story is a long, painful story and you will find, in some ways, a sordid story. She found herself in something like an emotional prison, guarded by this young man, from which there seemed to be no escape."

Defence attorney Aubrey Melford Stevenson

Ruth Ellis was born in the backstreets of Rhyl, North Wales, on the 9th of October 1926, the fourth of six children to parents Arthur and Bertha. The family subsequently relocated to South London. In 1943, aged 17, Ellis started work as a photographer's assistant, which introduced her to the vibrant, sometimes sleazy, nightlife of London clubs and brought her into contact with Canadian and American troops on leave from World War II.[1] To look the part, Ellis dyed her dark hair platinum blonde, and wore tailored dresses, heavier makeup, and pearls.

She became romantically involved with a French-Canadian soldier named Clare Andrea McCallum, and their relationship took a significant turn when Ellis discovered she was pregnant. He proposed marriage, but she discovered that McCallum was already married and had a family in his home country. Shortly before Ellis's 18th birthday, she gave birth to a baby boy, Clare Andrea, known as Andy. In 1950, she married dentist George Johnston Ellis, and the following year gave birth to a baby girl, Georgina. George refused to acknowledge the child as his, and he and Ruth soon separated.

Ellis delved into the world of modelling, posing in lingerie for risqué postcard photographs. She also became a hostess at various London clubs, enticing patrons to buy pricey drinks, a task she carried out with poise and charm. One of the clubs she worked at was Carol's, where she first encountered David Blakely, 24, an attractive, public-school-educated, aspiring racing driver relying on the financial support of his affluent family.

Shortly after Ellis's 27th birthday in 1953, Blakely began regularly staying at her flat at 44 Egerton Gardens, Knightsbridge, despite having two homes of his own and being engaged to a woman named Mary Dawson. The flat was near The Little Club, a members-only establishment managed by Ellis. The relationship was stormy, and Blakely was often violent, resulting in Ellis receiving black eyes, cut lips, and bruised arms. Matters escalated when Ellis found herself pregnant with Blakely's child in December. Receiving no support from him, she resorted to a backstreet abortion. The tragic saga continued in March 1955 when Ellis discovered she was pregnant once again, prompting a callous response from Blakely, who gave her a blow so severe that it led to a miscarriage.[2]

On the night of the 10th of April Ellis tracked down Blakely at The Magdala Tavern, Hampstead, Northwest London, having spotted his car parked outside. As he was leaving, she took out a .38 calibre Smith & Wesson Victory Model revolver from her handbag and fired five shots. Witnesses later told of their shock as she attempted to fire at him again while he lay on the ground. The bullet ricocheted off the pavement, striking a bystander.

In the aftermath, Ellis calmly turned to Blakely's friend, Bertram Clive Gunnell, and said, "Will you call the police, Clive?" In a nearby pub, off-duty police officer Alan Thompson was enjoying a drink when the sound of gunfire reverberated in the street. He ran outside and saw Blakely fatally wounded and Ellis holding the gun.[3] She was arrested and taken to Hampstead police station. Blakely was pronounced dead on arrival at New End Hospital. He had sustained one gunshot wound to the left hip, one to the left shoulder blade, and one to the right leg.

The next day, Ruth Ellis was cautioned and charged with murder. She replied: "I understand." When the charge was read, she responded, "Thanks."[4] Ellis was granted legal aid and represented by Aubrey Melford Stevenson, along with Seabag Shaw and Peter Rawlinson. She pleaded not guilty to the murder charge, and the trial began at the Old Bailey on the 20th of June 1955. That morning, Ellis entered the courtroom, hair her signature platinum blonde. She was wearing a black suit with astrakhan fur on the lapels and pockets and a white silk blouse.[5] Her defence team had suggested she tone her appearance down for her trial and dye her hair a more natural shade, but Ellis opted against it.

As the trial began, Stevenson directly addressed the jury: "There is no question here that this young woman shot this man. But we ask you to return a verdict of manslaughter, not of murder."[6] Ellis's defence centred on the argument that intense jealousy had significantly affected her mental state, leading to a state of provocation. Stevenson emphasized that this was the first time this defence had been presented in a court of law in the UK.

He continued: "Ruth Ellis's story is a long, painful story and you will find, in some ways, a sordid story. She found herself in something like an emotional prison, guarded by this young man, from which there seemed to be no escape." Stevenson described Blakely as "a most unpleasant person" but said that he had "become an absolute necessity" to Ellis.[7] Stevenson's gaze moved from juror to juror as he said, "However brutally he [Blakely] behaved, and however much he spent of her money on various entertainments of his own, and however much he consorted with other people, he ultimately came back to her and always she forgave him."[8]

Prosecutor Christmas Humphreys depicted Ellis through a starkly different lens. He said to the jury: "In 1954 and 1955, she was having simultaneous love affairs with two men, one of whom was Blakely, and the other a man called Desmond Edward Cussen." He further argued that Blakely had been attempting to end his involvement with Ellis, noting, "Ms Ellis was angry at the thought that he was leaving her, even though she had another lover at the time."

Humphreys added that, after Ellis's arrest, she had made a full confession to the murder. He quoted her as saying, "I put the gun in my bag . . . I intended to find David and shoot him. I saw him and he turned away from me . . . I shot him." During this confession, Ellis recounted that Blakely managed to run for a few steps before she fired another shot, adding, "I fired a third shot. I don't remember firing any more, but I must have done." Humphreys asserted that, in early 1955, Ellis had told Blakely's friend Seaton Findlater that he was trying to leave her, but she was trying to stop him from doing so.

The prosecutor proceeded to give an account of events over the Easter Sunday weekend, saying that Blakely went to stay with Findlater. The purpose, he said, was to break off the relationship with Ellis. On Good Friday, Ellis was with Cussens. She called Findlater in the evening and asked if Blakely was with him. Findlater lied and said that Blakely wasn't. Around midnight, Cussen drove Ellis to Findlater's apartment at 29 Tanza Road, Hampstead. Blakely and Findlater were awoken by the sound of Ellis smashing Blakely's car windows with a hammer. They called the police and she left.

At about 3 a.m., they awoke again to the sound of Ellis hitting the windows of the car a second time. Police were called back to the apartment and Ellis sent on her way. "On Sunday – the all-important day," said Humphreys, Blakely, Findlater, and others were throwing a party at the flat. David, Findlater and another man, Bertram Clive Gunnell, went to The Magdala to buy more beer. They stayed there for about half an hour. At about 9 p.m., Ellis appeared outside. Fifteen minutes later, Blakely, Findlater, and Gunnell left the public house. As they approached the car, Ellis opened fire at Blakely.

Witness testimony began with Desmond Edward Cussen, 33, a former R.A.F. officer, now a director of his family's tobacco business, who described his relationship with Ellis. He disclosed that their relationship had begun approximately two years earlier. Cussen recalled that on Good Friday he chauffeured Ellis to Findlater's flat. When she returned, she told him that the police had been summoned after she had smashed Blakely's car windows. On Easter Sunday, Ellis and her ten-year-old son Andy spent most of the day at Cussen's flat. He drove her home to 44 Egerton Gardens around 7 p.m. When questioned by defence attorney Stevenson about his feelings for Ellis, Cussen candidly admitted, "I was terribly fond of her."

Cussen claimed that Ellis expressed a desire to break with Blakely on multiple occasions, yet she continued to return to him, even after Cussen proposed marriage. He had seen bruises and marks on Ellis's body on several occasions, which he helped her conceal with make-up. He once accompanied Ellis to Middlesex Hospital due to their severity.

Blakely's friend Seaton Findlater recalled visiting a flat in Marylebone Road with Gunnell and Blakely some months before the shooting. Ellis was there, and Blakely asked him if he "could assist him to leave her". Humphreys asked what Ellis said to that, and Findlater replied, "I cannot remember the exact words, but she was rather sarcastic, about him needing some help to leave her." He also testified about Ellis smashing Blakely's car windows on Good Friday evening.

Findlater and Blakely's friend Bertram Clive Gunnell described the shooting of Blakely. He said that they had just come out of The Magdala, recalling, "I went round to the passenger seat of the Vanguard [Blakely's car]. The door was locked so I had to wait for David Blakely. While I was waiting, I heard two bangs and a shout of 'Clive'." Gunnell said he went round to the back of the car and saw Blakely lying on the floor with Ellis nearby holding a gun.

Mr L. C. Nickolls, director of the police laboratory at Scotland Yard, testified that one shot was fired from just three inches away and had left powder marks on the back of Blakely's jacket.

Dr Duncan Whittaker provided insights into Ellis's psychological state at the time of the shooting. According to him, Ellis was "very disturbed" and that the situation she found herself in was "absolutely intolerable for her". Addressing the jury, he suggested that women prioritized emotional connections more intensely than men, finding it challenging to disassociate their sexual experiences from the bond with a partner. He also claimed that women were more susceptible to hysterical reactions, particularly in the context of infidelity, leading them to temporarily lose their "critical faculties" and try to solve the problem at a more "primitive level".[9] He believed Ellis both hated and loved Blakely, and that she exhibited some level of emotional immaturity. Despite this, he said he believed that she was sane at the time of the shooting.[10]

The Old Bailey fell silent as the defence called Ruth Ellis. Questioned about her relationship with David Blakely, she said that they became romantically involved just two weeks after they first met in August 1953. Shortly after their meeting, Ellis became the manager of The Little Club, Knightsbridge, and took the flat above the club for £10 a week. Blakely came to live with her. She recalled, "I was still married, and he was engaged to another young woman. He slept at my flat nearly every night but spent the weekends at Penn in Buckinghamshire." Ellis was asked by Stevenson whether she was in love with Blakley at the time, and she replied, "Not really." She said that after her abortion, she wanted to break off the relationship, but Blakely "didn't like the idea of ending our affair at all".

Ellis recounted that she began a relationship with Cussen later that year, despite persistent pressure from Blakely to marry him. She remembered, "He [Blakely] told me that he would never have any happiness if we didn't get married. He told me that he had broken his engagement off." According to Ellis, this marked the beginning of Blakely's increasingly possessive and jealous behaviour.

Despite Blakely's initial impression of wealth, after calling off his engagement, Ellis claimed that she was left shouldering the financial responsibilities, purchasing his clothing, covering his cigarette and drinks expenses, and providing him with money. When asked by Stevenson whether Blakely ever provided an explanation for his financial difficulties, she replied, "I knew racing cars were very expensive." Whatever little money Blakely had, he was funnelling into his career. She recounted a specific incident in 1954 where Blakely said he was going to take his own life after his father cut off his allowance. She recalled, "I gave the barmaid at the club instructions that if he came to the bar, he was to be allowed to drink without paying."

As Ellis continued to support Blakely's expensive lifestyle, his jealousy towards other patrons at the club grew increasingly apparent. By October 1954, he became physically violent towards Ellis. "He only hit me with his fists or hands, and I bruise very easily." She said that she tried to end her relationship with Blakely multiple times and had even moved in with Desmond Cussen for a couple of months because she thought it was the only way of "breaking up the affair". Nonetheless, she found herself repeatedly drawn back to Blakely and, later that year, they moved into a flat together at 44 Egerton Gardens, near The Little Club.

While Blakely was jealous about Ellis's interactions with other men, he engaged in numerous affairs. Ellis recalled an occasion when she remained outside one woman's residence all night, aware that Blakely was inside. Blakely did not leave the premises until 9 a.m. the following morning. When Stevenson enquired about her emotional state during this period, Ellis admitted, "I was getting jealous of him. I had done what he wanted, given up my business [she lost her manager's job partly because of Blakely's enormous unpaid bar tab] and left my friends, and it was my turn to become jealous of him." Ellis said she told Blakely they were finished and asked for his key to the flat, but he refused to hand it over. He returned to their flat about a week later. Stevenson probed her decision to reconcile with him. Ellis responded, "Because I was in love with him."

In March 1955, Ellis found out she was pregnant. She recalled,

"At the end of March, we had a fight and Blakely became very violent. I had a miscarriage." In early April, she recounted that she went with him to the motor racing at Oulton Park, but his car broke down on the way. Ellis informed the jury that Blakely blamed her, citing an earlier remark she had made that his treatment of her would bring him no luck. When they returned to London, Ellis had to stay in bed with a cold. During two consecutive nights, Blakely returned home in the early hours. When Stevenson enquired about her emotional state during this time, she candidly replied, "I felt nothing but contempt for him."[11]

The next evening brought a noticeable shift in Blakely's demeanour. Ellis said that he exuded a sense of contentment, discussing the prospect of marriage with apparent enthusiasm. He presented Ellis with a promotional photograph of himself in his racing driver gear, a poignant token of affection. As the photo was shown in court, Ellis was visibly moved, wiping away tears with a handkerchief. On the back, Blakely had written: "To Ruth, with all my love, from David." The couple spent the next two days going to the cinema and discussing their future plans.

On Good Friday morning, they parted on good terms. Blakely told Ellis he was going for a drink with friends but arranged to pick her up at 8 p.m. to join the group. However, the appointed hour came and went, and Blakely was notably absent. Ellis recounted her growing anger. Around 9:30 p.m. she telephoned Findlater to ask if he knew where Blakely was. Findlater laughed and nonchalantly remarked, "Oh, he's all right," before saying that Blakely wasn't with him. Ellis then contacted Cussen, asking him to drive her to Findlater's flat.

Ellis continued, "He drove me there, and I saw the car outside. I was furious and rang the doorbell, but they would not answer it, though I rang and rang." She proceeded to dial their number from a nearby call box, only to have them abruptly disconnect the call. Frustrated and angry, she resorted to smashing the windows of

Blakely's car. Reflecting on that moment, she confessed, "I was simply furious. I wanted to see David – I wanted to tell him to jump in the lake or something silly of that kind."

The next day, Ellis said she went to Tanza Road and just watched Findlater's flat. She recollected: "Like a typically jealous woman. I thought there was something going on that I should know about." Through an open window, she overheard what appeared to be a party, hearing Blakely's voice and a woman's laughter. That night, she saw a light go on in the Findlater's nanny's room. Around 12:30 a.m., the blind was pulled down. The party was still in full swing, but she could no longer hear Blakely or the giggling woman. Stevenson asked Ellis: "Rightly or wrongly, what did you think was happening?" Ellis replied, "I thought it might be that David was up to one of his old tricks again. I thought he might be having an affair with the nanny."

Ellis returned home that night but said she didn't sleep. She told the hushed courtroom: "I was very upset, and I had the peculiar idea that I wanted to kill David." Stevenson enquired, "We have heard in evidence that you took a revolver to Hampstead [to The Magdala]. Is that true?" Ellis answered, "I don't really know. I was very upset." She went on to recount the harrowing moments when she approached Blakely outside The Magdala pub the following evening and fired the fatal shots.[12]

Cross-examining, Humphreys asked Ellis just one question: "When you fired that revolver at close range into the body of David Blakely, what did you intend to do?" With unwavering conviction, Ellis declared, "It is obvious. When I shot him, I intended to kill him." Humphreys concluded his brief cross-examination, expressing his gratitude to Ellis for her cooperation before resuming his seat. His ten-second cross-examination stands as one of the shortest on record in any murder trial.

The trial lasted a mere two days. Strikingly unconventional for murder trials in the UK, both the prosecution and defence opted against presenting any closing arguments. Mr Justice Havers assumed the responsibility of summing-up the case, directly addressing the jury, which was comprised of ten men and two women. He emphasized that, even if they were to accept every aspect of Ellis's testimony, it failed to establish any viable defence against the charge of murder. He continued, "It is my duty to direct you the evidence in this case does not support a verdict of manslaughter on the grounds of provocation. It is not therefore open to you to bring in a verdict of manslaughter on the grounds of provocation."[13] He found no evidence that Ellis was insane at the time of the crime and added that jealousy was no defence under the law to the charge of murder.

The jury retired. They returned after just twenty-five minutes and found Ruth Ellis guilty of the murder of David Blakely. During sentencing, Mr Justice Havers, addressing Ellis, remarked: "The jury has convicted you of murder. In my view it was the only verdict possible."[14] Ellis received the jury's verdict with composure. Moments later, a fleeting smile graced her lips as she glanced towards the prison nurse. She was escorted to the holding cells, where the judge granted her father permission to visit her.

Ruth Ellis was handed a mandatory death sentence and transferred to Holloway Prison. There she awaited her execution by hanging, scheduled for the morning of the 13th of July. There was no appeal by her legal team.

Ellis's mother, Bertha, later said that her daughter told her she didn't want her sentence commuted to manslaughter. She recollected Ellis telling her, "It's no use, mother, I was sane when I did it. And I meant to do it, and I won't go to prison for ten years or some and come out old and finished."[15]

Ellis garnered widespread support throughout the nation, with figures such as Ellis's local MP, George Rogers, advocating clemency. Rogers spoke for many observers when he said: "She's a mother and a woman and to hang a woman is abhorrent to millions."[16] The renowned novelist Raymond Chandler agreed commenting, "I am deeply shocked that this woman will be hanged until death. And in Britain."

Volunteers organized a petition, signed by over 50,000 people, to send to Home Secretary Gwilym Lloyd George. Ellis's new solicitor, John Bickford, was inundated with phone calls from people asking him to demand a reprieve from the Home Secretary and wrote a seven-page letter to the Home Secretary setting out the grounds for a reprieve. He explained that Ellis was an alcoholic so couldn't be fully responsible for the murder.[17] However both the petition and Bickford's letter were rejected, and, on the 11th of July, Gwilym Lloyd George affirmed that the execution would proceed as planned on the 13th.

On the 12th of July, solicitor Victor Mishcon and his clerk, Leon Simmons, visited Ellis at Holloway Prison to draw up her will. During their discussion, Ellis disclosed that Desmond Cussen had not only supplied her with the murder weapon but also showed her how to use it the weekend before the murder. After the meeting, Mishcon drove straight to the Home Office with this new information. The Home Secretary controversially ruled that this made no difference to the verdict, and even showed the murder was premeditated.

At 8:45 a.m. the next morning, Albert Pierrepoint, the appointed public executioner, along with his assistant, roused Ellis from her cell. Beneath a crucifix adorning her cell wall, she took communion. She declined breakfast but accepted a glass of brandy offered by a wardress. While drinking it, she asked, "Will they blindfold me?"[18] Learning that a white hood would be placed over her head, she made her way to the execution chamber, covering the short distance with measured steps.

Beyond the prison walls, a congregation numbering hundreds of people had assembled. Numerous voices rose in protest against the death penalty, while others prayed. The impending execution marked a rare instance of the implementation of capital punishment upon a woman in the United Kingdom, where 90 per cent of women sentenced to death ultimately received reprieves.

Some remained optimistic that Ellis's documented suffering and emotional turmoil, stemming from Blakely's mistreatment, could serve as compelling grounds for a commutation of her sentence. However, systemic inadequacies within the legal system at the time failed to accommodate women's experiences of gendered equality.

At 9:17 a.m., a notice was displayed outside the prison walls, officially confirming Ruth Ellis's execution by hanging. According to staff at Holloway Prison, she was "the calmest woman who ever went to the gallows". The aftermath of her execution galvanized widespread support for the abolition of the death penalty in the United Kingdom, which was halted ten years later. Notably, Ellis's case etched an indelible mark in history as she became the last woman to receive the death penalty in the United Kingdom.

Desmond Cussens subsequently emigrated to Australia and died in 1991. He denied ever giving Ellis the gun with which she shot David Blakely. In 2003, Ruth's sister, Muriel Jakubait, launched a posthumous appeal against Ellis's sentence, asking for it to be commuted to manslaughter owing to undue provocation and diminished responsibility. The appeal failed, the court ruling that the verdict was consistent with the law as enforced at that time.[19]

Ruth Ellis's tragic story and controversial end has inspired numerous books, plays, TV dramas, and documentaries, as well as the movie *Dance With a Stranger* (1985), starring Miranda Richardson as Ruth Ellis and Rupert Everett as David Blakely.

---

[1] *Watford Observer* – "A Fine Day for a Hanging" https://www.watfordobserver.co.uk/news/nostalgia/crimelibrary/ruthellis/
[2] *Crime Magazine*, 29 February 2012 – "Ruth Ellis: Love, Lust and Death on the Gallows"

[3] *Birmingham Gazette*, 29 April 1955 – "I Saw Model Shoot my Friend"

[4] *Liverpool Echo*, 11 April 1955 – "Man Found Shot Near Public-House"

[5] *Evening Post*, 20 June 1955 – "Murder? Not Guilty Says Blonde"

[6] *Evening Standard*, 20 June 1955 – "Model Tells Jury of Shooting Drama"

[7] *Birmingham Evening Mail*, 20 June 1955 – "Woman Was in an Emotional Prison – QC"

[8] *Evening Standard*, 20 June 1955 – "I Took the Gun and Shot Him"

[9] *The Daily Telegraph*, 21 June 1955 – "Shot Lover: Models Says, 'I Intended to Kill Him'"

[10] *Birmingham Evening Mail*, 20 June 1955 – "Disturbed in Mind"

[11] *Evening Standard,* 20 June 1995 – "It Was My Turn to Become Jealous – Model Tells Jury"

[12] *Evening Standard*, 20 June 1955 – "Models Tells of Shooting"

[13] *Evening Standard*, 21 June 1995 – "The Love and Jealousy of Ruth Ellis"

[14] *Evening Standard*, 21 June 1955 – "Death Sentence Passed on Model"

[15] *Sunday Dispatch*, 26 June 1955 – "Woman Who Wants to Die"

[16] *Daily Herald*, 1 July 1995 – "I Begged Ruth Ellis to Ask for Mercy – MP"

[17] *Daily Herald*, 11 July 1955 – "Ruth Ellis Will Know Today"

[18] *Daily Mirror*, 14 July 1955 – "The Last Hours of Ruth Ellis"

[19] *Daily Mail*, 9 November 2003 – "Hanged Ruth Ellis Appeal Dismissed"

Death Wish

Gary Gilmore was arrested and charged with the robbery and murder of two men in Utah in 1976. The case quickly gained widespread media attention not only for the senseless nature of the murders – both men complied but were killed regardless – but also for Gilmore's unprecedented request for the death penalty following his conviction. His insistence on being executed and refusal to appeal his sentence led to a moral dilemma that propelled the case into the annals of criminal history.

"Gary Gilmore was perhaps the only death-row inmate to ever appear in person before the Utah Supreme Court. He stood there and told them, 'Don't you have the guts to carry out the sentence? I'm willing to accept it.'"

Jack Ford, KSL reporter

On the night of the 19th of July 1976, 24-year-old Max Jensen was working the night shift at the Sinclair gas station located at 175 E. 800 N, Orem, Utah. Around 11:20 p.m., a concerned customer contacted the police, reporting the absence of staff at the station. By the time the police arrived, the customer had discovered Max's lifeless body in the restroom. He had sustained two gunshot wounds to the head, and the money changer typically worn by attendants was missing from his belt.[1] It was estimated that around $150 was missing.[2]

The following evening, Debbie Bushnell was in her home attached to the City Center Motel in Provo, Utah, where her husband, Bennie, 26, served as manager. Shortly after 10:30 p.m., she heard two gunshots. Alarmed, she rushed into the motel and found her husband lying face down with two bullet wounds to the head. The motel's cash box, containing approximately $100, was conspicuously absent. Debbie promptly contacted both the police and paramedics but, despite their attempts at CPR, Bennie was declared dead on arrival at hospital.

Moments before Bennie was shot, Peter Arroyo, a tourist from California, was standing outside the motel. Through a window, he saw a man with a gun in one hand and the motel's cash box in the other. Two gunshots caused Peter to retreat into the courtyard shadows. Seconds later, the armed man emerged from the motel clutching the cash box and took off in the direction of the Standard gas station on the corner of University and Third.³

Earlier that evening, Martin Ontiveros, a mechanic at the station, had been approached by a dark-haired, bearded man who requested a lube job for his white 1969 Ford pickup. The man seemed drunk and wandered off in the direction of the City Center Motel. The same man reappeared later to pay for the service. Martin noticed that a makeshift, bloodstained bandage was now wrapped around his hand.

Martin had a habit of listening to a police radio scanner, so he knew that a murder had just occurred a couple of blocks away. He jotted down the man's licence number and called the police. Patrolman Ned Lee responded and noticed a trail of blood leading to or from a nearby bush. Hidden in the bush was a .22-calibre pistol.

Less than an hour later, police received another call, this time from a woman named Brenda Nicol. She told them that her cousin, Gary Gilmore, recently released from prison on parole into her custody, had called her and said that he needed immediate medical assistance after accidentally shooting himself in the hand. He said he couldn't go to hospital and asked her to pick him up at a friend's house. Instead, Brenda decided to call the police and report the incident.

The motel where the crime occurred was somewhere Gilmore had called home for a significant period. When Brenda heard the news of Bennie Bushnell's murder, she couldn't shake off the dreadful feeling that, despite her hopes that Gary might be rehabilitated, her cousin was the elusive killer sought by the police. Her fears soon proved justified. She would later recall, "I really felt guilty about the men Gary killed."⁴

Around 1:30 a.m., unaware that the police were already waiting, Gary Gilmore was arrested near the house of Kathryne Baker, the mother of his girlfriend Nicole, in Pleasant Grove, some twelve miles north of Provo. Detectives had already begun exploring the similarities between Bennie Bushnell's murder and Max Jensen's homicide the night before. Both victims were found face down with two gunshot wounds to the head. Moreover, they had both been killed with a .22 pistol, the same type of gun found by Patrolman Lee.

Later that day, Gilmore was formally charged with the murders of Max and Bennie. Judge J. Gordon Knudson instructed that Gilmore's mental competence to stand trial be assessed.[5] Gilmore subsequently underwent psychiatric evaluation at Utah State Hospital.

On the 21st of August, Gilmore was judged competent to stand trial. He entered pleas of not guilty to both first-degree murder charges. A two-week psychiatric evaluation conducted by Dr John C. Woods and Dr Robert Crist concluded that Gilmore possessed the capacity to fully assist in his defence and comprehend the legal proceedings. When Gilmore appeared in court, his team revealed they intended to pursue an insanity defence.[6]

Gilmore's trial for the murder of Bennie Bushnell, viewed as the strongest of the two cases, began at Provo's Fourth District Court. The trial for the murder of Max Jensen was set for a later date, depending on how long the first trial took. By the 6th of October, a jury composed of nine women, three men, and one alternate juror (in case one of the others became ill) had been selected. In an unprecedented move for Provo City Court, it was declared that, owing to the extensive pre-trial publicity, the jury would be sequestered. Security was tightened, with police stationed inside and outside the courtroom and spectators barred from carrying handbags, bags, or briefcases.[7]

Prosecutor Neal Wooton opened proceedings by asserting that Gilmore had committed the murder of Bennie Bushnell. Wooton recounted that in the process of discarding the murder weapon near the Standard station, Gilmore had accidentally shot himself in the hand. This proved his undoing, as the blood trail Gilmore left was noticed by an observant mechanic (Martin Ontiveros). He called the police, who soon found the murder weapon. The prosecutor continued, "They will tell you that they found a shell casing there." He said that this shell casing matched those found at the motel crime scene.

Michael Esplin, representing Gilmore, chose to forgo an opening statement.

The prosecution's first witness, Peter Arroyo, identified Gary Gilmore as the individual he had seen hastily departing the motel, clutching a gun and the cash box. Arroyo vividly recalled the moment, stating that he stood in the courtyard approximately ten feet away. "He actually stopped when he saw us. I looked right at him. I looked at the gun, and I looked up at his face to see what he was going to do with the gun." According to Arroyo, Gilmore made eye contact with him and then turned, retracing his steps back around the counter.

Mechanic Martin Ontiveros provided further incriminating testimony, positively identifying Gilmore as the individual who had picked up his truck at the station with a visible bloody hand shortly after the motel shooting. Patrolman Ned Lee detailed his discovery of the murder weapon in a bush. Photographic evidence of the gun was entered into evidence and shown to the jury.

Detective William Brown confirmed that the weapon had been dusted for fingerprints. Cross-examining, Esplin asked Brown whether he had found any prints, to which Detective Brown replied that he had found one. Esplin asked, "Did you transmit it to the laboratory?" Detective Brown responded that he did but that they "needed a better comparison". Sensing an opening, Esplin probed further, asking, "In other words they couldn't make a determination?" The detective replied, "Right."[8]

The prosecution summoned FBI agent Gerald Nielsen who confirmed that Gilmore bore a recent gunshot wound on his left hand at the time of his arrest. Drawing on his expertise in ballistics, Nielsen asserted that the gunshot inflicted on Bennie's head and the wound on Gilmore's hand had been caused by the same weapon – the gun discovered by Patrolman Lee.

Dr John M. Morrison, Utah's deputy chief medical examiner, confirmed that Bennie Bushnell's cause of death was a gunshot wound to the head. Dr Morrison's professional opinion, based on the presence of powder burns on Bushnell's skull, was that the gun had been pressed against Bushnell's skull.[9] In an attempt to challenge Dr Morrison's credibility, defence attorney Esplin asked if he had examined the murder weapon. Dr Morrison stood firm, asserting that specific details about the weapon or ammunition were unnecessary for him to draw his conclusions.

The prosecution concluded their case in less than two days. In response, Esplin declared that the defence would not be summoning any witnesses. Gilmore was unhappy with this decision, questioning, "Couldn't we have called somebody? Just for appearance's sake?"

In his closing argument, Esplin contended that the prosecution had failed to present sufficient evidence to establish Gilmore's guilt beyond a reasonable doubt. He suggested that the gun may have discharged accidentally, drawing a parallel with the subsequent incident in which Gilmore tossed the gun into a bush and received a gunshot wound to his hand. Esplin urged the jury, "If you have any reasonable doubt, then find the defendant guilty of a lesser crime or acquit him."[10]

Wooton countered Esplin's argument, maintaining that the prosecution had presented abundant evidence of Gilmore's intent to kill Bushnell. He highlighted Dr Morrison's testimony that the gun had been placed against Bushnell's head, something that couldn't have been done accidentally. Addressing the jury, he concluded, "Think about the case deeply and judge it fairly. Not only judge it fairly for Gary Gilmore but judge it fairly for

Bennie Bushnell, for his widow, for his child, and for a child yet unborn."

Around 10:15 a.m. on the 7th of October, the case was handed over to the jury to decide. By 11:40 a.m., they had given their unanimous verdict: Gary Gilmore was guilty of the murder of Bennie Bushnell. Gilmore displayed no discernible emotion, though he glanced towards his girlfriend, Nicole Baker. They had made up since the fateful row that may have triggered Gilmore's murder spree and she was seated in the gallery behind him. Following the guilty verdict, the jury was instructed to return in the afternoon for the sentencing phase of the trial.[11]

Judge Bullock made clear that the jury's task was to determine whether Gary Gilmore should receive a death sentence or life imprisonment. The prosecution advocated for a death sentence, with Wooton telling the jury that Gilmore had "learned to kill his victims" after a witness to his Oregon robbery had positively identified him. The defence pursued a sentence of life in prison.

Albert Swenson, a chemistry professor at Brigham Young University, testified that after Gary Gilmore's arrest, his blood alcohol content measured less than seven-hundredths of a gram per hundred grams of blood. This test was administered five hours after the shooting. According to Swenson, at the time of the murder, Gilmore would have been under the influence of alcohol, but not unaware of his actions.

Brenda, Gilmore's cousin recalled a phone conversation with Gilmore while he was in jail awaiting trial. She told Gilmore that his mother wanted to know whether the murder charge against him was true. Gilmore admitted, "Tell her that it's true."

Gilmore himself then took the stand and, contrary to all expectations, assumed full responsibility for Bushnell's murder, candidly recounting that he had drunk twelve cans of beer and consumed drugs that night following an argument with his girlfriend Nicole. He admitted entering the motel, brandishing his .22-calibre pistol, and instructing Bushnell to lie face down on the ground. Despite Bushnell's compliance, Gilmore pressed the gun to the back of his head and pulled the trigger. He explained, "I felt like there was no way that what happened could have been avoided. There was no other choice or chance for Mr Bushnell. It was something that couldn't be stopped."[12]

*

Cruelly abused by his parents Frank and Bessie, Gilmore had been in and out of detention of various kinds since the age of 12. His rap sheet included shoplifting, auto theft, delinquency of a minor, burglary, vagrancy, and rape.[13] Released on parole from Oregon State Prison in April, he had just completed 12 years of a 15-year sentence for assault with a deadly weapon.

After Gilmore's release from prison in Oregon – just twelve weeks before the murders – the trajectory of his life appeared positive for a time. However, this changed when he started dating 19-year-old Nicole Baker, who had been married twice before and had two young children. Gilmore became obsessively jealous. He started drinking heavily, taking drugs, and threatening anybody who even dared to say hello to her.

In the lead-up to the two murders, Gilmore fixated on acquiring a 1969 white Ford pickup truck. Val Conlin, owner of a used-car business in Provo, recalled, "It was an absolute obsession. I've never seen anyone want anything so bad in his life." Spencer McGrath, Gilmore's former boss at an insulation factory, revealed a disconcerting motive, stating, "Gary said he wanted the truck so he could steal more." There was a problem: Gilmore couldn't scrape together the $1,895 to buy it. Conlin proposed a solution, urging Gilmore to come up with the down payment.

On the 19th of July, Conlin allowed Gilmore to take the truck, after he promised to have the down payment in two days' time. That night, Gilmore killed Max Jensen in a robbery that netted only $125. The next evening, Gilmore was having trouble with the truck, so he took it to the Standard station. He then walked to the City Center Motel where Bennie Bushnell was robbed and killed.

According to three psychiatrists who evaluated Gilmore after his arrest, he exhibited traits such as "impulsiveness, rationalizations of his behaviour, low frustration tolerance, callousness, and an immediate need for gratification". The diagnosis was indicative of antisocial personality disorder, a condition that might have been exacerbated by the influence of alcohol and drugs. However, Gilmore did not meet Utah state's criteria for insanity.

During his testimony, Gilmore asserted that he had not been completely truthful with the psychiatrists because he had not confessed to the murders. He cited negative experiences with doctors during his time in prison, recounting instances when he had been restrained and subjected to electric shock therapy while chained hand and foot to his bed.[14]

The jury unanimously voted to sentence Gary Gilmore to death for the murder of Bennie Bushnell. Following their decision, Judge Bullock asked Gilmore which method of execution he preferred: hanging or shooting. Gilmore responded, "I prefer to be shot." He joined five other men on Utah's Death Row.[15] Hearing that his defence attorneys intended to appeal his death sentence, Gilmore fired them. He appeared in court on the 2nd of November and told Judge Bullock he wanted his death sentence carried out. "You sentenced me to die. Unless it's a joke or something, I want to go ahead and do it."[16]

The judge ordered that Gilmore should be shot by a firing squad at the Utah State Prison on the 15th of November. He also indefinitely postponed the Jensen trial, which had been scheduled to begin a week earlier. Gilmore's resolute pursuit of his own death played out against the backdrop of the contentious reinstatement of the death penalty in the United States in 1976 (it had been suspended in 1972). A legal battle began that cast a spotlight on the issue of capital punishment and attitudes to it in the Utah state legislature.

Despite Gilmore's steadfast insistence on his own death, his mother, Bessie, and lawyers from the American Civil Liberties Union urged Utah's Supreme Court to delay his execution. These efforts initially proved successful, resulting in multiple postponements. During this time, Gilmore made two suicide attempts while behind bars. He also persuaded Nicole to join him in a suicide pact. She took an overdose of sleeping pills, but a friend found her unconscious and she survived. A new date was eventually set for the 17th of January 1977, making Utah the first state in the Union to resume executions.

Shortly after 8 a.m. Gilmore was escorted from his cell to the execution chamber. He was strapped into a black-upholstered oak chair, with a black hood covering his face and a white target affixed to his heart. His request to be shot standing without a hood, which he deemed more dignified, was denied.

The firing squad was comprised of five volunteers armed with Winchester rifles. One of the rifles held a blank, so that none of the shooters could be certain which of them had fired fatal bullets. The warden read a legal order as Gilmore stared directly at him, calmly stating, "Let's do it." Moments later, the squad opened fire, aiming at his heart.[17]

Gary Gilmore's execution was the first carried out in the US in almost a decade, since that of Luis Monge in a Colorado gas chamber in 1967. Gilmore's death captured national attention, with former KSL reporter Jack Ford recalling, "Gary Gilmore was perhaps the only death-row inmate to ever appear in person before the Utah Supreme Court. He stood there and told them, 'Don't you have the guts to carry out the sentence? I'm willing to accept it.'"[18]

The repercussions of Gilmore's trial transcended the confines of the courtroom and execution chamber, leaving an indelible mark on popular culture. His last words, "Let's do it", inspired the iconic Nike slogan, "Just Do It", and Gilmore's image stared from the cover of *Newsweek* magazine. The case also spawned numerous books – notably the 1979 Pulitzer-Prize-winning true crime novel *The Executioner's Song* by Norman Mailer – a TV film, and the hit song (in the UK) "Gary Gilmore's Eyes" by The Adverts. Gilmore had donated his corneas for transplant surgery and the song was written from the point of view of a patient who had unwittingly received them.

---

[1] *Deseret News*, 20 July 1976 – "Attendant Murdered at Orem Gas Station"

[2] *The Ogden Standard-Examiner*, 21 July 1976 – "Utah Man Arrested After Motel Clerk, Attendant at Station Gunned Down"

[3] *Detroit Free Press*, 12 December 1976 – "He Killed Them So He Wouldn't Kill Me"

[4] *Los Angeles Times*, 11 January 1987 – "10 Years Later, Victims Can't Forget Gary Gilmore: Utah Killer Spurned Appeals, Demanded His Quick Execution"

[5] *Deseret News*, 7 August 1976 – "Defendant Faces Tests"

[6] *The Ogden Standard-Examiner*, 21 August 1976 – "Parolee Will Stand Trial in 2 Murders"

[7] *The Daily Spectrum*, 6 October 1976 – "Gilmore Trial Opens in Provo"

[8] *The Executioner's Song* by Norman Mailer

[9] *The Ogden Standard-Examiner*, 7 October 1976 – "First of Two Death Trials Goes to Jury"

[10] *Deseret News*, 8 October 1976 – "Firing Squad Decreed in Provo Slaying"

[11] *The Capital Journal*, 7 October 1976 – "Parolee Found Guilty in Death"

[12] *Los Angeles Times*, 15 November 1976 – "Utah Killer: 'I Just Take What I Want'"

[13] *Statesman Journal*, 30 July 1976 – "Gilmore's Record"

[14] *Statesman Journal*, 8 October 1976 – "Oregon Prison Parolee Gets Utah Death Term"

[15] *The Sacramento Bee*, 8 October 1976 – "Utah Firing Squad Ordered for Killer"
[16] *The Salt Lake Tribune*, 2 November 1976 – "Convicted Murderer Requests Firing Squad"
[17] *The Guardian*, 18 January 2022 – "Gary Gilmore Gets His Death Wish"
[18] *The Salt Lake Tribune*, 23 October 2004 – "Gilmore's Gun is the Prize for Best Essay"

Justice for the Ripper

Between 1975 and 1980, the women of West Yorkshire lived in fear as a serial killer dubbed the "Yorkshire Ripper" terrorized the area. He killed at least 13 women before he was finally unmasked as Peter Sutcliffe, a married lorry driver. The search for Sutcliffe was among the largest and most expensive manhunts in British history, costing around £4 million. The trial, which began in January 1981, not only unveiled the grim details of Sutcliffe's crimes, but also exposed the systemic shortcomings in the investigation that had allowed him to evade capture for so long.

"The crimes are horrible and sadistic, beyond our ordinary comprehension. Does it mean he must be mad, or just plain evil?"

Sir Michael Havers

Around 10:50 p.m. on the 2nd of January 1981, Sergeant Bob Ring and Police Constable Bob Hydes were conducting routine licence plate checks in Sheffield's red-light district. They came across a brown Rover P6 V8 with false plates in the Light Trades House driveway on Melbourne Avenue, Broomhill. In the driver's seat sat a man with dark, bushy hair, a moustache and beard. He was accompanied by a known sex worker, Olivia Reivers.[1]

The officers were struck by the resemblance between the man and the composite sketch of the serial killer known as the Yorkshire Ripper, who, since 1975, had been targeting sex workers and, more recently, women walking alone at night. The Yorkshire Ripper's method involved brutal assaults, primarily in the red-light districts of West Yorkshire cities. The attacks featured sudden, violent blows to the head, followed by further assaults on the victims' bodies. The Ripper Task Force, established to investigate the murders, had amassed over 30,000 files by this point.[2]

The driver of the car was 35-year-old Peter Sutcliffe and the officers decided to take him in for questioning. Before they set off, Sutcliffe requested permission to urinate in some bushes. He was subsequently transported to Dewsbury police station. Olivia Reivers, reflecting on her interaction with Sutcliffe, commented to the press shortly after Sutcliffe's arrest, "I was in the car with him for about 20 minutes. After only a few minutes, I realized there was something strange about him. He was very nervous."[3]

The next day, Sergeant Robert Ring, acting on a hunch, returned to the scene where Sutcliffe had been arrested. Near the spot where Sutcliffe had purportedly urinated, Ring discovered a knife, hammer, and rope. After Sutcliffe used the toilet at the police station, officers found another weapon in the cistern: a wooden-handled knife.

Following two days of interrogation, Sutcliffe confessed to being the Yorkshire Ripper, providing detailed accounts of the string of murders. He expressed relief, stating, "I'm glad it's all over. I want to tell my wife myself. I don't care about myself, just my family."[4]

On Monday the 5th of January, Sutcliffe appeared at Dewsbury Magistrates Court, charged with the murder of 20-year-old Jacqueline Hill, the Yorkshire Ripper's thirteenth victim. He appeared composed and showed no outward signs of emotion. In the street outside the court, however, an angry crowd of several hundred people had gathered. Some displayed signs advocating Sutcliffe's execution, while others tried to spit at him as he exited the courtroom, his head covered by a blanket.

The following month, on the 20th of February, Sutcliffe faced an additional 12 counts of murder and seven counts of attempted murder. To avoid the scenes that occurred during his initial court appearance in January, he was covertly brought into court at dawn. Citing "special circumstances", the trial was relocated to London's Old Bailey (the Central Criminal Court of England and Wales), less than half a mile from the Whitechapel area where Jack the Ripper operated in the late 19th century.

Access to the courtroom was restricted, with only 50 members of the public admitted. Surviving victims of the Yorkshire Ripper were among those attending. Sutcliffe was represented by James Chadwin and Sidney Levine, while the attorney-general Sir

Michael Havers, the British government's chief law officer, led the prosecution.

On Wednesday, the 29th of April, Peter Sutcliffe entered the courtroom and was escorted to the glass-enclosed wooden prison dock. When asked to enter a plea, he responded, "Not guilty of murder, but guilty of manslaughter on the grounds of diminished responsibility."[5] Judge Leslie Boreham rejected the plea and ordered the jury of six men and six women to determine whether Sutcliffe was guilty of murder, or the lesser charge, which would result in detention in an institution as opposed to life in prison.

Prior to the start of the trial, detectives had received widespread criticism for their inability to catch Sutcliffe. Detective Constable Andrew Laptew defended the investigation, asserting that criticism was unwarranted. In 1979, Laptew had previously identified Peter Sutcliffe as the Yorkshire Ripper. He had interviewed Sutcliffe after his car had been spotted 46 times in the red-light districts where the serial killer most often operated. Laptew's belief that Sutcliffe was the Yorkshire Ripper was based on various witnesses describing the killer's height, build, hairstyle, and the distinctive gap between his front teeth. However, amidst the investigation of numerous other leads, Laptew's suspicions went unheeded. After the interview, Sutcliffe went on to commit five more attacks, claiming the lives of three additional women.[6]

On the 5th of May, a jury consisting of six men and six women took their seats at the Old Bailey. For the prosecution, Sir Michael Havers provided key details about the murders, controversially observing, "The last six attacks were on totally respectable women."

Havers went on to add that Sutcliffe suffered from paranoid schizophrenia and believed he was on a divine mission to kill sex workers. "He said, in short, that he had messages from God to kill prostitutes and that what he was doing was a divine mission."

Havers disclosed that psychiatrists examining Sutcliffe agreed that he was temporarily insane during the murders, leaving it to the jury to determine his state of mind. Havers added, "The doctors might have been deceived by this man, that he fought to pull the wool over their eyes with a clever and premeditated story."[7] Havers pointed to evidence supporting this, such as Sutcliffe telling his wife after his arrest (their conversations were recorded) that "if he could make people believe that he was mad, he would do only ten years in a loony bin".[8]

Havers informed the jury that mention of a "divine mission" only surfaced in Sutcliffe's eighth interview with a psychiatrist, emphasizing that in his sixteen-hour confession to police, Sutcliffe had never brought up his "mission". While Havers acknowledged that this didn't disprove Sutcliffe's diminished responsibility plea, he asserted that it presented strong evidence to the contrary.

Havers pointed out that Sutcliffe only sexually assaulted one victim, Helen Rytka. He then read out notes from Sutcliffe's confession, in which he stated that he had not intended to kill his first victim, sex worker Wilma McCann, in October 1975, "but she was mocking me and it grew and grew until I became a beast".

Sutcliffe also said that a motorcycle accident in his late teens, in which he hit his head on a lamppost, might have influenced his subsequent actions, and that his hatred of sex workers began when he was swindled by one in 1969. He also said that he remembered all his victims' names, "They are all in my brain reminding me of what a beast I am. I know I would have gone on and on. And now I am glad I have been caught." Havers then read aloud the rest of the 34-page statement that Sutcliffe had made following his arrest, going into detail about every single murder and attempted murder he had committed.

The prosecution's first witness, Donald Sumner, recounted the motorcycle accident he and Sutcliffe had experienced 16 years earlier. "We had a puncture while we were going along and came off the bike. Peter went into a lamppost and I went sliding down the road." Following Sumner's brief testimony, Sutcliffe's friend

Trevor Birdsall took the stand. He recalled an incident in 1969 when he and Sutcliffe were driving through Bradford's red-light district. Sutcliffe asked him to stop the car and got out. He soon returned and admitted hitting a woman with a stone inside a sock.[9] "I asked him where he had been, and he said he had followed a woman to a house somewhere. He said that he had hit her."[10]

The woman had jotted down Birdsall's number plate and a few days later the police contacted him. Birdsall acknowledged that Sutcliffe was with him in the car but did not mention Sutcliffe's admission. Sutcliffe later told Birdsall he had talked to the police and that everything was all right. Sutcliffe had indeed spoken to the police, confessing to the assault on the woman, who chose not to press charges.

On the night of the 15th of August 1975, Birdsall was in Halifax with Sutcliffe when Sutcliffe spotted Mrs Olive Smelt who was walking home alone after a night out with friends. Sutcliffe got out of his car, followed Olive down a side road, and engaged her in conversation before assaulting her with a hammer and slashing her lower back with a knife. The attack was interrupted and Sutcliffe fled back to his car. Miraculously, Olive survived and reported that her attacker had a Yorkshire accent.

During cross-examination by defence attorney Chadwin, Birdsall noted that when Sutcliffe returned to the car after the attack on Olive and the previous assault on the woman in Bradford, he appeared "remarkably calm". Birdsall further stated that Sutcliffe seemed calm when he informed him a couple of days later that he had spoken with the police. Asked about Sutcliffe's general demeanour, Birdsall described him as generally quiet and somewhat shy, especially around women.

After reading about the attack the following day, Birdsall (who had not witnessed the actual assault) wondered if Sutcliffe could have been responsible. However, he did not to report his suspicions to the police at this time, or when news of the Yorkshire

Ripper's subsequent murders appeared in the newspapers and on television.

In June 1979 Birdsall heard an audio recording sent to police by a man calling himself "Wearside Jack". The tape, which was widely broadcast, was initially thought to be from the Yorkshire Ripper. (Twenty-five years later the message was revealed to be a hoax perpetrated by John Samuel Humble, who was sentenced to eight years in prison for perverting the course of justice.) The voice on the tape sounded nothing like Sutcliffe, allaying Birdsall's concerns.

However, Birdsall's suspicions of Sutcliffe intensified after the murder of 20-year-old Leeds University student Jacqueline Hill, the Yorkshire Ripper's thirteenth victim, on the 17th of November 1980. Following the murder, the police released a description of the vehicle they believed the killer was driving that matched Sutcliffe's car at the time, a brown Rover 3.5 saloon. Birdsall testified that on the 25th of November, he wrote an anonymous letter to the police conveying his suspicions, which was ignored. The following day, he visited Bradford police station in person. Although the police made a report of the ensuing conversation, it inexplicably went missing.

Another witness, Ronald Barker, who lived next door to the parents of Sutcliffe's wife, Sonia, had accompanied Sutcliffe to pubs on several occasions during 1977. Returning home after one outing, he recounted falling asleep in the car. On waking up, he realized they were in a run-down part of Leeds called Chapeltown, and Barker asked why. He remembered, "Peter was driving, and I think he mentioned something about this being Ripper Country. The car stopped, and Peter got out." Barker said that Sutcliffe was gone for about twenty minutes. Unbeknownst to Barker, during two of these excursions, Sutcliffe had killed one woman and severely injured another. During cross-examination by the defence, Barker stated that Sutcliffe never appeared different on returning to the car, and that he still had difficulty believing Sutcliffe could be the Yorkshire Ripper.

Testimony was then presented about the knife, hammer, and rope discovered near where Sutcliffe was arrested, and the knife in the lavatory cistern at the police station. Detective Sergeant Desmond O'Boyle, who had interviewed Sutcliffe on the day of his arrest, then took the stand. He said Sutcliffe denied being the Yorkshire Ripper and claimed he was out that night because he was fed up being "nagged" by his wife at home.[11] O'Boyle said that Sutcliffe was initially reluctant to provide a blood sample, prompting him to ask, "Why? Are you the Ripper?" Sutcliffe denied the accusation and ultimately consented to the test.

Following O'Boyle's testimony, the court adjourned for the day. The following morning, hundreds of protesters had assembled outside the Old Bailey. Several brandished signs accusing Sir Michael Havers of condoning the murder of sex workers and perpetuating harmful stereotypes by drawing a distinction between them and "respectable women" during his opening statement.

The proceedings recommenced at 9 a.m., and attention shifted to Detective John Boyle, one of the officers to whom Sutcliffe confessed being the Yorkshire Ripper. Boyle recounted the unforgettable moment when Sutcliffe uttered, "About the Yorkshire Ripper. Well, it's me," and described how, after Sutcliffe was charged with the murder of Jacqueline Hill, he said, "I am glad I have been apprehended because I was totally out of my mind when I committed this and other acts."

Boyle said that Sutcliffe went on to describe each of his murders, telling the detective, "I had the urge to kill any woman. The urge inside me to kill girls was now practically uncontrollable. It sounds a bit evil now."[12] In his confession, Sutcliffe said he had an urge to kill sex workers and felt satisfaction after each murder. Boyle testified he believed that Sutcliffe's satisfaction came from "one less prostitute" in the world.

Responding to a question from Chadwin, Boyle acknowledged that, in his experience, Sutcliffe was among the easiest and most cooperative suspects he had ever interviewed. Despite being given the opportunity to have a solicitor present for his confession, Sutcliffe politely declined.[13]

During the trial, it emerged that detectives had interviewed Sutcliffe nine times concerning the Yorkshire Ripper murders before his final arrest. Additionally, his car had been observed in the red-light districts of Leeds, Bradford, Sheffield, and Manchester on 60 occasions. Sutcliffe explained that he had avoided arrest because his wife had provided him with alibis for the murders. "These occasions were weeks – sometimes months – after the event. My wife would agree that we were at home as we were practically all of the time."[14]

Prison hospital officer John Edward Leach, assigned to monitor Sutcliffe, testified that on the 28th of January, he noted that Sutcliffe refused to discuss the murders, except to mention that he was "possessed" while committing them. Less than a week later, Sutcliffe expressed a desire to "rid the country of prostitutes". Leach testified that, during a visit by his wife, Sonia, Sutcliffe had said he would be in prison for a long time unless he could "convince people" he was "mad". On the 11th of February, Leach documented Sutcliffe's claim of hearing voices in his head.[15] Another officer, Frederick Edwards, said that Sutcliffe had informed him that doctors considered him disturbed, a diagnosis Sutcliffe allegedly found amusing. Edwards recalled Sutcliffe rocking back and forth on his chair, asserting that he was as normal as anyone else.

Sir Michael Havers then declared that the prosecution had presented all their witnesses and rested their case.

It was now the defence's turn. In an unexpected twist, James Chadwin summoned Sutcliffe to testify. Clad in a light-grey suit, an open-necked blue shirt, and light-brown boots, Sutcliffe admitted to killing thirteen women and attempting to kill seven others. Responding to his attorney's enquiries, Sutcliffe recounted that, at the age of 20, while working as a gravedigger, he had heard "God's voice" speaking to him.[16]

When asked if he ever doubted the divine nature of the voice, Sutcliffe admitted to briefly questioning it after reading in a newspaper that he had killed a woman who was not a sex worker. He explained: "I was convinced by the messages I received that they were prostitutes. I felt it was all right and was persuaded I wasn't wrong because God doesn't make mistakes. The newspapers do."[17]

Sutcliffe informed the jury that he had been grappling with depression since around 1965 or 1966, triggered by a motorcycle accident. His depressive state intensified when, in 1969, he temporarily broke up with Sonia, then his girlfriend (they did not marry until 1974). He recounted, "I was so depressed, in fact, that this led to my first encounter with a prostitute."[18] On this occasion, a sex worker refused to return £5 from the £10 he paid, leading Sutcliffe to call the assignation off. Despite this, she took his money. After returning home, he claimed to hear the voice of God blaming sex workers for all his troubles.

Four weeks later, Sutcliffe attacked his first sex worker while cruising with his friend, Trevor Birdsall. When Chadwin asked why, Sutcliffe responded, "Because it was what I had to do. It was my mission. I had been told they were the scum of the earth and had to be got rid of."[19] From September 1969 until 1975, Sutcliffe said he had not harmed any sex workers, adding that he took a night job to "keep away" from his "problem". Before attacking Anna Rogulskyj – who survived – on the 5th of July 1975, he claimed to have heard voices reminding him of his mission.

Sutcliffe then went into detail about his other murders and attempted murders. He said that he had no fear of being caught. He believed he was guided and protected by God. He had "lost count" of how many times police had interviewed him but said that it was "many times". Recalling an encounter with an officer who seemed convinced of his guilt, Sutcliffe said: "One of them said they knew it was me and that he had no doubts at all. But he went away. One officer had a picture in front of him with my footprint on it."[20]

Sutcliffe spent the entire day in the witness box. Resuming his testimony next morning, Chadwin questioned why he hadn't mentioned his alleged divine mission when confessing to detectives. Sutcliffe insisted, "I didn't want them to find out about the mission. I was by no means convinced that it was finished."[21] Chadwin asked Sutcliffe if he thought he was "mad" or whether there was anything "wrong" with him mentally. He responded that he didn't, adding that he didn't think he would spend less time in custody if he was deemed to be mentally ill.

Cross-examining, Havers probed inconsistencies in Sutcliffe's testimony. He questioned the varying explanations Sutcliffe had given police and doctors regarding the attack on his first murder victim, Wilma McCann, on the 30th of October 1975. Sutcliffe initially claimed to police that he had killed her in a fit of temper but later asserted to doctors that he had left home that night with the intent to kill a sex worker. Havers asked, "Was it because you realized that what you had said about McCann would not be of much help to you if you wanted to pull the wool over the doctors' eyes?" Sutcliffe insisted it wasn't, stating that he hadn't told police the truth.

Disputing Sutcliffe's assertion that God had instructed him to kill sex workers, Havers highlighted the fact that six of his victims were not sex workers, suggesting a broader motivation. He stated: "Had you got to the stage where your lust for killing meant that everybody that you saw, if in a quiet spot, could meet their death at your hands?" Sutcliffe denied this. Havers then asked him why he never killed his victims in his car. Sutcliffe replied that there would have been evidence all over the car, to which Havers responded, "Well done. Stop there. There would be blood all over the car. It would make your detection more likely. A messy job to get rid of it. That's what I'm getting at. Your capacity for control."[22]

By this observation, Havers intended the court to understand that Sutcliffe was fully aware that what he was doing was wrong.

After Sutcliffe concluded his testimony, Chadwin called on Dr Hugo Milne, a forensic consultant psychiatrist at Bradford Hospital. With experience of examining approximately two hundred killers and a keen awareness of attempts to feign mental illness, Dr Milne's opinion was that Sutcliffe was not malingering, but afflicted with schizophrenia of a paranoid type. A 35-page report outlining symptoms of schizophrenia, including uncontrollable impulses, preoccupation, and paranoia regarding sex workers, grandiose ideas, hallucinations, depression, misidentification, and over-controlled behaviour – an abnormal ability to remain completely calm in the most stressful of situations – was read out for the jury. Chadwin then asked Dr Milne whether he considered Sutcliffe a danger. Dr Milne bluntly replied, "Not dangerous. Extremely dangerous."[23]

During cross-examination by Harry Ognall for the prosecution, Dr Milne acknowledged that Sutcliffe's claim of hearing God while working as a gravedigger fifteen years earlier had never been disclosed until he spoke with psychiatrists after his arrest. Ognall questioned whether Sutcliffe might have been prompted to discuss such messages by the nature of the psychiatrists' questions. Dr Milne admitted the possibility of Sutcliffe attempting to deceive but maintained his belief in the sincerity of Sutcliffe's statements.

Following Dr Milne's testimony, the defence called Dr Malcolm MacCulloch, the medical director of Park Lane special hospital in Liverpool. Like Dr Milne, he attested to Sutcliffe's paranoid schizophrenia, having reached this diagnosis in just half an hour. He said he diagnosed it as soon as Sutcliffe told him that Manchester was a "wicked place" and that he needed to go to the city and kill a sex worker.[24] He outlined the eight "first-rank signs" aiding in his diagnosis, noting that Sutcliffe exhibited four, including bodily hallucinations, influence of thought, delusional perception, and passivity.

The trial entered its third week on the 18th of May with the defence presenting their final witness: Dr Terence Kay, a consultant forensic psychiatrist specializing in prisoners at Leeds and Wakefield prisons. Dr Kay also diagnosed Sutcliffe with paranoid schizophrenia after eight interviews, stating in court, "I felt safe in the diagnosis, but was uneasy because of other factors." When discussing the murders with Sutcliffe, Dr Kay noted a discrepancy between Sutcliffe's nonchalant demeanour and the gravity of the topic. Additionally, prison officers, who had continuous contact with Sutcliffe, informed Dr Kay that Sutcliffe was "out to fool them all".[25]

With the defence resting, it was time for closing arguments. Havers posed the jury a key question: "The crimes are horrible and sadistic, beyond our ordinary comprehension. Does it mean he must be mad, or just plain evil?" He cast doubts on Sutcliffe's claim of hearing voices from God, suggesting this was merely a convenient excuse.

In his closing arguments for the defence, Chadwin said to the jury, "If you are persuaded by the evidence that it is more probable than not that, at the time of the killings, Sutcliffe was suffering from a disease of mind that subsequently impaired his responsibility, then that is enough." Chadwin painted Sutcliffe as "a man with a diseased mind" who genuinely believed he was on a mission from God to kill sex workers. He also refuted that there was any kind of underlying sexual motivation in the murders.[26]

After five hours and fifty-five minutes, the jury returned with a majority verdict of 10 − 2, which the judge accepted. Peter Sutcliffe was found guilty on all thirteen murder counts and seven attempted murder counts. Judge Boreham sentenced him to life in prison with a recommendation that he serve at least thirty years.

Despite this, the judge expressed little likelihood of Sutcliffe ever being released. Some victims' relatives, including Doreen Hill, mother of victim Jacqueline Hill, called for the death penalty. She commented, "I would like him to be hanged. I could kill him

Who Wielded the Axe?

A portrait of Lizzie Borden, c.1890.

A cover of the *Illustrated Police News* dramatically depicts Lizzie Borden's acquittal on 20 June 1893.

The hatchet head that could have been the weapon used in the 1892 murders of Andrew Borden and his second wife Abby.

The Borden family home in 1892.

VIEW OF THE VICINITY OF THE MURDERS.

I. Borden house.
II. Borden barn.
III. The well.
IV. Fence with barbed wire on top.
V. Side entrance.
VI. Churchill residence.
VII. Dr. Bowen's house.
VIII. Dr. Chagnon's house.
IX. Kelley house.
X. Yard from which officers watched the Borden house.
XI. Kelley's barn.
XII. Pear orchard.

A contemporary drawing of the Borden neighbourhood in Fall River, Massachusetts.

Stage actor and model
Evelyn Nesbit, c.1900,
four years before her
marriage to Harry
Kendall Thaw.

Sheet music of a 1913 song that
appears to justify Thaw's
murderous actions.

Architect Stanford White,
a victim of Thaw's jealousy
in June 1906.

Thaw lunching in his cell in Manhattan's "The Tombs"
prison following White's murder. Thaw's wealth
ensured he was treated well.

Brighton Trunk Murderer

The crime scene at 47, Kemp Street, Brighton showing the trunk in which Mancini hid Violet's body.

A police officer displays the trunk Mancini bought in hopes of concealing Violet's murder.

Toni Mancini, pictured here in 1934, did not confess to murder until 1976.

Mancini's partner and victim Violet Saunders, a.k.a Violette Kaye, c.1933.

Crime of Passion

Ruth Ellis with her lover, racing driver David Blakely, at the Little Club, London, 1955.

Official notices of the death of Ruth Ellis, attached to the doors of Holloway Prison, 13 July 1955.

Controversy surrounding the case and the verdict attracted large crowds on the day Ruth Ellis was hanged.

Death Wish

Double murderer Gary Gilmore arrives at court in Utah under guard, December, 1976.

Gilmore's drawing of his girlfriend Nicole Baker and her child. The text reads: "LADY MADONNA LITTLE MOTHER MY ELF MY WIFE O, MY LIFE!"

Reporters gather around the chair in which Gilmore sat to face a firing squad on 17 January 1977. The hood Gilmore wore is draped over the back of the exhibit.

THE RIPPER'S VICTIMS

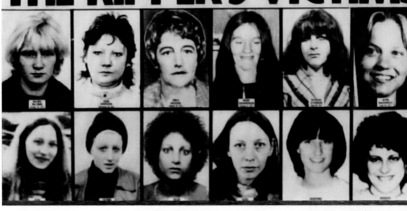

Twelve of Yorkshire Ripper Peter Sutcliffe's
13 murder victims.

The Yorkshire Ripper trial at London's Old
Bailey sparked furious protests, especially
by female sex workers.

Serial killer Sutcliffe pictured
before his arrest.

The Dingo Trial

The discovery of Lindy's daughter's jacket helped prove that a dingo was the culprit.

Lindy Chamberlain faces the press on 21 August 1989, eleven months after she and husband Michael were finally cleared of killing their child.

Michael and Lindy Chamberlain display a photo of mother and baby on the steps of the Alice Springs courthouse, February 1981.

The Little Girl Murderer

Murder suspect Tsutomu Miyazaki is escorted to Tokyo District Court, 20 August 1989.

Police investigate the site in Itsukaichi, Tokyo, where one of Miyazaki's victim's remains was found.

Traders were not slow to cash in on the furore surrounding Simpson's trial for the murders of his ex-wife Nicole and her friend Ron Goldman.

Police mugshot of football star and actor O.J. Simpson.

A fleet of patrol cars follows the white Ford Bronco containing Simpson in a slow-speed chase, 17 June 1994.

O.J. Simpson and Nicole at the opening of the Harley Davidson Cafe, NYC, 19 October 1993.

myself."[27] At the time, capital punishment in the UK had been suspended; it was abolished in 1998.

Sutcliffe commenced his life sentence at HM Prison Parkhurst, but in March 1984, he was transferred to Broadmoor Hospital, a high-security psychiatric facility in Berkshire, England. Despite being found sane by the jury, Sutcliffe had received a further diagnosis of paranoid schizophrenia during his incarceration. Home Secretary Leon Brittan informed Parliament of the move, citing Sutcliffe's deteriorating mental condition, which posed a potential threat to prison staff.[28]

Given the nature of his crimes and the danger he presented to fellow inmates, Sutcliffe was only allowed minimal contact with other prisoners. Despite these measures, he experienced multiple attacks, including a strangulation attempt and a stabbing incident that resulted in damage to his right eye. Throughout the years, Sutcliffe made various unsuccessful attempts to appeal his sentence and secure parole. In 2010, the High Court imposed a whole life tariff on Sutcliffe, ensuring he would never be released.

On the 12th of November 2020, aged 74, Peter Sutcliffe passed away at the University Hospital of North Durham. An inquest attributed his death to complications related to COVID-19, noting that he had refused to shield in prison despite having multiple underlying health conditions.

---

[1] *The Yorkshire Post*, 28 March 2019 – "How and Where Was the Yorkshire Ripper Caught?"

[2] UPI, 7 January 1981 – "Ripper Case Came Down to Police on the Beat"

[3] *The Ottawa Citizen*, 6 January 1981 – "Ripper Suspect 'Model Son'"

[4] UPI, 6 May 1981 – "Yorkshire Ripper Murders Described"

[5] *Daily Press*, 29 April 1981 – "Sutcliffe Says He Is Yorkshire Ripper"

[6] UPI, 4 May 1981 – "A Detective Who Wrote a Report in 1979 Naming Peter Sutcliffe"

[7] *The Guardian*, 23 May 1981 – "The Sudden Dilemma of the Prosecution"

[8] *The Daily Telegraph*, 9 May 1981 – "Sutcliffe Spoke of Deal Over Trial, Says Prison Officer"

[9] *Western Daily Press*, 7 May 1981 – "Sutcliffe's Road Crash"

[10] *Manchester Evening News*, 7 May 1981 – "My Pub-Crawl Nights Out with Sutcliffe"

[11] *The Daily Telegraph*, 8 May 1981 – "Victim Sits Quietly as Old Bailey Hears of the 'Shy, Quiet, Unaggressive Man'"

[12] *Hull Daily News*, 8 May 1981 – "The Ripper: I Had Urge to Kill"

[13] *Evening Post*, 8 May 1981 – "The Ripper Said He Was So Sorry"

[14] *Western Daily Press*, 9 May 1981 – "The Ripper's Offer to Set His Wife Free"

[15] *Huddersfield Daily Examiner*, 9 May 1981 – "Killer Laughed at Doctors When They Thought him Mad"

[16] *Cambridge Evening News*, 11 May 1981 – "Ripper: I Heard Voice of God"

[17] *Birmingham Evening Mail*, 11 May 1981 – "Ripper in Box"

[18] *Evening Standard*, 11 May 1981 – "The First Time I Met Sonia – on Valentine's Day"

[19] *Birmingham Evening Mail*, 11 May 1981 – "I Heard Voice so Many Times – I Had to Go On"

[20] *Daily Post*, 12 May 1981 – "It Was a Miracle the Police Didn't Catch Me Earlier"

[21] *Huddersfield Daily Examiner*, 12 May 1981 – "Killings Were on God's Signal, Claims Ripper"

[22] *The Guardian*, 13 May 1981 – "Nothing Wrong With My Mind, Says Sutcliffe"

[23] *The Daily Telegraph*, 14 May 1981 – "Ripper's Madness Was Obvious to Suspicious Psychiatrist"

[24] *Manchester Evening News*, 15 May 1981 – "Doctor Tells of City Link Over Ripper 'Illness'"

[25] *Western Daily Press*, 19 May 1981 – "Voice Said No to Sutcliffe Suicide Bid"

[26] *The Daily Telegraph*, 20 May 1981 – "Is Ripper Mad or Just Plain Bad? Asks Prosecution"

[27] *Huddersfield Daily Examiner*, 23 May 1981 – "Ripper Faces a Life of Isolation in Prison"

[28] UPI, 27 March 1984 – "Yorkshire Ripper Transferred to Mental Hospital"

The Dingo Trial

In 1980, while on a family camping trip in the Australian Outback, Lindy Chamberlain claimed that her nine-week-old daughter, Azaria, had been snatched from their tent by a dingo. Her account captured the public's imagination and thrust the case into the media spotlight. The narrative took a dark turn as Lindy found herself accused of murdering her own child. Her trial became a national spectacle and the fodder for cheap jokes, before eventually exposing flaws in the forensic investigation and Australian legal system.

"The dingo had its shoulder halfway out of the tent and was shaking very vigorously and I thought it might have had a shoe or something and I called out to get out of the tent."

Lindy Chamberlain

On the 16th of August 1980, Lindy and Michael Chamberlain along with their three children – two-month-old Azaria, four-year-old Reagan, and six-year-old Aiden – set up camp at Uluru (formerly Ayers Rock), a sandstone monolith within the Northern Territory's Uluru-Kata Tjuta National Park. That weekend, the campsite hosted two or three hundred people, and the Chamberlains, seasoned campers, made good use of their limited space by arranging their sleeping bags head-to-toe.

Originating from the western Queensland town of Mount Isa, where Michael served as a Seventh Day Adventist minister, the Chamberlain family went exploring the next morning, driving to Maggie Springs, a natural waterhole. While taking in the view, Lindy observed a dingo "standing silently, watching us all".[1] The family returned to the campsite, and Michael recalled, "We put Azaria to bed in her carry basket. The barbecue was about 20 metres from our tent where our second child, Reagan, was asleep."

According to Michael, he and Lindy were standing around the barbecue beneath a shelter when he heard what sounded like a whimper coming from their tent. "We spun around and saw a shape just like a dingo slinking out of the tent." Michael and Lindy later said it appeared to have something in its mouth, but it was too dark to see clearly.[2] The couple chased after the animal, but it vanished into the night. Finding the tent empty, Lindy yelled, "Has anybody got a torch, a dingo's got my baby!"

Campers grabbed flashlights and began searching the area as word of the disaster spread. Police from Alice Springs arrived, followed by rangers and trackers. They were assisted by sniffer dogs and more than a hundred tourists who were camping in the area. A police spokesman commented, "There are dingo lairs everywhere. If the baby has been taken into a cave, the possibility of recovery is almost nil."

On the 25th of August, Azaria's jumpsuit, disposable nappy, onesie, and booties were discovered by tourists in a rock crevice some 600 metres from the spot where the Chamberlain family had been camping. The items were torn and bloodstained and found not far from several dingo lairs.[3]

As the search for Azaria focused on the area where her clothing had been found, the Chamberlains found themselves the target of local rumours that they had killed their daughter. Lindy complained to *The Sydney Morning Herald*, "The latest rumour going around is that my husband has been charged with the baby's murder and that my baby was a sacrifice for our religion."[4] The couple's religious beliefs were also focused on in various prejudicial ways. It was even suggested that the name "Azaria" meant "sacrifice in the wilderness", although the Chamberlains said it meant "Helped by God", which is correct.

In December 1980, an inquest into Azaria's death was held, and Magistrate Denis Barritt of Alice Springs concluded that Azaria was attacked by a wild dingo in her family's tent while asleep, clearing Lindy and Michael of any responsibility. Barritt also noted that Azaria's body was taken from the dingo's possession and disposed of by an unknown person or persons.[5]

However, after police discovered what appeared to be traces of blood in the Chamberlain's car Chief Minister and Attorney General Paul Everingham filed a motion in November 1981 to overturn the inquest's findings. A second inquest commenced in Alice Springs on the 14th of December 1981, leading to Lindy being charged with murder with Michael as an accessory.

Media coverage of the case was often intrusive. One article from *The Sydney Morning Herald*, on 20 January 1981, summed this up. It was titled "Home Was a Nightmare of Idle Gossip: 'A Medieval Witch-Hunt'". Lindy said her young son, Aidan, was harassed at school, and that rumours began circulating that Azaria was a human sacrifice. One headline from *The Age* on 12 February 1981, read: "Detective: Azaria's Mother Rejected Hypnosis Request." Another from *The Sydney Morning Herald* on 11 February 1981, proclaimed: "Doubts on Dingo Theory." The following week, another story in *The Sydney Morning Herald* was headlined: "The Dingo Case – Fact and Fiction Create a Mystery." There was also speculation that Lindy Chamberlain may have been suffering from post-natal depression – a baseless supposition that would persist for decades. (It was still being voiced – to a Sky News reporter – as a possible explanation for the crime by former Northern Territory chief minister Stephen Hatton as late as 2017.)[6]

Lindy and Michael Chamberlain arrived in Darwin, the capital of the Northern Territory, on the 6th of September 1982, for their trial at the Supreme Court. Owing to the interest the case had excited, the courtroom was equipped with two television cameras broadcasting the proceedings to an adjacent building. The Chamberlains were represented by John Phillips, a prominent Melbourne attorney with experience of over one hundred and fifty murder trials. Ian Barker led the prosecution, and Mr Justice Muirhead presided over the case.[7]

On the 13th of September, Lindy and Michael pleaded not guilty to the charges. Lindy was seven months pregnant, and had earlier requested a postponement, but her request was rejected. Philip Lefevre, Deputy Minister of the Northern Territory Supreme Court, addressed the assembled media, noting, "It is probably the first time in the history of courts in Australia that we have had a situation like this." He specified that only one representative from each media organization would be allowed in the courtroom at any given time and prohibited the use of cameras and recording devices.[8]

In his opening address, Prosecutor Ian Barker accused Lindy of concocting a "fanciful lie" with her claim that Azaria was taken by a dingo during their camping trip. The prosecution posited an alternative narrative: Lindy had killed her daughter in the front passenger seat of the family car, which was parked near their tent.

The prosecution based this hypothesis on the fact that, since the initial inquest, traces of blood had been discovered in the car. Barker said that scientific evidence indicated the blood was freely flowing, and he also noted that there were signs that efforts had been made to clean it up. He added that blood on Azaria's clothing suggested that her throat had been slashed. Addressing each juror, Barker remarked, "If she was killed in the car, one can forget the dingo story." As for Michael, the prosecutor accused him of assisting Lindy to enable her to escape punishment.

Barker said that, in the two inquests, Michael had claimed to have heard a cry resembling "someone being squeezed", but that Lindy did not hear the sound. Despite this, she ran to the tent, declaring that a dingo had taken her baby.[9] Barker admitted that the evidence against the couple was circumstantial. "Quite obviously, if there had been an eyewitness, the case would have been much shorter." Barker refrained from presenting a motive for Lindy killing her daughter, as Australian law did not require the prosecution to establish one.

Camper Sally Lowe took the stand. On the 17th of August, she remembered seeing the Chamberlains at Uluru and, in the evening, having a 45-minute conversation with Lindy in the barbecue area. Lindy, holding Azaria with what Sally described as a "new mum glow", seemed entirely at ease as the barbecue heated up. According to Sally, Lindy showed no signs of distress or unease. Lindy briefly went to put Azaria to sleep in the tent, an absence of only six to ten minutes.[10]

Sally testified that she distinctly heard "the baby cry – quite a serious cry" shortly before Lindy hurried back to the tent, claiming to have seen a dingo slinking away into the night. Sally staunchly rejected the prosecution's assertion that it would have been impossible for her to hear Azaria's cry from the tent.

Sally also vehemently denied the possibility that Azaria might already have been dead during the barbecue. Both she and her husband, Gregory John Lowe, claimed to have had a clear view of Azaria before Lindy took her to the tent, confirming she was alive. Sally then detailed her discovery of a pool of wet blood, some 8 by 16 centimetres in size, inside the tent, along with some blankets that were strewn about. Sally added that Lindy had no traces of blood on her clothing.

During cross-examination, defence attorney Phillips probed the prosecution's suggestion that the Chamberlains had "ample opportunity" to clean their car of blood. Sally adamantly stated that she had not seen the couple near the car. Sally's husband, John Lowe, backed up his wife in his own testimony, recalling his search for Azaria with Michael in the bush. He said that there was nothing in Michael's actions to indicate he "lacked urgency" as the prosecution had implied. He and Michael had searched for about half an hour "at full pelt", occasionally returning to the campsite to see if there was any news.[11]

Judith and William West next took the stand with Judith recounting camping near the Chamberlains that night. She recalled hearing a "throaty growl" from a dingo in the vicinity of their tent. Approximately five to ten minutes later, she heard Lindy's desperate cry that a dingo had taken her baby. Judith also remembered seeing Michael and Lindy walking away together for about ten minutes during the search. When they returned, she observed Michael offering a blessing and saying a prayer, but she stressed that neither of them were holding anything, certainly not the body of their daughter. William corroborated her account, adding that he overheard Michael comforting Lindy with the words, "We can handle this, we are people of God" as she broke down.

Following their testimony, Constable Francis John Morris, the police officer in charge during the search for Azaria at Uluru took the stand. He expressed his belief that a dingo possessed the strength to carry off a baby, citing his own observations of dingoes carrying large kangaroo carcasses in the bush.

Constable Morris described examining Azaria's clothing, discovered about 6 kilometres from the campsite a week after her disappearance. He confirmed finding a few spots of blood on a purple blanket inside the tent where Azaria had been sleeping. Expanding his search, he discovered additional blood spots on a sleeping bag positioned midway between Azaria's bassinet at the back of the tent and the campsite entrance. During cross-examination, Barker questioned Constable Morris about the absence of a pool of blood or blood-soaked fabric, as described by Sally. He denied having observed this.[12]

Senior park ranger Derek Arthur Roff revealed that, two weeks' earlier, he had alerted his superiors about the potential threat posed to children and babies by dingoes in the area. Roff informed the court that he had specifically instructed searchers to be on the lookout for signs of anything buried, as dingoes were known to bury their prey. He also recalled a pre-disappearance conversation with the Chamberlains about a particular dingo that had been spotted near the campsite.

Following Azaria's disappearance, Roff observed drag marks on a sand ridge just above the tent. He informed the court that Aboriginal trackers had traced the tracks of a notably large dingo for approximately 5 kilometres. The trackers identified pawprints that matched those found at the drag marks above the tent, adding a layer of corroborating evidence to the defence's case.[13]

Tourist Edwin Murray Haby testified that the dingo tracks began no more than 100 metres away from the tent. He described the tracks leading to an oval-shaped depression in the sand, which, according to Haby, could have been made by the dingo putting something down. He stated that marks in the depression strongly suggested the presence of an object, possibly a knitted jumper or woven fabric. Adjacent to it, he noted what seemed to be a drop of blood or saliva.[14]

Camper Wallace Victor Goodwin then gave his account of the moment he found items of Azaria's clothing: "The grow suit was laying on its back with the feet facing out towards the roadway. The top of the grow suit was facing in towards the Rock [Uluru]. Its feet were sticking up in the air. The singlet [onesie] was inside the grow suit." When shown a photograph of the clothing on the ground, Goodwin said that the photo was taken after the clothing had been moved, asserting, "That is nothing like the way the clothing was found."[15]

In September 1981, shortly after Azaria's disappearance, detectives had searched the Chamberlains' home, removing possessions the family had taken to Uluru. These items included their yellow car, a Holden Torana, which the prosecution said revealed blood spots upon examination. Detective Sergeant Graeme Charlwood said that Michael Chamberlain informed him about a brown-and-white camera bag used during the camping trip, which he promptly handed over. The prosecution said that traces of blood were discovered in the bag's zipper teeth, claiming that Lindy had hidden the baby's body in the bag. Cross-examining, Phillips asked, "That bag there is what the Crown said is incriminating to the Chamberlains, isn't it?" Charlwood responded that it was.[16]

Subsequently, Keyth Thomas Lenehan was called as a defence witness. He recounted an incident on the 17th of June 1979, when he was involved in a road accident and Michael Chamberlain – who Lenehan did not know – had kindly come to his aid, driving him to

Cairns Base Hospital. Lenehan recalled that he was bleeding from a head wound sustained during the accident, leaving traces of blood in the Chamberlains' car. The defence proposed that the blood discovered in the Chamberlains' vehicle was Lenehan's, challenging the prosecution's theory that Azaria had been killed in the car.

To bolster its case, the prosecution called Dr Kenneth Brown, a forensic dentist. He testified to discovering a "distortion" about 5 centimetres below Azaria's onesie neckline. Dr Brown argued against dingo bites, stating the damage lacked expected additional tooth marks. However, he admitted under cross-examination that holes in Azaria's jumpsuit were consistent with tooth damage and acknowledged the possibility of the front hole resulting from Azaria's body being placed on a ground projection.[17]

Dr Andrew Charles Scott, a forensic biologist, testified that Azaria's blood was evenly distributed around her collar and stained almost all sections of her jumpsuit. He suggested that Azaria had been held generally upright during the blood flow. This was corroborated by Dr Anthony Neal Jones, a pathologist, who said it was his opinion that Azaria's throat had been slashed while she lay on her back. Sergeant Frank Cocks claimed the damage to Azaria's clothing resembled that caused by scissors found in the Chamberlains' car; subsequent examination of the scissors, however, revealed no traces of blood. Their graphic testimony proved extremely upsetting for Michael, prompting an early adjournment by the judge.[18]

The following day, Dr Scott highlighted the scarcity of blood in the Chamberlains' tent – he said it was insufficient to support the idea of a dingo carrying a bleeding baby. He also pointed to the absence of saliva traces on Azaria's clothing and her sleep basket. On the adult mattress from the Chamberlains' tent, he found a small amount of "foetal blood", roughly a teaspoon in volume. When questioned about the source, he acknowledged the possibility of it originating from an adult with a rare haemoglobin condition but deemed it improbable.

Under cross-examination by the defence, Dr Scott was asked whether it was possible the dingo picked up Azaria by her matinée jacket, which was never found. Dr Scott admitted, "You can postulate that if a child was carried by a dingo by the matinée jacket, the saliva would obviously be on the matinée jacket."

The prosecution's focus returned to the evidence found in the Chamberlains' car and camera bag, with Professor Michael Chaikin from the University of New South Wales testifying that three tufts found in the bag resembled Azaria's jumpsuit. He asserted that the jumpsuit damage was likely caused by sharp scissors, not a dingo's teeth.[19] Senior Constable James Metcalfe explained that the bloodstains discovered in the car were mainly under the dashboard on the passenger side and beneath the front passenger seat. Forensic biologist Joy Kuhl confirmed that the blood spots in the car and on the camera bag zipper originated from a baby less than three months old. However, following standard practice at the time, the laboratory slides from the car and the camera bag tests had been destroyed after her examination. This meant that the Chamberlains' defence team never had access to them to run their own tests.[20]

On the 14th of October, the defence began presenting its case, with Phillips informing the jury of its intention to challenge the prosecution's evidence. Lindy Chamberlain, the first defence witness, took the stand wearing a powder-blue maternity dress. Tearfully, she vehemently denied any involvement in her daughter's death. Lindy took the jury through the family's camping trip, recounting the crucial moment she saw the dingo: "The dingo had its shoulder halfway out of the tent and was shaking very vigorously and I thought it might have had a shoe or something and I called out to get [it] out of the tent."[21] When she ran to the tent and saw that Azaria was gone, it dawned on her that the dingo had been carrying her baby.

Over two dozen witnesses gave evidence for the remainder of the day, some attesting to the Chamberlains' good character and the profound grief the couple experienced after their daughter's death. Others shared accounts of their interactions with dingoes at Uluru. Lorraine Beatrice Hunter testified that the night before Azaria disappeared, her son had been attacked by a dingo. The defence then called their own forensic experts, including Professor Keith Campbell Bradley, who disputed the prosecution's claim of Azaria's throat being slashed with scissors. He explained that circumferential bleeding around the neck was common in operations where puncture-type wounds (such as those inflicted by a dog or a dingo's teeth) were inflicted on patients' necks.

Professor Barry Boettcher, head of the department of biological sciences at Newcastle University, challenged Joy Kuhl's testimony regarding the blood in the car and camera bag. He criticized her testing method for potentially producing false positives for foetal haemoglobin and suggested the substances found weren't blood at all. He was supported by forensic expert Richard Nairn and biochemist Finley Cornell, who also questioned Kuhl's findings. Cornell pointed out discrepancies in blood typing, highlighting that the blood believed to be Azaria's was categorized as PGM, while Kuhl identified the blood in the car as PGM 1+, the same type as Lenehan's.[22]

Cornell added that he had conducted iso-electric focusing tests on six carpet samples from the Chamberlains' car, and none revealed the presence of proteins found in blood. He highlighted the high sensitivity of the tests, capable of detecting about half a drop of blood on an area "the size of a 20-cent coin".

Leslie Colin Harris, president of the Dingo Foundation, expressed his belief that a dingo could seize small prey, like Azaria, by the head, vigorously shaking it to break the neck before quickly retreating. To illustrate the animals' adeptness, he recounted an incident where a dingo entered his home and extracted 2.5 kilograms of scotch fillet from plastic and paper wrapping, leaving the packaging nearly undamaged.[23]

The trial concluded with 72 witnesses having given evidence and with nearly 3,000 pages of evidence recorded.

In closing arguments, defence attorney John Phillips challenged the prosecution's case, asserting that the crowded campsite left no room for secretive actions by Lindy or Michael, such as concealing Azaria's body. He criticized the prosecution for failing to establish a motive in two years. Prosecutor Ian Barker, in the prosecution's summation, acknowledged the absence of a motive but emphasized what he termed the "massive" body of evidence presented to support Azaria's murder by her mother. Barker declared the dingo story was preposterous, stating, "It's not capable of belief, and if it can't be believed, there's only one alternative."[24]

Summing up the case, Justice Muirhead cautioned the jury of nine men and three women against venturing into uncharted territory by speculating on Lindy's alleged post-natal depression, accurately stating that there was no evidence to support such claims. As the courtroom buzzed with chatter, the prevailing sentiment was that Lindy and Michael would be acquitted. However, to the surprise of many, the jury unanimously found Lindy Chamberlain guilty of Azaria's murder, resulting in a life sentence. Michael Chamberlain was found guilty of being an accessory after the fact and received an 18-month suspended sentence. Despite high hopes, two appeals against Lindy Chamberlain's conviction were both denied.

The "Dingo Baby" trial proved to be the final case in the Northern Territory to be determined by the unanimous vote of all twelve jurors. Following the trial, subsequent legislation introduced a new precedent, requiring only a majority of 10–2 for a conviction. It also secured its place in Australian legal history as the first trial to be televised in the country.

The case deeply engaged the public's attention, fuelled by the starkly divided opinions surrounding it. On 13 November 1982, *The Sydney Morning Herald* posed the question, "Why is the nation obsessed with Lindy?", contending that the case had given rise to lingering, unanswered questions. Despite the conviction, some felt that the case remained unsolved, pointing to the absence of any discernible motive, the lack of eyewitnesses, and the intricate timing required to execute such a crime. In the wake of Lindy Chamberlain's conviction, a "Free Lindy" movement sprang up. *The Daily Telegraph* reported on 3 November 1982, that thousands of signatures had been collected. Despite this, according to an article in *The Sydney Morning Herald* from 24 November 1985, 55.4 per cent of people believed that she was where she belonged – behind bars.

Then in February 1986, Azaria's missing matinée jacket was finally unearthed near a dingo's lair at the base of Uluru. The discovery prompted Northern Territories' Attorney General Paul Everingham to order Lindy Chamberlain's release from prison and initiate a fresh investigation. The case reached the Supreme Court in 1988, where it was revealed that the blood inside the Chamberlains' car could have been any substance, the likeliest explanation being a sound-deadening compound from a manufacturing overspray common in cars of that era. This revelation cast new light on the case and prompting a re-evaluation of the evidence.

On the 15th of September 1988, Lindy and Michael Chamberlain's convictions were quashed, marking the end of a long legal battle. In 1992, Lindy and Michael were awarded AU$1.3 million in compensation for their wrongful convictions.

Following their acquittal, Lindy displayed unwavering determination in reclaiming her reputation and seeking justice for her daughter. Despite enduring persistent public scrutiny and criticism, she emerged as a passionate advocate for legal reform and the rights of those wrongly accused. She was particularly determined to overturn her acquittal and establish that Azaria had been taken by a dingo. Finally, an inquest in 2012 definitively ruled that a dingo had snatched the child and established Lindy and Michael's innocence.

The case not only became fodder for one-liners on popular TV shows like *Seinfeld* and *Frasier*, but also inspired the 1985 book *Evil Angels* by John Bryson, on which the 1988 film *A Cry in the Dark*, starring Meryl Streep as Lindy Chamberlain, was based. Lindy chronicled her experiences in a 1990 autobiography titled *Through My Eyes*, the 2004 miniseries *Through My Eyes*, and in her 2015 autobiography *A Dingo's Got My Baby: Words That Divided a Nation*.

---

[1] *The Sydney Morning Herald*, 17 January 1981 – "The Azaria Mystery"
[2] *The Albuquerque Tribune*, 18 August 1980 – "Wild Dog Steals Baby in Australia"
[3] *The Sydney Morning Herald*, 25 August 1980 – "Missing Baby's Clothes Found"
[4] *The Sydney Morning Herald*, 4 September 1980 – "Rumours Harass Family of Ayers Rock Baby"
[5] *The Age*, 21 February 1981 – "The Azaria Finding"
[6] https://www.nzherald.co.nz/world/chamberlain-dingo-didnt-take-baby-says-former-australian-politician/
VRFSABLKQNO4REHHRU6MI7TSCI/
[7] *The Age*, 11 September 1982 – "The Chamberlains, Self-Made Hermits in a Town that Couldn't Care Less"
[8] *The Age*, 13 September 1982 – "Press Pilgrimage is a $1 Million Bonanza"
[9] *The Monitor*, 13 September 1982 – "Bizarre 'Wild Dog' Killing Trial Opens"
[10] *The Sydney Morning Herald* 15 September 1982 – "Chamberlains Break Down in Court"
[11] *The Age*, 15 September 1982 – "Menacing Growl: Witness"
[12] *The Sydney Morning Herald* 16 September 1982 – "Dingo Strong Enough to Carry a Baby, Policeman Tells Trial"
[13] *The Age* 17 September 1982 – "Witness Describes Jump-Suit Find"
[14] *The Age* 16 September 1982 – "Witness Says He saw Canine Tracks"
[15] *The Sydney Morning Herald*, 17 September 1982 – "Dingoes at Ayers Rock Bolder Now, Court Told"
[16] *The Sydney Morning Herald*, 21 September 1982 – "Witness Tells of Bleeding in Chamberlains' Car"
[17] *The Age*, 24 September 1982 – "Small, Pointed Object Caused Distortion in Azaria's Singlet: Dentist"

[18] *The Age*, 25 September 1982 – "Azaria Generally Upright When Bleeding: Doctor"

[19] *The Age*, 28 September 1982 – "Some Jumpsuit Damage Caused by Sharp Scissors, Scientist Tells Trial"

[20] *The Age*, 7 October 1982 – "Camera Bag Test Slides Destroyed: Biologist"

[21] *The Sydney Morning Herald*, 14 October 1982 – "Crying Mrs. Chamberlain Denies She Cut Baby's Throat in Car"

[22] *The Age*, 19 October 1982 – "Pastor Describes Birth Rites"

[23] *The Sydney Morning Herald*, 20 October 1982 – "Expert Tells Trial of Dingo Killing Method"

[24] *The Age*, 27 October 1982 – "Guilt Evidence Massive: QC"

The Little Girl Murderer

Japan is a nation with a generally low crime rate, and the murder of children in particular is exceptionally rare. However, between August 1988 and June 1989, four girls between the ages of four and seven were abducted, murdered, and mutilated in Tokyo and Saitama Prefecture. The case became known as the "Little Girl Murders" and caused widespread moral panic as the police scrambled to identify a suspect before he struck again. Eventually, a 26-year-old man named Tsutomu Miyazaki was arrested. The marathon trial took seven years to complete. It raised questions regarding the potential influence of media on individuals with disturbed mental states and also attitudes to capital punishment in the Japanese courts.

———————

"When the rat man appeared, I couldn't understand what was going on, and the next thing I knew, something that looked like a mannequin had fallen down."

Tsutomu Miyazaki

———————

On the 23rd of July 1989, a nine-year-old girl from Hachioji, a suburb near Saitama, rushed home in a state of panic. She frantically recounted a disturbing encounter to her father. A man had accosted her and her younger sister in a park, enticing them to a secluded wooded area. Fortunately, the girl had managed to break free.

The girl's father, a 35-year-old office worker, sprinted to the wood. There he encountered a man taking photographs of his nude six-year-old daughter beside a stream. The father confronted him, and the man fled and hid among the trees. The father contacted police, and after a short period, the man emerged from the wood and was arrested. He was identified as 26-year-old Tsutomu Miyazaki, who worked at his father's print shop.

At Hachioji police station, Miyazaki confessed not only to the incident involving the sisters, but also to the murder of five-year-old Ayako Nomoto, who had vanished on the 6th of June. Miyazaki said that he had coerced the young girl into his car and driven her to a river. When she made fun of his "deformity", he killed her. (Miyazaki was born with radioulnar synostosis, a rare condition that causes the fusion of the two bones in the forearms.)

As corroborating evidence Miyazaki sketched a map of the Okutama district in western Tokyo. Following his directions, police ventured to the outskirts of a national park where they discovered Ayako's skull. The police suspected that Miyazaki was responsible for three other murders, including that of four-year-old Mari Konno in August 1988, seven-year-old Masami Yoshizawa in October 1988, and four-year-old Erika Namba in November 1988. The girls' kidnappings had flooded local media, and police had called these "European-American style" crimes a symptom of a breakdown in Japanese society.[1]

Miyazaki was charged with murder and abandonment of a human body. A search of his bedroom at his parents' home uncovered stacks of pornographic comics, magazines, and video-tapes, some depicting graphic images of child abuse. The police also discovered several cameras, along with recording and editing software. One officer remarked to the media, "We are going to screen them all carefully. Quite frankly, we're afraid of what we might find."[2]

As the investigation continued, Miyazaki confessed to the murders of Mari and Erika. He divulged that he had strangled Mari, burnt her remains, and left them on her parents' doorstep. He also admitted strangling Erika and leaving her lifeless body on a mountainside. A couple of days later, he confessed to the killing of Masami. Miyazaki also revealed that he had videotaped their lifeless bodies so "I could see them again and again".[3]

Miyazaki was charged with the additional murders and made his initial appearance in the Tokyo District Court on the 30th of March 1990. The case had gained intense public attention, drawing a crowd of almost fifteen hundred people outside the courthouse, vying for one of the fifty spectator seats. Miyazaki admitted most of the charges. However, he denied the murders were premeditated. The courtroom was shocked when Miyazaki nonchalantly informed the judge that he had consumed the flesh of one of his victims, stating, "On the whole, my feeling was that I did them in a daydream."[4]

Miyazaki's father refused to hire a defence attorney for his son, saying, "It wouldn't be fair to the victims." Miyazaki was appointed two attorneys from the public defender's office, Junji Suzuki and Keiji Iwakura. According to Suzuki, the only reason he agreed to take on the challenging case was because he staunchly opposed capital punishment. He announced, "We want to build enough of a case for the judge to sentence Miyazaki to life in prison."

In contrast to the Western jury system of justice, Japan employs a predominantly judge-based approach. Trials for complex cases can span years, with multiple hearings. The initial session of Miyazaki's trial commenced on the 18th of April 1990, and focused on his mental state during the murders. His team argued insanity, while Miyazaki contended that he was a product of a modern society where computers, comic books, television, and videotapes served as substitutes for reality, nurturing dangerous fantasies.

Miyazaki's attorneys said that he suffered from a congenital brain disorder and led a secluded life. Despite living with his parents, Miyazaki had a distant relationship with them. His main family companion was his grandfather; after his grandfather's death and cremation, Miyazaki consumed some of his ashes in an attempt to maintain their closeness. His defence also suggested that the death of Miyazaki's grandfather triggered a nervous breakdown, leading to the manifestation of his violent fantasies.

Taking the witness stand, Miyazaki explained how he lured his first victim, four-year-old Mari Konno, into his car and drove to an isolated mountain park outside Iruma city in Saitama Prefecture, where he strangled her. After dismembering Mari, he took her head back to his home, doused it in gasoline, and set it ablaze. Miyazaki admitted to sleeping beside his victims' corpses and consuming their blood. He also said that he had confessed to the murders by sending a letter to the Tokyo headquarters of *Asahi Shibun* – one of Japan's most widely read newspapers – under a woman's name to mislead the police. He also admitted sending a box containing Mari's remains to her family.

After his grandfather's cremation, Miyazaki said that he had brought pieces of calcinated bone home and eaten them in his bedroom. He also asserted that the murders occurred within "a lasting dream" and involved the appearance of a "rat man". "When the rat man appeared, I couldn't understand what was going on, and the next thing I knew, something that looked like a mannequin had fallen down."[5] Despite Prosecutor Kensaku Iuchi's assertion that the murders were sexually motivated, Miyazaki insisted that the girls were sacrifices. He believed that by killing them, he could bring his grandfather back to life.[6]

Testimony concerning Miyazaki's personality was presented. An unnamed man, a former classmate in high school, informed the judge, "He never had a girlfriend. He was weird." A former co-worker from the printing company where Miyazaki worked, testified, "Unless you talked to him, he never said anything. He ate his lunch separate from others, and he went straight home after lunch." Family counsellor Yutaka Masuda characterized Miyazaki as "a man with a 'Lolita complex' [a fascination with underage girls, particularly among much older men] – someone who might have been made to feel inadequate".

The contents of Miyazaki's bedroom provided further insight into his personality and motives. He had amassed thousands of anime comics and videotapes, including recordings of children's TV shows that he had shared with his grandfather. Miyazaki's obsessions extended to collecting violent pornographic videotapes. Additionally, he had a penchant for photographing unsuspecting women. Throughout the presentation of evidence, Miyazaki nodded off several times.

After a couple of days, the trial was suspended so that Miyazaki could undergo psychiatric evaluations by Saitama Prefecture. These focused on his abnormal behaviours – which also included animal abuse – and the consumption of his grandfather's remains. The Japanese media nicknamed Miyazaki the "Otaku Murderer", referencing the Japanese cultural phenomenon of *otaku* – individuals with an obsessive interest in anime, manga, and video games. The *Shukan Post* declared, "Tsutomu Miyazaki Dwells Within Us," shedding light on the psychological abnormality of *rori-kon*, a Japanese-English term for a "Lolita Complex". The article esti-mated that approximately 300,000 people in Japan were "latent *rori-kon* fans".[7]

In March 1992, a panel of five psychiatrists and one clinical psychologist concluded that Miyazaki had a personality disorder. However, their opinions differed on his ability to distinguish right from wrong. One of them, Hideo Hosaki, asserted that Miyazaki bore full responsibility for the murders but suggested that a death sentence might be inappropriate due to the "enormous social impact".[8]

On the 18th of December Miyazaki's attorney requested a re-examination by the three psychiatrists who initially deemed Miyazaki competent. Suzuki declared, "The more we see of him, the more we think he lives in a different world. We felt the report did not establish Miyazaki's mental capabilities beyond reasonable doubt, so we asked for a second evaluation."[9]

This re-examination spanned two years, concluding in December 1994. During this period, one expert diagnosed Miyazaki with schizophrenia, while two others diagnosed him with dissociative identity disorder. Although the details of the examination were not extensively discussed, all the experts concurred that he was compe-tent and understood that his actions were wrong. Dr Ishil, one of the psychologists, expressed his belief that Miyazaki was primarily a paedophile and secondly a killer. He commented, "Killing was an extension of his interest in little girls, a way of possessing them."

Miyazaki remained incarcerated while awaiting his next court hearing. Suzuki remarked on Miyazaki's time in jail, noting, "He's perfectly happy. He is allowed to read comics all day." Miyazaki returned to court on the 7th of October 1996, and during this trial session, the prosecution urged for a death sentence, asserting: "There is no room for sympathy for the defendant's motive. His rehabilitation is impossible."[10] Before court adjourned for the day, Miyazaki remarked to the judge: "I want to go home early."[11]

On the 14th of April the following year, Miyazaki reappeared at the Tokyo District Court for the conclusive session of his protracted trial. Presiding Judge Kenjiro Tao declared Miyazaki guilty and determined him to be mentally sound enough to be held accountable for the series of murders.[12] Miyazaki displayed minimal reaction in response to the verdict. He scanned the courtroom with a distant expression before jotting something down in his notebook. Following the sentencing, Miyazaki's team lodged an appeal.

The appeal finally reached the Tokyo High Court on the 21st of December 1999. Miyazaki's team did not dispute his guilt but argued that he was legally insane at the time of the murders. They requested additional psychiatric examinations and suggested that Miyazaki might have been coerced into confessing. Miyazaki, seemingly uninterested in the proceedings, rested his chin on one hand and doodled with the other. When called to testify, he claimed that he had been compelled to confess through intimidation and accused the police of framing his motives as sexual owing to his possession of explicit photographs and videos of young girls.[13] Miyazaki's appeal was ultimately denied.

In January 2006, The Supreme Court upheld the death penalty for Miyazaki. Presiding Justice Yokiyasu Fujita rejected the defence's argument that Miyazaki was mentally incompetent at the time of the murders. He ruled that, while Miyazaki had an extreme character disorder, it did not absolve him of criminal responsibility. "The atrocious murder of four girls to satisfy his sexual desire leaves no room for leniency."[14]

In the days leading up to the ruling, Miyazaki had written a letter to the Supreme Court saying that he was not guilty of the murders, adding, "I think I did something positive." He claimed that his victims came to him in his dreams and thanked him, and that they were happy. He additionally wrote a letter to the magazine, *Sou*, after the sentence was upheld, criticizing his impending execution: "When the footboard comes off and you fall, you are thrown into a place of terror."[15]

During that period, Japan was accelerating its pace of executions due to mounting concerns about violent crime. On the 17th of June 2008, Minister of Justice Kunio Hatoyama signed Miyazaki's death warrant; he was hanged at the Tokyo Detention House on the same day. His execution occurred alongside those of Shinji Mutsuda, who had been convicted of robbery and murder, and Yoshio Yamasaki, who had taken two lives for the insurance money. A 2020 government survey revealed that over eighty per cent of the Japanese population supported the death penalty for murder in extreme circumstances, such as those involving rape, robbery, or multiple homicide.

---

[1] *San Francisco Chronicle*, 12 August 1989 – "Arrest in 'Western' Murders That Shocked Japan"

[2] *The Toronto Star*, 11 August 1989 – "Confessed Killer Linked to Tokyo Child Murders"

[3] *Honolulu Star-Bulletin*, 3 September 1989 – "Shocked Japan Re-Examines Laws on Graphic Violence"

[4] *The Daily Telegraph*, 31 March 1990 – "Kidnap Killer Confesses to Eating Child Victim's Flesh"

[5] *Yahoo Japan*, 18 September 2023 – "The 'After' of People Whose Lives Were Ruined by Tsutomu Miyazaki"

[6] *The Japan Times*, 23 January 2006 – "Killer's Motives Remain in the Dark"

[7] *LA Times*, 19 September 1982 – "Sordid Serial-Killing Case Exposes the Other Side of Innocence in Japan"

[8] *Yomiuri Shimbun*, 14 April 1997 – "Tokyo District Court Certifies Death Penalty for Defendant Miyazaki for Kidnapping and Murder of Four Young Girls as Fully Responsible"

[9] *The Silencing of the Lambs* by Charles T. Whipple

[10] *Huddersfield Daily Examiner,* 7 October 1996 – "Mutilating Murders Man Deserves to Die"

[11] *Yomiuri Shimbun*, 26 December 1996 – "Serial Child Kidnapping and Murder Case Defendant Tsutomu Miyazaki, Tokyo District Court to Be Sentenced in April"

[12] *The Daily Herald-Tribune*, 14 April 1997 – "Japanese Child-Killer Sentenced to Hang"

[13] *The Japan Times*, 27 January 2000 – "Serial Killer Claims He Was Forced into Confessing"

[14] *ABC News*, 18 June 2008 – "Japan Confirms Execution of Cannibal Killer"

[15] *238 Death Row Inmates' Last Words*, Tetsujin Nonfiction Editorial Department, Tetsujinsha

O.J. SIMPSON, 1994

"The Trial of the Century"

On the 17th of June 1994, millions watched in astonishment as the former NFL superstar O.J. Simpson led the LAPD on a slow-speed car chase through Southern California. The chase unfolded shortly after he had been ordered to turn himself in for charges related to the murders of his ex-wife, Nicole Brown Simpson, and her friend, Ronald Goldman. Along the route, people waved homemade signs in anticipation of Simpson's arrest. Eventually, he surrendered, marking the beginning of a high-stakes trial for the double homicide. This legal spectacle would become one of the most renowned and extensively covered trials in American history, earning the title of "The Trial of the Century".

———————

"If I put this knit cap on, who am I? I'm still Johnnie Cochran with a knit cap. O.J. Simpson in a knit cap from two blocks away is still O.J. Simpson."

Defence Attorney Johnnie Cochran

———————

On the 12th of June 1994, at approximately 10:20 p.m., Pablo Fenjves was disturbed by a dog persistently barking in his Los Angeles Brentwood neighbourhood. About twenty-five minutes later, Steven Schwab encountered a large white Akita with bloodstained paws while walking his own dog. Despite appearing alone and agitated, the Akita followed Schwab back to his home. Neighbour Sukru Boztepe and his wife offered to shelter the dog for the night, but it remained restless. Around midnight, they walked the dog, which led them to a townhouse at 875 South Bundy Drive. There, Boztepe discovered a woman's lifeless body, barefoot and lying face down in a pool of blood at the bottom of a short flight of steps leading to a path up to the front door.[1]

Boztepe immediately contacted the police who soon discovered a second body, that of a man, near a tree and fence. The victims were identified as 35-year-old Nicole Brown Simpson, the former wife of NFL player Orenthal James "O.J." Simpson, and her 25-year-old friend, Ron Goldman. Both had been stabbed, with Nicole's head nearly severed. In bushes nearby, police came across a blue knit cap and a bloodstained black leather glove.

During their turbulent seven-year marriage, Simpson had pleaded "no contest" to assaulting Nicole in 1989. Despite divorcing in 1992, reports suggested that they were attempting a reconciliation, having just attended their daughter Sydney's dance recital earlier that day.

Police took Simpson in for routine questioning at Parker Center in Downtown Los Angeles and obtained a search warrant for his vehicle and his $1.2 million mansion just two miles from Nicole's condo. During the interview, Detective Tom Lange noted a cut on Simpson's left hand.

Simpson was released pending investigation and voluntarily provided a blood sample for comparison with crime scene evidence. Forensic experts discovered small, reddish-brown droplets outside his home leading to a point some fifty feet from the garage.[2] A bloodstained glove matching the one discovered at the crime scene was found near a guesthouse on his property. Simpson swiftly enlisted lawyer Robert Shapiro, forming a "dream team" that included Johnnie Cochran, F. Lee Bailey, and others.[3] Shapiro said to reporters, "At the same time this murder took place, O.J. was at home waiting to get into a limousine to take him to the airport."[4]

However, after Simpson's DNA was found at the crime scene, he was charged with the double murder on the 17th of June. Simpson, who was staying at his friend Robert Kardashian's home, agreed to surrender by 11 a.m.; however, the police postponed this until noon for a mental health evaluation due to reports of Simpson's disturbing behaviour, which included updating his will and writing suicide notes. When noon passed without Simpson turning himself in, the LAPD declared him a fugitive.

Police visited Simpson's home but discovered that he had left with Al Cowlings, a former NFL player, in his white Ford Bronco. Shapiro held a news conference during which Kardashian read parts of a note Simpson had written: "Don't feel sorry for me. I've had a great life, great friends. Please think of the real O.J. and not this lost person." Investigators traced Simpson's phone to Interstate 5 in Orange County, and a slow-speed pursuit ensued with Simpson in the back seat, holding a gun to his head, threatening suicide.

The televised pursuit, spanning about two hours and 60 miles of

Southern California freeways, captivated millions of viewers. Spectators, both on TV and in person, witnessed the event unfold, with some holding banners and shouting phrases such as "The Juice is loose!"[5] ("Juice" was Simpson's NFL nickname, derived from his initials.) The pursuit eventually ended peacefully at Simpson's mansion in Brentwood, where he surrendered to police.

The incident became a defining moment in the case, heightening public interest, and setting the stage for the subsequent trial, slated for January 1995. The jury was sequestered in the second week of January, with Judge Lance Ito advising them, "We will try to make this something less than an experience of going into incarceration, but it won't be a picnic."[6]

Deputy District Attorneys Marcia Clark and Christopher Darden, assisted by Prosecutors Hank Goldberg and William Hodgman, led the prosecution. Johnnie Cochran, known for his expertise in police brutality and civil rights cases, replaced Robert Shapiro as the lead defence attorney, though Shapiro remained on the team. Cochran was supported by F. Lee Bailey, Robert Kardashian, and others, at a cost estimated between $3 million and $6 million.[7] Court TV televised the trial using closed-circuit TV in the courtroom, a relatively new development permitted after a 1981 Supreme Court ruling.

The trial began on the 24th of January. Outside the courtroom, a carnival-like atmosphere prevailed, as a lengthy line of people braved blustery weather to pass through metal detectors and enter the C.S. Foltz Criminal Courts Building. News reporters mingled with the crowd, and vendors peddled popcorn and macabre souvenirs, including "Dateline, O.J." t-shirts for $10 apiece. One seller, Keith Davidson, reported selling a dozen despite the dreary weather.[8]

Shortly before 9 a.m., Deputy District Attorney Christopher Darden confidently outlined the prosecution's intention to provide compelling blood and fibre evidence linking Simpson to the murders. Photographs of the crime scene appeared on the large courtroom television screen; however, Judge Ito ordered that it should be disconnected from the television feed reaching the outside world.

Darden claimed that it was the jealous, ugly "other side" of Simpson that the public never saw that killed Nicole Brown Simpson because "he couldn't have her". As for Ron Goldman, Darden maintained that he was killed by Simpson simply because he "got in the way". (It transpired that Nicole had left her glasses at a restaurant and Goldman was returning them to her). Prosecutor Marcia Clark chimed in, saying that on the night of the murders, Simpson's whereabouts for more than an hour were not accounted for.[9]

Darden continued, telling the jury, "The face we will expose to you in this trial is the one that Nicole Brown encountered almost every day of her adult life. A batterer, a wife-beater, an abuser, a controller. You'll see the face of Ron and Nicole's murderer."[10] Simpson sat with his defence attorneys, a shocked expression on his face. He raised an eyebrow, shook his head, and took notes. At one point, he exclaimed, "That's a lie!"

After the prosecution's opening statements, defence attorney Johnnie Cochran took the floor. He argued that Simpson had fallen victim to "a rush to judgment" by detectives who had mishandled evidence and dismissed a witness account that supposedly mentioned four men near the scene. Cochran declared, "The evidence will show that O.J. Simpson is an innocent man wrongfully accused." He pledged to bring forth witnesses contradicting the prosecutor's timeline of events.[11] Cochran provided a different alibi for Simpson than the one earlier presented: that he was swinging a golf club in his front yard.

Cochran also vehemently contested prosecution claims portraying Simpson as a violent, murderous, controlling man. Instead, he said that Simpson was a compassionate individual who showered money, gifts, and employment opportunities not only on Nicole but also on her family members. Furthermore, he said evidence would show that Simpson was suffering from acute rheumatoid arthritis in his wrists on the day of the murders and wouldn't have been able to carry them out. The trial's opening statements reportedly attracted an audience of 50 million viewers.

The first witness, Sharon Gilbert, a 911 operator and dispatcher, recounted an incident that occurred on the 1st of January 1989, at approximately 4 a.m. While on duty, she received a distress call from a screaming woman, identified as Nicole, during which sounds of someone being physically assaulted were audible in the background. Gilbert promptly dispatched a unit to the residence Nicole shared with O.J. Simpson. Upon arrival, Detective John Edwards encountered a highly agitated Nicole at the door, who exclaimed, "He's going to kill me!" Edwards enquired who was going to kill her, and she responded, "O.J.", before clarifying she meant "the football player". Edwards recalled that Nicole had a "hand imprint" on her throat as well as a cut lip and bruises on her face.[12]

Edwards quoted Simpson as saying, "I don't want that woman in my bed anymore. I got two other women." Edwards told Simpson he was going to be arrested but allowed him to re-enter the home to get dressed, but Simpson sped off.[13] He was eventually tracked down and pleaded no contest to spousal battery and served 30 days in jail, completed 120 hours of community service, and served two years of probation. Simpson's defence team had unsuccessfully tried to prevent this testimony from being presented.

The jury was then presented with another 911 call, from 1993, during which Nicole said, "My ex-husband has just broken into my house and he's ranting and raving outside in the front yard." A juror appeared to wince as Nicole's voice became more and more hysterical. The prosecution also unveiled items from a safe deposit box, including a letter in which Simpson documented the 1989 attack on Nicole. In the letter, he wondered "how I got so crazy".[14] Another letter Nicole had kept was presented in which Simpson appeared full of remorse, telling her, "How wrong I was for hurting you".[15]

Ron Shipp, a friend of Simpson for 26 years and a former LAPD officer, testified that Simpson had confided to him the day after the murders that he had dreams of killing Nicole. Shipp said he hadn't told police because he didn't want to get involved. Eventually, Shipp detailed the conversation to Sheila Weller, who was writing a book about the case. The prosecution argued that Shipp's account showed Simpson's influential ties with the LAPD, asserting that this dynamic left Nicole feeling powerless. Under cross-examination by the defence, Shipp was portrayed as a lying hanger-on with a drinking problem.

Early in the trial, two eyewitnesses claimed to have seen four men near Nicole's home on the night of the murders. Leif Tilden reported seeing them between 10 and 10:30 p.m., describing them as college students. Mary Anne Gerchas also reported seeing four men, specifying that two appeared Hispanic and the others Caucasian. District Attorney Marcia Clark discredited Gerchas' account, labelling her a "known liar and a Simpson case groupie". Gerchas was later arrested during the trial for defrauding a hotel of $23,000.[16]

The prosecution called Nicole's sister, Denise Brown, to testify about Nicole and Simpson's stormy relationship. She recounted an incident in a crowded bar where he grabbed her crotch and declared, "This belongs to me." Denise described another occasion where Simpson threw her against a wall and then ejected her from the house. She also mentioned that Simpson had a "frightening" look in his eyes at his and Nicole's daughter's recital just hours before the murders. The defence challenged Brown's credibility. They revealed she had first denied Nicole was abused by Simpson, but then changed her opinion, citing newfound awareness. They also presented a video showing a cheerful Simpson kissing Denise at the recital.

The prosecution turned to the night of the murder, with witness Pablo Fenjves testifying that he heard a dog howling near Nicole's home just after 10 p.m., implying that that was the time of the murder. Officer Robert Riske said there was no sign of forced entry or ransacking at the home, and recounted finding a bloody glove close to Ronald Goldman's body, along with a knitted cap. During cross-examination, he admitted that some detectives walked near the bodies without protective gear and that the telephone hadn't been checked for fingerprints before being used.

Officer Riske also admitted not inspecting trash cans, the water temperature in a bath, or a melting cup of ice cream. The defence argued these oversights could have helped to establish a more accurate timeline. The medical examiner and coroner, Dr Lakshmanan Sathyavagiswaran, said that he was unable to pinpoint the time of the murders, estimating it as between 9 p.m. and 12:45 a.m.

During Detective Tom Lange's testimony, the defence continued to probe the investigation. Lange stated that owing to the absence of blood on Nicole's bare feet, she was likely killed first. In contrast, Ronald had blood on his shoe soles, indicating proximity to Nicole's blood. Under cross-examination, Detective Lange said that coroner's assistants had washed off blood spots on Nicole's back, despite his request for analysis and that they had failed to preserve her stomach contents. He admitted that standard procedures, such as placing plastic bags on the victims' hands to preserve potential evidence under their fingernails, were not followed, and that he was called back to the crime scene three weeks later to collect a smear of blood from the gate that he had been ordered to take the day after the murders.

The defence argued that an "assassin or assassins" were responsible for the double murder. However, Detective Lange replied that a drop of blood containing a mixture of Nicole and Ronald's blood had dripped from the killer's knife onto Ronald's shoe, suggesting a single killer. The detective also refuted the theory that the murders may have been drug-related, emphasizing that no drug paraphernalia had been found in Nicole's or in Ronald's home.

On the 13th of February, the jury visited the locations where Nicole and Ronald's bodies had been found; they also visited Simpson's mansion. Crowds gathered, with a man displaying a sign reading "Free O.J." and distributing orange juice.[17]

Back in court, testimony shifted to Simpson's reaction to Nicole's death. Detective Ron Phillips claimed that Simpson never enquired about the details of her death. For the defence, Cochran suggested that Simpson was groggy from overnight travel to Chicago, having slept only an hour. Detective Phillips, under cross-examination, admitted that Simpson had in fact asked, "What do you mean she's been killed?" when presented with his police report.

When the jury was presented with the blood-spattered leather glove and blue ski cap, they leaned forward in their seats, craning their necks to get a better view. Seeing the hat, Simpson turned to Shapiro and silently mouthed, "That looks too small for me."[18]

The following week featured crucial testimony from one of the defence's key witnesses, Rosa Lopez, who was employed as a housekeeper adjacent to Simpson's Brentwood mansion; however, she was called by the prosecution. She had claimed in her 29th of July statement to have observed Simpson's white Ford Bronco parked haphazardly near his home twice on the night of the murders – around 8:15 p.m. and around 10:15 p.m.

During cross-examination, prosecutor Maria Clark exposed a contradiction in Lopez's previous statement. While Lopez had stated she was walking her employer's dog around 10:15 p.m. or 10:20 p.m., she had omitted any mention of the Bronco. This undisclosed detail led to an adjournment, affording the prosecution more time to question Lopez. On her return to the stand, Lopez admitted being influenced by Simpson's investigators to alter the time of her Bronco sightings and confessed uncertainty about the exact time after 10 p.m. when she saw the car parked.

One of the most highly anticipated moments of the trial came when Detective Mark Fuhrman took the stand. Portrayed by Simpson's legal team as a racist who could have manipulated evidence to incriminate Simpson, they proposed that he had discovered two gloves at the crime scene and planted the second one at Simpson's home. Witness Kathleen Bell, who claimed to have encountered ex-Marine Fuhrman at a Marine recruiting office in the mid 1980s, had written a letter to Simpson's team claiming the detective had told her, "When he sees a 'N-word' driving with a white woman, he would pull them over". Detective Fuhrman denied ever meeting Bell.[19]

In a cliffhanger ending to the trial week, Detective Fuhrman then presented a large shovel, a jumbo plastic bag, and a soiled white towel found in Simpson's Bronco. The implication was that Simpson was planning to murder and bury Nicole but was interrupted by Ronald Goldman.

When Detective Fuhrman returned to court the following Monday, he testified finding a bloody glove among leaves and twigs behind Simpson's mansion, near a guesthouse, the morning after the murders. "This glove didn't have any signs of dirt or twigs or leaves on it," he said. Cross-examining, the defence suggested that he planted the glove to implicate Simpson. Fuhrman adamantly denied this, shooting back, "No, I saw one glove."[20]

The next prosecution witness, Detective Philip Vannatter, presented photos depicting blood smears inside Simpson's Bronco and drops of blood leading to his home. Detective Vannatter testified that Simpson had cuts on the middle finger of his left hand in the wake of the murders and a swollen knuckle. He theorized that Simpson had cut his hand during the murders, and then left a trail of blood into his own home. Simpson's lead counsel Robert C. Baker asked Simpson to show the jury his left finger, as Shapiro suggested his knuckle was always "swollen due to a medical condition and not any laceration".[21] Forensic pathologist Dr Werner Spitz put forward a new explanation for cuts on Simpson's left hand. He opined that the wounds were fingernail gouges that could have been inflicted by Nicole Simpson or Ronald Goldman as they tried to break free of a chokehold.

Lead prosecutor Marcia Clark called the actor and radio personality Brian "Kato" Kaelin to the stand. He was living in one of Simpson's guesthouses at the time and recalled hearing a bump on a wall about 10:45 p.m on the night of the murders. Kaelin went on say that earlier that day Simpson had told him that he and Nicole had had an argument at their daughter's dance recital. He also said Simpson tried to get him to provide an alibi for the evening, telling him, "Kato, you know I was in the house."[22] Kaelin also said that he saw Simpson that night outside the house about 9:35 p.m., and that he was wearing a dark sweatshirt.

After Kaelin's testimony, limo driver Allan Park revealed that, from 10:22 p.m. to 10:49 p.m. on the night of the murders, he failed to spot Simpson's Bronco during three passes of his house – Simpson was supposed to be meeting him outside. Assigned to drive Simpson to the airport to catch a flight to Chicago, Park finally buzzed the gate at 10:56 p.m., but received no response. He observed a 6-foot-tall, 200-pound Black man entering the house, prompting another buzz. Simpson, claiming to have overslept, assured Park he would be out shortly. Park testified that Simpson carried four bags to the airport, but skycap James Willias reported he only checked in two bags – a bag containing clothes and a golf bag—and that Simpson was also carrying a duffel bag. The prosecution suggested that Simpson had stashed bloody clothing in the fourth bag, and disposed of it in an airport trash can; however, no fourth bag was ever found.

On the 21st of April, the trial faced a setback when 13 jurors revolted owing to a disagreement with Judge Ito's decision to reassign three sheriff's deputies who had been deputed to look after the jury. After a four-day break, the trial resumed. DNA evidence took centre stage, with criminalist Renee Montgomery of the

California Department of Justice Crime Lab revealing that blood swatches from the crime scene walkway and samples found on the back gates showed DNA consistent with Simpson's. In his Bronco and on the right-hand glove at his home, mixtures of DNA matching Simpson, Nicole, and Ronald were discovered. The blood on Simpson's driveway also matched his DNA.[23] In his bedroom, blood on a pair of socks came back as a match to Simpson and Nicole.

LAPD criminalist Susan Brockbank and FBI Special Agent Doug Deedrick, experts in hair and fibre analysis, testified that the glove found at the crime scene was a match for the one discovered at Simpson's home. Hairs found on Nicole, Ronald, the gloves, and the blue knit cap were consistent with Simpson. Dark blue cotton fibres matching the sweatshirt Simpson wore at the dance recital were found on the victims, although this sweatshirt was never discovered. Additionally, fibres from a 1993–1994 Ford Bronco, similar to the one Simpson owned, were present on the victims, the cap, and both gloves.

FBI shoeprint expert William J. Bodziak said that prints found at the crime scene and inside Simpson's Bronco were from a rare pair of size 12 Bruno Magli shoes. A significant challenge for the prosecution arose when it was revealed that such shoes had not been found at Simpson's home. To counter this, Bodziak compared the shoeprints to a pair of Reebok trainers found in a cupboard, stating, "For all practical purposes, the shoes are identical in the size and shape features." [24] Barry Scheck, one of Simpson's attorneys, produced a photograph of Detective Fuhrman walking through a puddle of blood at the crime scene and suggested that he had broken into the Bronco and planted the footprint there.

In the trial's pivotal moment, Simpson attempted to put on the leather gloves the prosecution claimed he used in the murders. Struggling to put them on, he asserted, "They're too small." When Darden expressed scepticism, Simpson sarcastically suggested, "Do you want to try them?" The prosecutor then asked him to straighten his fingers and put them in the glove, demonstrating a snug fit.

According to Richard Rubin, former vice president of glove-maker Aris Isotoner, the right glove had shrunk "well below" the extra-large size on the tag, and Simpson couldn't get the left glove on owing to damage to the lining. Rubin noted that in their original condition, the gloves would easily fit someone of Simpson's size.[25] Rubin was also shown photographs and videos of Simpson working at NFL games, and identified a pair of gloves he was wearing as the same brand as the bloodstained glove found at the murder scene and the one found at Simpson's home.

After 23 weeks of prosecution testimony, it was the defence's turn. Swiftly aiming to restore Simpson's image, they called his 25-year-old daughter, Arnelle, who was living at a guesthouse at Simpson's home. She characterized Simpson as a caring father who continued to support Nicole even after their breakup, bringing her soup during an illness. She emphasized his generosity, mentioning the guesthouses he built for his children. Arnelle refuted claims that she had ever seen her father wearing a dark sweatshirt, contradicting Kaelin's testimony, and that she never saw blood on her father's driveway on the night of the murder.[26]

Simpson's mother, Eunice, confirmed that her son suffered from rheumatoid arthritis. She described him as "very upset and shocked" on learning about Nicole's murder. Songwriter Carol Connors and interior designer Mary Collins attested that they had been with Simpson in the days before the murders, noting his normal demeanour. The defence then called Danny Mandel, who claimed to have walked past Nicole's home shortly before 10:30 p.m. and seen no signs of blood or bodies, casting doubt on the prosecution's timeline. Under cross-examination by Clark, Mandel admitted he wasn't scrutinizing every house he passed. His date, Ellen Aaronson, told the court, "On the street there was nothing. It was an extremely quiet evening – out of a movie."

According to Robert Heidstra, who lived near Nicole, he was walking his dogs half a block from her home at 10:35 p.m. on the day of the murders, when her dog began barking wildly. Approximately five minutes later, he heard a man shout out – he couldn't make out any words – followed by two male voices arguing and a gate slamming. His testimony supported the defence's assertion of the possibility of two assailants, raising doubts about the feasibility of Simpson committing the murders before being driven to the airport at 11 p.m. However, Heidstra also bolstered the prosecution's case by mentioning that, after hearing the male voices, he had seen a white Ford Bronco speeding away from Nicole's home.

Francesca Harmon, another neighbour, testified that she left a dinner party near Nicole's home at 10:20 p.m. and saw nothing unusual. Denise Pilnak, a local resident, stated that she and her friend, Judy Telander, were on her porch around 10:20 p.m and the street was quiet. But around 10:33 Pilnak heard a dog barking. During cross-examination by Clark, she admitted initially telling detectives that this occurred at 11:30 p.m.[27] Following Pilnak's testimony, Judge Ito excluded evidence supporting the defence's alternative theory – that Colombian drug lords killed Nicole and Ronald in a mistaken attempt on the reality-show celebrity Faye Resnick's life. (Resnick had once briefly stayed with Nicole while undergoing treatment for cocaine addiction.) The judge deemed this theory "highly speculative" with no supporting evidence from the defence team.[28]

Following this setback, the defence called lawyer Mark Partridge, who shared a flight with Simpson from Chicago to Los Angeles in the hours following the murders. Partridge recalled Simpson making calls for information regarding Nicole's death and giving an autograph to a fan. As Partridge testified, Simpson appeared to wipe tears from his eyes.[29] Partridge also mentioned noticing a cut on the middle knuckle of Simpson's left hand, a detail corroborated by Hertz Corp. executive Raymond Kilduff, who testified seeing an injury on Simpson's left middle finger while driving him to the airport in Chicago.

Dr Robert Huizenga, who examined Simpson three days after the murders, suggested that the left-hand injury likely resulted from broken glass rather than a knife. Describing Simpson as physically compromised, with problematic knees, achy ankles, and limited motion in his arms and wrists, the doctor noted signs of potential rheumatoid arthritis, a condition that ran in the family. Despite these issues, Dr Huizenga maintained that Simpson could still hold a knife. When Deputy District Attorney Brian Kelberg, the prosecution's medical expert, raised the possibility of malingering, the doctor, drawing on his experience as a former team physician for the Los Angeles Raiders, asserted his ability to identify individuals exaggerating injuries.

The prosecution rebutted Dr Huizenga's testimony by presenting a video of Simpson working out in May before the murders. The videotape was taken for his *Minimum Maintenance Fitness for Men* video and featured Simpson stretching, lunging, and doing push-ups. Throughout the video, Simpson complained about his "bad knees" but lead prosecutor Marcia Clark said the tape showed he could lift his arms above his head and throw "jabs and uppercuts" similar to the movements the killer would have made. When cross-examined, Dr Huizenga admitted that Simpson's arthritic wrists would not have prevented him from yanking back Nicole's head by her hair and slashing her throat, as long as she was immobilized.

The defence then focused on Simpson's Bronco, presenting testimony from tow-truck driver John Meraz, who claimed that, following the murders, the vehicle was moved, left unlocked, and never fully secured in the tow yard. He further admitted to stealing credit card receipts to show off to fellow workers and said he saw no blood or fingerprint dusting in the vehicle, bolstering the defence's assertion of evidence tampering. Cross-examining, Clark showed Meraz a picture of dusting powder on the Bronco, and Meraz responded he was farsighted and not wearing his glasses.

Police photographer Willie Ford testified that he did not observe a bloody sock in Simpson's bedroom when he videoed it the day after the murders. The prosecution argued that the socks had already been taken as evidence, but the defence suggested their absence could indicate potential later planting by detectives.[30] Detective Bert Luper then testified that he saw criminalist Dennis Fung collect the socks before the scene was documented on videotape. Forensic expert Herbert MacDonell asserted that the blood on the sock was not spattered but applied through "direct compression".[31]

In response to the prosecution's blood evidence, the defence called toxicologist Frederic Rieders, who testified that a chemical preservative from the police crime lab was present on the bloody sock and in the blood on Nicole's home's front gate. The defence argued that the presence of this preservative suggested a frame-up, highlighting that the same lab stored blood from both Simpson and Nicole. They proposed that if detectives wanted to frame Simpson, they could have smeared blood samples on the evidence. Microbiologist John Gerdes also criticized the police lab, testifying that he found serious sloppiness in specimen-handling procedures, posing a significant risk of cross-contamination. Gerdes stated, "I found that the specimen-handling procedures were done in such a manner there [was] a tremendous risk of cross-contamination."[32]

The defence then turned back to Detective Fuhrman and the racist statements he allegedly made. It was revealed that Judge Ito's wife, Margaret York, had previously served as the detective's superior officer. The prosecution initially urged Judge Ito to recuse (disqualify) himself owing to a potential conflict of interest, but later withdrew the request due to concerns that it might lead to a mistrial.

The defence obtained videotaped interviews with Detective

Fuhrman from Laura Hart McKinney, a filmmaker and screen-writing professor working on a screenplay about the LAPD. Detective Fuhrman's lawyers unsuccessfully attempted to block the admission of these tapes in court. When played, the defence argued the tapes undermined Fuhrman's credibility, revealing numerous racial slurs, use of the "N-word" 41 times, descriptions of police brutality against Black suspects, and misogynistic remarks. Fuhrman made references to "planting evidence" and suggested that such practises were common in the LAPD.

As the trial neared its conclusion, Judge Ito informed the jury that they had the option to consider the lesser charge of second-degree murder. This suggestion arose in response to the defence's insistence on an "all or nothing" approach, urging judgment solely on first-degree murder charges. Judge Ito then requested that Simpson officially declare his decision not to testify in his own defence for the record. Standing from his seat, Simpson proclaimed, "I did not, could not, and would not have committed this crime." On the other side of the room, Ronald Goldman's father clenched his fists, muttering bitterly, "Murderer. Murderer."[33]

Delivering her closing argument, Prosecutor Marcia Clark discredited Detective Fuhrman as a racist; however, she also derided the defence's contamination conspiracy theory as "far-fetched" and asserted that the blood evidence unequivocally proved Simpson's guilt. With unwavering determination, she addressed the jury: "At the conclusion of all of our arguments. When you open up the windows and let the cool air blow out the smokescreen that's been created by the defence, with the cool wind of reason, you will see that the defendant has been proven guilty, easily, beyond a reasonable doubt."[34]

When presenting his closing arguments, defence attorney Johnnie Cochran introduced a pair of undersized black leather gloves reminiscent of those linked to the case. Attempting to fit his hands into them, he struggled and then grappled to remove them – a symbolic reference to the earlier trial moment when Simpson faced a similar glove challenge. Cochran proceeded to don a blue ski cap resembling the one discovered at the crime scene and asked rhetorically, "If I put this knit cap on, who am I? I'm still Johnnie Cochran with a knit cap. O.J. Simpson in a knit cap from two blocks away is still O.J. Simpson." With a grin, he pulled off the hat and declared, "If it doesn't fit, you must acquit."

The jury reached a surprisingly swift verdict after less than four hours of deliberation, acquitting O.J. Simpson on two counts of murder and releasing him after 15 months of incarceration. According to Alan M. Dershowitz's book *America on Trial*, the country came to a standstill to witness the live verdict. During that time, long-distance telephone calls dropped by 58 per cent, electric consumption surged, water usage decreased as people hesitated to leave their seats, and trading volume on the New York Stock Exchange dropped by 41 per cent.[35]

Despite being acquitted of the murders, Simpson faced a civil trial in 1997 following a wrongful death lawsuit filed by the families of Nicole Simpson and Ronald Goldman. In this trial, he was found liable for their deaths and mandated to pay $33.5 million in compensatory and punitive damages. Despite his legal troubles, Simpson continued to stay in the public spotlight, making frequent appearances on television and in various media outlets. However, public opinion regarding his guilt remained sharply divided.

In 2007, Simpson found himself in legal trouble once again when he was arrested in Las Vegas on charges of armed robbery and kidnapping. The incident unfolded as he, along with a group of men, confronted sports memorabilia dealers in a hotel room, allegedly to take back his own memorabilia that he claimed had been stolen from him. Subsequently, he was sentenced to 33 years in prison, ultimately serving only nine years.

---

[1] *The Mercury News*, 1 July 1994 – "Bloody Paws Led to Slaying Site Simpson Case"

[2] *The Journal Times*, 14 June 1994 – "O.J. Simpson Questioned in Ex-Wife's Death"

[3] *The Orlando Sentinel*, 26 June 1994 – "Lawyers Add to Star Quality of Incredible Simpson Saga"

[4] *Boston Herald*, 16 June 1994 – "Simpson Gets a New Lawyer and Alibi"

[5] *Los Angeles Times*, 17 June 2019 – "How the O.J. Simpson white Bronco Chase Mesmerized the World"

[6] *USA Today*, 10 January 1995 – "Jury Told to Pack for a Long Trial"

[7] *St. Louis Post-Dispatch*, 5 February 1997 – "Jury Blames Simpson in Beating and Killing of Goldman"

[8] *Daily News of Los Angeles*, 24 January 1995 – "Sidewalk Hoopla Takes Stage"

[9] *Chicago Sun-Times*, 24 January 1995 – "Trial Starts with O.J.'s Other Side"

[10] *Daily Breeze*, 24 January 1995 – "Prosecutor: Jealous O.J. Turned Killer"

[11] *The Mercury News*, 25 January 1995 – "Facts Were Ignored in 'Rush to Judgement'"

[12] The State of California vs. O.J. Simpson

[13] *The Seattle Times*, 31 January 1995 – "First Trial Witnesses Tell of Nicole's 911 Call"

[14] *Akron Beacon Journal*, 3 February 1995 – "Jury Hears Tape of Enraged O.J."

[15] *St. Louis Post-Dispatch*, 3 February 1995 – "O.J. Wrote Nicole 'How Wrong I Was' for 1989 Beating"

[16] *The Times*, 10 February 1995 – "Key Evidence in O.J. Simpson Trial Shows Lone Killer"

[17] *The Dallas Morning News*, 13 February 1995 – "Simpson Jurors Tour Murder Site"

[18] *Boston Herald*, 18 February 1995 – "Notorious Glove, Cap Make First Appearance"

[19] *Delaware County Daily Times*, 10 March 1995 – "Yesterday's Developments in the O.J. Simpson Case"

[20] UPI, 13 March 1995 – "OJ Lawyers Suggest Cop Planted Glove"

[21] *The Charlotte Observer*, 21 March 1995 – "Jury Gets a Look at Simpson's Finger"

[22] *The Toronto Star*, 23 March 1995 – "Witness Says O.J. Hoped He Would Give Solid Alibi"

[23] *Los Angeles Times*, 24 May 1995 – "2nd State Scientist Backs DNA Results"

[24] *The Times*, 20 June 1995 – "Expert Links Size of Shoe Prints to O.J."

[25] *The Hamilton Spectator*, 17 June 1995 – "Glove Found at Scene of Killings Shrank"

[26] UPI, 10 July 1995 – "O.J.'s Family Members Called to Stand"

[27] *Daily Breeze*, 12 July 1995 – "Neighbor Recalls 2 Male Voices"

[28] The Augusta Chronicle, 14 July 1995 – "Judge Rejects Defense's Drug Theory"

[29] *Waterloo Region Record*, 14 July 1995 – "An Agitated Simpson Still Gave Autograph, Witness Tells Court"

[30] *St. Louis Post-Dispatch*, 20 July 1995 – "Witness: O.J.'s Bronco Unsecured"

[31] *Sun Sentinel*, 28 July 1995 – "Expert Says Blood on Sock Was Applied, not Spattered"

[32] *The Hamilton Spectator*, 3 August 1995 – "L.A. Police Lab Work 'Sloppy'"

[33] *The Journal Times*, 23 September 1995 – "O.J. Tells Court He's Innocent"

[34] *The Augusta Chronicle*, 27 September 1995 – "Jurors Urged to Rely on 'Cool Wind of Reason'"

[35] *America on Trial: Inside the Legal Battles That Transformed Our Nation* by Alan M. Dershowitz

Repeat Offender

Home is supposed to be a place of safety. However, the security of the family home proved a tragic illusion for 12-year-old Polly Klaas, abducted from her bedroom by a habitual criminal named Richard Allen Davis. His subsequent trial for murder featured an unconventional and controversial defence. The case also had a profound impact on the public's awareness of child abduction and prompted the enactment of California's "Three Strikes" law.

"I won't be asking you to acquit Mr Davis. We won't be offering any excuses for what Mr Davis did, but we will be asking you to convict Mr Davis of what the evidence shows."

Defence Attorney Barry Collins

It was a quiet night in the peaceful community of Petaluma, California on the 1st of October 1993. Twelve-year-old Polly Klaas was having a slumber party at 427 Fourth Street with two of her friends, Kate and Gillian, when at about 10:30 p.m., Richard Allen Davis, armed with a knife, entered the house through the unlocked back door. Davis had a lengthy criminal record, with three prison terms totalling 14 years. In 1976, he was convicted of kidnap and assault and served five years. In 1984, he was convicted of kidnapping, robbery, first-degree burglary, and assault and served eight years of a 16-year sentence.[1]

Polly opened her bedroom door to find him standing there. He ordered the girls not to scream or "I'll slit your throats". He tied and gagged them and then left with Polly.[2] Kate and Gillian wriggled free and woke up Polly's mother, Eve, who called the police.

The abduction galvanized the local community. Vast numbers of volunteers assisted in the search for Polly. Posters featuring her face were printed in the thousands. Scores of people wore purple ribbons, her favourite colour, as a sign of hope she would be found safe and well. Based on Kate and Gillian's description of Davis, a sketch was drawn up by forensic composite artist Jeanne Boylan depicting a dark haired, bearded man.

The case began to unravel for Davis just hours after he took Polly. Babysitter Shannon Lynch observed his white Pinto wagon stuck in a ditch near the residence of her employer, Dana Jaffe, on Pythian Road, Santa Rosa. Sheriff's Deputies Mike Rankin and Thomas Howard ran Davis's plates, unaware of the recent kidnapping over in Petaluma, and found nothing unusual. However, noticing an opened bottle of beer in the car, they filled out a Field Interrogation card that included Davis's details.

Several weeks later, on the 27th of November, Jaffe found torn, child-sized, red knitted tights, an inside-out, adult-sized dark sweatshirt, and a knotted piece of white silky cloth resembling a hood on her grounds. Nearby, an unused condom and wrapper were discovered by police. Forensic testing at the FBI's crime laboratory in Washington, D.C., confirmed that the hood-shaped cloth matched pieces found in Polly's bedroom.

Detectives revisited the Field Interrogation card and arrested Davis at his sister's home in Ukiah, California. He was held on parole violations at the Mendocino County Jail in Ukiah, while detectives continued their investigation and search for Polly. Marc Klaas, Polly's father, declared, "We understand there has been an arrest . . . but no sign of Polly has been found. Our work will not be done until we find Polly."[3]

The search continued, and on the 4th of December, after he was told that his DNA had been found in her bedroom, Davis confessed to kidnapping and strangling Polly. He subsequently led detectives to her body in a shallow grave in a wooded area south of Cloverdale.[4] On the 8th of December, Davis was formally charged with the kidnapping and murder of Polly, as well as attempted lewd acts on a child, robbery, burglary, assault, and false imprisonment.

As Judge Robert Dale read out the charges, Davis appeared relaxed, grinning several times during the proceedings. His casual demeanour sharply contrasted with public defender Bruce Kinnison's statement that Davis seemed suicidal and had "cried periodically" during their conversations. Kinnison told Ohio's *Dayton Daily News*, "I've dealt with other people accused of these kinds of crimes and they always had a way of deflecting the responsibility. I was really surprised at how direct he was. He was immediately remorseful."[5]

On the 22nd of December, Davis entered a barely audible not guilty plea to all charges. Following a three-day preliminary hearing, Judge Robert Dale ordered him to stand trial, expressing scepticism about parts of Davis's confession, especially his claim of marijuana and alcohol impairing his memory of Polly's kidnapping.[6] Prosecutors announced that they were seeking the death penalty against Davis if convicted.

Before the trial began, Superior Court Judge Lawrence Antolini imposed a ban on cameras in the courtroom other than to take photographs before proceedings began each day.[7] This was partly due to the excessive media coverage surrounding the then-current O.J. Simpson trial. He stated, "We are presently seeing media saturation of a trial in Southern California. They are more interested in Simpson than any soap opera or sports. They are television groupies for the Simpson case."[8] In September 1995, after two months of jury selection, Judge Antolini, seeking a more impartial jury, decided to move the trial from Sonoma to Santa Clara County. The change of venue came with a change of judge, as Antolini was replaced by Santa Clara Superior Court Judge Thomas Hastings.

A jury of six men and six women was selected and opening statements began in the Santa Clara County Hall of Justice with Prosecutor Greg Jacobs on the 17th of April 1996. He detailed the evidence implicating Davis, including his DNA found on Polly's bunk bed, and his confession that led to the discovery of her body. The most dramatic moment came when the 911 call made by Polly's mother was played. She was heard exclaiming, "Apparently, a man just broke into our house, and they said he took my daughter. She's not here. I didn't even hear anything." At one point, she handed the phone to Polly's friend Kate who described a man armed with a knife tying them up before taking off with Polly.

Prosecutor Jacobs said that Polly's body was too decomposed for conclusive evidence of sexual assault, but told the jury that her stretch miniskirt was pulled up above her waist and an unused condom and wrapper were found nearby.[9] The prosecutor asserted that Davis's primary goal that night was to sexually assault and then kill Polly. During Davis's confession, he had been equivocal about sexually assaulting her, telling detectives, "I hope I didn't do nothin' with her. I don't think I did anything to her."[10]

Defence attorney Barry Collins took the floor for his opening statement. In an unusual move, Collins admitted that his client was guilty of the murder of Polly but announced plans to contest a specific allegation: that Davis had sexually assaulted her. Addressing the jury, he said, "I won't be asking you to acquit Mr Davis. We won't be offering any excuses for what Mr Davis did, but we will be asking you to convict Mr Davis of what the evidence shows." He highlighted that no evidence of a sexual assault could be found, and while the pathologist said this was due to advanced decomposition, Collins said that even Egyptian mummies embalmed for centuries had yielded DNA evidence.

Collins's strategic admission aimed to temper the jury's potential outrage over the forthcoming testimony, with the hope of saving Davis from a death sentence. However, it sent shockwaves through the courtroom, catching everyone off guard. Expressing his surprise, Marc Klaas stated, "I was really blown away by that. It doesn't make much sense to me. Good Lord, two-and-a-half years and millions of dollars and it turns out that they're going to admit that he did it anyway." Prosecutor Cliff Harris also criticized the defence's approach, noting that while it wouldn't alter their case, it could expedite the trial proceedings.[11]

Testimony then got underway with Polly's mother recounting the events of the night her daughter was abducted. The anguish etched across her face was unmistakable as she detailed asking the girls to keep the noise down and not stay up too late. She recalled, "And

Polly said, 'Good night, Mommy,' and that was the last time I saw her." Jacobs prompted her to identify the pair of red tights discovered on Pythian Road, which she confirmed belonged to her daughter.[12]

Polly's friends, Kate McLean and Gillian Pelham, testified after Eve. They recalled the slumber party, Davis's attack, and Polly's abduction in confident and animated tones. Gillian told the court, "He said, 'Don't scream or I'll slit your throats.' I thought it was some sort of joke because I didn't think that that sort of thing really happened." They both described how all three were ordered to lie face down on the floor before he bound them, pulled pillowcases over their heads, and gagged them. They remembered that Davis said he wanted to find valuables and took Polly out of the room with him and told them by the time they counted to one thousand, she would be back.

Both girls avoided looking at Davis until they were asked by the prosecutor to identify him. Kate said she couldn't positively identify him. Gillian was more assertive, maintaining that he was the man who disrupted their slumber party and abducted Polly.

Following the girls' testimonies, Kamika Milstead, a teenage neighbour, took the stand and recounted an incident on the evening of Polly's abduction. She described peering out of her bedroom window and spotting a man resembling Davis sitting in a car across the street. A thin man approached the car and engaged Davis in conversation, seemingly gesturing towards the Klaas residence. As this unknown man moved away, Milstead saw Davis retrieve a bag from his car – which, the prosecution contended, held the fabric used to bind Polly and her three friends.

During lunch break, prosecutor Jacobs downplayed Milstead's testimony: "I'm not saying Davis didn't have contact with people that night." He suggested that Davis may have just been familiarizing himself with the neighbourhood, refuting speculation that two people might have been involved in Polly's abduction and murder. He also pointed out that Milstead's testimony didn't fit with the evidence, as she identified Davis's car as a grey, four-door Honda with primer patches, whereas his car was actually a white 1979 Ford Pinto.

Two other teenagers, Thomas Georges and Taleah Miller, recalled seeing Davis in the neighbourhood on the night Polly was abducted. Taleah was being dropped off home after seeing a movie but waited for Davis to walk past before she got out of the car, telling the court, "He was just kind of scary looking. He just kind of stood out."[13] Sean Bush, who was visiting friends near Polly's house, said he saw Davis walk up to the back door and open it.[14] All of them said that Davis didn't appear to be intoxicated.

All of the testimony focusing on Davis's movements that night was an effort by Jacobs to undermine his story that he was high on drugs and alcohol at the time of the kidnapping. Davis had claimed he didn't remember a thing, until he found himself driving around the Sonoma Valley with Polly in the front seat.

Another witness, Daryl Stone, claimed he saw Davis in two parks near Polly's home the weekend before, and the prosecution sought to show this meant that he had specifically targeted Polly and been stalking her. Stone also said that he saw Davis again on the night of Polly's abduction, cruising the neighbourhood in his car. Under defence cross-examination by Collins, Stone revealed he hadn't mentioned his earlier sightings of Davis when interviewed by the FBI in November 1993.[15] Stone also said that the man he saw had tattoos on his arms, which prompted Judge Thomas Hastings to tell Davis to pull up his sleeves, revealing intricate blue tattoos.

During Davis's confession, he had claimed that he had never been in Petaluma before, but Stone's testimony cast doubt on this. Another witness, Barbara Fugate Horne, also testified that she had seen him in the area in mid-September. She maintained that she saw him with a woman and what she thought was a small child at Walnut Park, one of the parks where Stone had claimed to have seen him. She later saw him on a bench with a tall, thin man – the second reference to an unknown man. According to the prosecution, the police had tried but failed to identify him.[16]

Eleven-year-old Stephen Butts testified that he had encountered Davis in Wickersham Park, around the corner from Polly's home, three weeks before the kidnapping. He said that Davis was drunk and vomiting at the time. When he asked if Davis was okay, Davis responded sharply, "Get the hell away from me, you stupid kid." Similarly, Harvey Podstata, who was working on some commercial paintings across the street from Wickersham Park, testified he had seen Davis in the area twelve or fifteen times over about ten days the summer before Polly was kidnapped.[17] "He was dressed poorly. His whole demeanour was that of a person you would look at twice, and probably you would be frightened of him."[18]

Outside the courtroom, Collins expressed his belief that well-intentioned witnesses may have mistakenly identified others in the area as Davis, possibly influenced by a subconscious desire to aid in his conviction. When the trial proceeded the next morning, Davis's confession was played aloud. He said he had never been to Petaluma before and had no recollection of abducting Polly because he was "toasted". The next thing he remembered was driving around with her in the front seat. "If I let her go, I'd be going back to the joint." Without showing any emotion, he said that he had strangled her with a piece of cloth.[19]

Davis also claimed that he had hidden Polly in nearby bushes after his car got stuck in a ditch in the hours after he abducted her and before the police arrived. "I went back a half an hour later and was lucky to find her," he said, before adding, "Well, I guess it was unlucky ... unlucky for her." The prosecution didn't believe this part of Davis's confession. They believed that Polly was already dead.

When Deputy Thomas Howard testified about helping Davis to get his car out of the ditch, he said he thought he smelled alcohol on Davis's breath but felt that it was "a routine traffic call". He said that once Davis was out of the ditch, they escorted him out of the private driveway and told him to leave the area. Davis just pulled over to the side of the road, but since it was a busy night, Deputies Howard and Rankin left the area. Marc Klaas made some choice comments following Howard's testimony, saying, "These deputies really dropped the ball."[20]

On the 3rd of May, the jury revisited 427 Fourth Street, the site of Polly's abduction two and a half years earlier. In another van and guarded by numerous police officers and a helicopter, Davis accompanied them. Subsequently, the jury proceeded to Pythian Road, although they were unable to view the area where Polly's remains were discovered because it had been transformed into an impromptu memorial park.[21]

The following morning, Dr A. Jay Chapman, the pathologist who performed Polly's autopsy, detailed his findings in matter-of-fact tones. He revealed that Polly's skull was located at a distance from her body, with her hair detached. Some of her skin exhibited mummification, while other parts had reduced to skeletal remains. He added that Polly's advanced decomposition made it impossible to determine her exact cause of death, but he noted that pieces of cloth and rope found in her hair indicated she was strangled. He further testified that it was impossible to detect the presence of semen because there was no "identifiable remnant of any organ". However, Polly's legs were splayed, and her clothing pushed above her waist. Chapman's testimony proved so distressing that most of Polly's family left the courtroom. Marc tearfully commented to reporters, "This is terrible stuff. My Lord, I've got an image of Polly in my mind, and I can't let that go."[22]

Even though Davis had already confessed to Polly's murder, FBI DNA expert Harold Deadman testified that Davis's DNA was discovered in Polly's bedroom. Trish Phan, a lab technician from the California Men's Colony at San Luis Obispo, where Davis had been incarcerated before the abduction, testified about extracting a blood sample from him. She explained to him that the DNA in the blood could indicate whether he was the perpetrator of a sexual crime. Prosecutor Jacobs, commenting outside the court, suggested that Davis was aware that DNA from blood or semen could incriminate him, citing the discovery of a condom at the alleged site of Polly's sexual assault.[23]

The prosecution then tried to prove that the condom belonged to Davis, calling on Jeannette Marie Turner, the former owner of a shop named Seductions in Ukiah. She said that either on the day of or the day before the abduction of Polly, Davis had purchased a packet of Rough Rider condoms, the same brand found at Pythian Road.[24] The prosecution then called Frances Mays, who tearfully recalled that, on the 24th of September 1976, she was abducted by Davis – an ordeal that, prosecutors said, had similarities to Polly's abduction. She said that he came up behind her as she walked to her car, put a knife to her back, and forced his way into her car. He drove to a remote spot, "unzipped his pants and exposed himself to me." Seconds later, a car happened to pass slowly by. She managed to grab Davis's knife, unlock the door with her other hand, and chase after the car.[25] She subsequently reported the incident to police; Davis was arrested and convicted.

Forensic psychiatrist Dr Park Dietz, known for assessing the serial killer Jeffrey Dahmer and would-be presidential assassin John Hinckley Jr, was the prosecution's last witness. He hadn't interviewed Davis but, based his conclusions on Davis's extensive criminal history and mental evaluations. Dr Dietz asserted that Davis fit the profile of a sexual deviant with fantasies of victimization, emphasizing a pattern of abduction, hostage-taking, and control through threats or weapons. He characterized Davis's actions during Polly's kidnapping as indicative of "paraphilia", a condition marked by enduring patterns of unusual sexual arousal.[26] He suggested Davis had stalked Polly before abducting her, confidently telling the court, "He is like the director of a play, where he writes the script, sometimes even giving the victims lines to speak, and choreographs every move".[27]

The first defence witness was parole agent Thomas Berns, who said that on the 15th of October 1993, parole officials had decided to downgrade Davis's level of supervision from "high control" to "control service" which meant fewer supervisory contacts. Defence attorney Lorena Chandler said that it was clear parole officials hadn't "supervised him well" adding that they "kind of set him up for failure, and now they want to kill him for it".[28] The defence next called Detective Michael Meese, who pointed out inconsist-encies in Turner's testimony about selling Davis condoms. She had told detectives she knew it was either on the 30th of September or on the 1st of October 1993, because those were the only two days she worked. However, in phone interview with defence attorneys, she said she worked in the store all summer, and that the condom was a different brand.[29] (It would never be established how the condom came to be there, when it was left, or who dropped it.)

The defence's case was short owing to the fact that they had set their sights on the penalty phase of the trial when they hoped to influence the jury not to condemn Davis to death. During closing arguments, the prosecution maintained that Davis had targeted Polly in particular, stalked her, and then made the decision to kill her. "He weighed his going back to prison with Polly's life," said Prosecutor Greg Jacobs.[30] As he promised from the start of the trial, defence attorney Barry Collins did not ask for an acquittal. Instead, he asked the jury to convict Davis on everything, *except* the charge of attempting a lewd act on a child: "I'm not asking you to let Mr Davis off on anything or excuse his conduct in any way." [31]

The jury returned with their verdict after deliberating for about twenty hours over four days, finding Richard Allen Davis guilty on all counts. As the verdict was read aloud, Davis winked, kissed the air, and then raised his two middle fingers to the television cameras that had been granted access to record the verdict. Marc commented on the gesture outside court, saying, "He was showing us what he is, just a contemptible little punk who's been flipping off society since day one."[32] Many within the courtroom, and those who watched live on TV, speculated that the gesture would come back to haunt Davis during the trial's penalty phase.

On the 2nd of July, the courtroom brimmed with anticipation as Davis, flanked by his defence team, prepared to defend his life. Chandler argued that his troubled past, marked by abandonment and incarceration, made him a "damaged human being" undeserving of death. She suggested that "dark forces" had made him the man he was, and detailed his childhood yearning for a mother who abandoned him, followed by a grim adolescence and a life spent behind bars. In contrast, Jacobs urged the jury to consider the heinous nature of Polly's murder and its profound impact on her family.

The prosecution opened proceedings by calling several of Davis's previous victims, whose testimonies unveiled the deep scars left by Davis's actions. Marjorie Mitchell recounted a horrifying assault on the 17th of December 1976 that resulted in 30 stitches after Davis struck her with a poker. Mays repeated the details of her own abduction in 1976. Selina Varich recounted a traumatic experience on the 30th of November 1984, where she was assaulted and abducted. Davis drove her to a Mountain View bank and forced her to withdraw $6,000. Hazel Frost described an encounter on the 20th of December 1976, when Davis abducted her and held a shotgun to her neck. Each of these brave women revealed that, since the attacks, they had grappled with fear, sleeping with the lights on, and feeling apprehensive if approached by strangers on the street. The intention behind their testimony was to establish a pattern of Davis's violent behaviour persisting for years prior to the abduction and murder of Polly.[33]

Subsequently, the prosecution presented photographs of Polly's mother and sister, Annie, taken by the police on the 2nd of October

1993. The images depicted them huddled together in an oversized living-room chair their faces etched with grief. Polly's father Marc then provided a heart-wrenching account of the immense loss of his daughter. "Every time I see a pretty little 12-year-old girl, I am reminded of Polly." He described her as a happy and intelligent girl who had many interests, and fondly reminisced about teaching her to swim and play basketball. He added that Polly had some fears: "She was afraid of the dark. She was afraid of being alone. She was afraid that a bad man would come and take her in the night."[34]

The prosecution rested its case, and the defence began its effort to save Davis from a death sentence, calling on his 91-year-old grandmother, Norma Watson Johnny. She described him as a "nice little boy", "cute", and "lovable". Johnny appeared to try and catch Davis's eye from time to time, but he didn't return her gaze. Davis's aunt, Irene Davis, and Pearl Willhite who cared for him as a child, also testified, in a defence attempt to show that "dark forces" subsequently shaped Davis's life, turning him from a sweet little boy to a "damaged human being". Testimony was presented about how Davis's longshoreman father, Robert Davis, worked day and night and was rarely home. When he was, he was strict and intimidating. Davis's mother, Evelyn, was portrayed as an alcoholic who showed little affection towards her five children.

After Davis's parents separated, he and his siblings experienced a fragmented upbringing, shuttling between grandmothers' homes and their father's residences. Their mother remained uninvolved with the children except for Davis's oldest brother. Johnny revealed that Davis became involved with drugs after their father relocated the family to San Mateo County. Outside the court, Prosecutor Jacobs was sceptical about the defence's tactics. "I'm kind of watching to see what the dark forces that were mentioned in the opening statements are."[35]

Davis's defence called witnesses from his prison past as an inmate worker at the California Department of Corrections. James Park, a long-time prison system administrator, testified that the only time Davis was a productive member of society was during his time in prison. Patrick Schmidt, his former vocational sheet-metal instructor, highlighted Davis's success in the program. Engineer John Kellerman noted that Davis's reputation as a good worker secured him a temporary position in the prison's repair shop.[36]

Psychologist Lorelei Sontag testified that Davis had endured an abusive childhood. On two occasions his mother held his hand over an open flame. In addition, his father physically assaulted him, once punching Davis so hard that he crashed through a sheetrock wall. During cross-examination, Prosecutor Cliff Harris claimed that Davis's childhood wasn't as harsh as described and emphasized that his siblings had become productive members of society.[37] Davis's sister, Darlene Schwarm, however, discussing their childhood, recalled that their father had broken Davis's jaw on one occasion. (No mention was made during the trial of the young Davis's habit of attacking stray animals as a precursor to his violent crimes.)

The prosecution was seeking a death sentence while the defence hoped for a sentence of life in prison. Davis's fate was soon in the hands of the jury. They deliberated for some twenty-one hours before announcing that Davis deserved to die for the abduction and murder of Polly Klaas. Marc couldn't hide his relief at the verdict, clenching his fist in victory and exclaiming, "Yes!" from the public gallery. Davis simply smiled and spoke quietly with his team. The jury foreman, Brian Bianco, later commented, "We sentenced a man to death. I can't feel good about it. But on the other hand, I feel it was the right decision, so I don't feel bad about it." Polly's grandfather, Joe Klaas, also shared his thoughts on the verdict, stating, "We've been going to hell with Davis. He can go the rest of the way alone."[38]

Davis was formally sentenced to death on the 27th of September 1996. He stood up in court and vigorously criticized his defence attorneys. He also denied he had molested Polly, exclaiming, "The main reason I know I did not attempt any lewd act that night was because of a statement the young girl made to me while walking up the embankment: 'Just don't do me like my dad.'" Spectators in the courtroom gasped in shock. A close friend of Marc's, San Jose City Attorney Mike Groves shouted, "Burn in hell, Davis," as Marc attempted to launch himself at his daughter's killer. Prosecutor Greg Jacobs commented that no such claim had ever been made during the case, nor was there a single piece of evidence to support it.

Following Davis's outburst, Superior Court Judge Thomas Hastings confirmed the death sentence. He had the ability to reduce the sentence to life in prison without parole but said that Davis's behaviour made it "easy" to impose the death sentence.[39] Davis appealed his sentence in June 2009, but it was upheld by the California Supreme Court.

In the wake of Davis's conviction, public outrage, with Polly's father, Marc, at the forefront, led to the implementation of California's Three Strike Law on the 8th of March 1994. This means that persons convicted of an offence who have two other serious convictions – like Davis – will serve a mandatory sentence of 25 years to life or triple the usual sentence for the offence, whichever is greater.[40]

Richard Allen Davis remains incarcerated on California's Death Row in the Adjustment Center at San Quentin State Prison.

---

[1] *San Francisco Chronicle*, 10 December 1993 – "Richard Allen Davis – How Suspect Became 'Quintessential Convict'"

[2] *Akron Beacon Journal*, 7 October 1993 – "Town Takes Action"

[3] UPI, 1 December 1993 – "Suspect in Klaas Kidnapping Named"

[4] *Austin American-Statesman*, 6 December 1993 – "Town Mourns After Girl's Body Found"

[5] *Dayton Daily News*, 8 December 1993 – "Polly's Killer 'Sad'"

[6] *News & Record*, 14 May 1994 – "Suspect in Girl's Death to Stand Trial for Murder"

[7] *The Press Democrat*, 7 March 1995 – "No Camera in Davis Trial"

[8] *The Press Democrat*, 7 September 1995 – "Cameras Barred from Davis Trial"

[9] *The Columbian*, 17 April 1996 – "Klaas Jury Hears 911 Abduction Tape"

[10] *The Sacramento Bee*, 17 April 1996 – "Voices from the Past Opens Klaas Trial"

[11] *Daily News of Los Angeles*, 18 April 1996 – "Defence Says Suspect Killed Klaas"

[12] *The Press Democrat*, 18 April 1996 – "Lawyer Admits Davis Guilty"

[13] *San Francisco Chronicle*, 19 April 1996 – "Klaas Jury Told of Mystery Man"

[14] *The Press Democrat*, 19 April 1996 – "Witnesses Saw Davis in Neighborhood"

[15] *Contra Costa Times*, 19 April 1996 – "Allen Prosecutors Build Stalking Case in Quest for Death Penalty"

[16] *Contra Costa Times*, 23 April 1996 – "Others Saw Davis Near Klaas' Home"

[17] *The Press Democrat*, 23 April 1996 – "3 Witnesses Recall Davis Sightings"

[18] *San Francisco Chronicle*, 23 April 1996 – "Stalking Theory Bolstered by Witnesses in Polly Case"

[19] *Contra Costa Times*, 24 April 1996 – "Davis Told Police Polly Had to Die if he Were to Stay Free"

[20] UPI, 24 April 1996 – "Davis Acted Normal During Stop"

[21] *The Press Democrat*, 3 May 1996 – "Jury Visits Crime Scenes Davis Returns to Petaluma"

[22] *Contra Costa Times*, 7 May 1996 – "Autopsy Testimony at Davis Trial Sends Klaas Family from Court"

[23] *San Francisco Chronicle*, 9 May 1996 – "Hair Found in Polly's House Was from Davis, FBI Expert Says"

[24] *Contra Costa Times*, 15 May 1996 – "Prosecution Witness Says She Sold Davis Condoms"

[25] *Daily Breeze*, 16 May 1996 – "Attack by Klaas' Confessed Killer Detailed"

[26] *The Mercury News*, 22 May 1996 – "Davis Fits Profile of Deviant, Sex-Crimes Expert Testifies"

[27] *San Francisco Chronicle*, 22 May 1996 – "Davis Stalked Polly, Sex Crime Expert Says"

[28] *The Press Democrat*, 29 May 1996 – "Davis Defese Testimony Wrapping up"

[29] *San Francisco Chronicle*, 29 May 1996 – "Defense Opens in Klaas Case"

[30] *The Orlando Sentinel*, 11 June 1996 – "Prosecutor: Davis Killed Polly Klaas to Avoid Prison"

[31] Contra Costa Times, 12 June 1996 – "Davis' Lawyer Seeks an Acquittal Only on Molestation"

[32] *The Charlotte Observer*, 19 June 1996 – "Davis is Found Guilty of Polly Klaas Murder"

[33] *Contra Costa Times*, 3 July 1996 – "Davis Victims Tell of Fears, Pain Suffered 20 Years Later"

[34] *Contra Costa Times*, 4 July 1996 – "Marc Klaas Describes Life of Pain without his Polly"

[35] *The Press Democrat*, 11 July 1996 – "Grandmother: Davis 'Nice Boy' Aunt, Caretaker Also Recall Children, Parents"

[36] *The Press Democrat*, 12 July 1006 – "Witnesses Praise Davis' Prison Value"

[37] *Contra Costa Times*, 16 July 1996 – "Psychologist Says Abuse from Parents Destroyed Davis"

[38] *Akron Beacon Journal*, 6 August 1996 – "Jury Chooses Death for Child's Murderer"

[39] *Philadelphia Daily News*, 27 September 1996 – "A Vicious Insult from a Vile Killer"

[40] *San Francisco Chronicle*, 8 March 1994 – "Three Strikes Signed into California Law"

"I Think I Killed Someone"

Record producer Phil Spector's "Wall of Sound" revolutionized 1960s pop music creating a lush and dramatic sonic experience. Spector had left an indelible mark on the music industry, producing records for the likes of The Ronettes, Ike and Tina Turner, The Beatles, George Harrison, and John Lennon, before his life took a dark turn. In 2003 he was arrested in connection with the death of B-movie actor Lana Clarkson, found shot dead at his home. Spector's trial not only captured public attention but also shifted the narrative surrounding him. Media outlets that once celebrated his musical achievements were now dominated by the tragic events surrounding Lana's murder and revelations about Spector's treatment of other women.

———————

"This is a trial of public interest. I always have a problem with commentators telling people what is going on, rather than letting the public see the trial for themselves."

Los Angeles Superior Court Judge Larry Paul Fidler

———————

In the early morning hours of the 3rd of February 2003, a gunshot shattered the peace of the wealthy suburb of Alhambra, Los Angeles, California. At 5:02 a.m., a 911 call came in from Adrian de Souza, chauffeur of 62-year-old record producer Phil Spector.

De Souza reported that he had recently dropped Spector off at his baroque mansion, known as the Pyrenees Castle, in the 1700 block of Grandview Drive. Spector was accompanied by Lana Clarkson, a 40-year-old actress best known for starring in the fantasy movie *Barbarian Queen* (1985). De Souza was sitting outside in Spector's Mercedes S430 limousine when he heard the sound of the gunshot coming from inside the house, after which Spector came outside with a gun in his hand and said, "I think I killed someone."[1]

Police summoned to Spector's impressive residence discovered Lana's lifeless body slumped in an antique chair in the marble foyer. She had suffered a gunshot wound to the mouth, resulting in shattered teeth, with the bullet traversing her spinal cord and skull. Beneath her left leg lay a .38 calibre Colt Cobra revolver. Spector was promptly taken in for questioning and the investigation was handed over to the Los Angeles County Sheriff's Department.

During questioning, Spector informed detectives that he had met Lana for the first time that night at the House of Blues on Sunset Strip, West Hollywood (now a luxury hotel named the

Pendry West Hollywood), where she worked as a hostess. At first, he rudely asserted that he had accidentally shot Lana; he later claimed she had taken her own life. At one point, he disparaged her for entering his home and allegedly "blowing her brains out".

Spector was booked on suspicion of murder but released that evening after posting a $1 million bond. He retained defence attorney Robert Shapiro, renowned for representing O.J. Simpson and who had previously represented Spector in various civil cases spanning seven years.[2] While Spector remained free on bail, the investigation into Lana's death continued. In early March, Spector circulated an email to friends asserting that he had been "cleared" of Clarkson's murder, and her death had been classified as suicide. Sheriff's Capt. Frank Merriman countered Spector's claims, publicly declaring, "If we had come to a conclusion as monumental as suicide, we would have a duty to say so publicly. We believe a crime occurred."[3]

The following month, Spector gave an interview to *Esquire* magazine in which he vehemently proclaimed his innocence and suggested that Lana had shot herself after consuming a bottle of tequila. During the interview, he asserted, "She kissed the gun. I have no idea why. I never knew her, never even saw her before that night. I have no idea who she was or what her agenda was." Spector accused police of orchestrating a "frame-up" and confidently stated, "If they had any evidence against me, I'd be sitting in jail right now."[4]

In September, investigators submitted their findings to state prosecutors tasked with deciding whether to pursue criminal charges against Spector. While the District Attorney's office deliberated, Spector's bail was extended. On the 20th of November, Spector appeared at the Los Angeles courthouse, shielded from photographers by his entourage. He was formally charged with Lana Clarkson's murder, to which he pleaded not guilty. Exiting the court that afternoon, Robert Shapiro announced the assembly of an expert group of scientific professionals for Spector's defence.[5]

Despite facing a murder charge, Spector remained at liberty on bail. In the ensuing year, he opted to replace Robert Shapiro with Leslie Abramson, a prominent and vibrant criminal defence lawyer renowned for her involvement in the murder trial of brothers Lyle and Erik Menéndez. Abramson was initially contemplating retirement but cited Spector as a unique case, declaring, "No other defendant would get me to give up my freedom. No other defendant was someone I considered an idol, an icon, and the definition of cool."[6] However, in August, Abramson resigned, and Spector enlisted the services of Bruce Cutler, an attorney known for his defence of mob boss John Gotti of the Gambino crime family.

Spector made a courtroom return towards the end of September 2004, facing an indictment for Lana's murder. During this brief appearance, he vehemently criticized prosecutors, likening them to "Hitler-like figures".[7] The indictment signalled Spector's progression to trial, though the trial date was delayed multiple times as Spector's team sought to exclude various pieces of evidence, including his incriminating statements that portrayed Lana's death as an accident.

Prior to the commencement of jury selection in March 2007, Los Angeles Superior Court Judge Larry Paul Fidler declared his decision to allow the trial to be televised, granting the media full coverage from gavel to gavel. Justifying his choice, he explained, "This is a trial of public interest. I always have a problem with commentators telling people what is going on, rather than letting the public see the trial for themselves."[8] Following a week of jury selection, a panel of nine men and three women was chosen from approximately 100 prospects.[9]

On the morning of the 25th of April 2007, Spector entered Room 106 of the Los Angeles Superior Court, dressed in a tan three-piece suit with a knee-length jacket, platform shoes, and a distinctive wide-collared purple shirt. He wore a blond wig, a departure from his previous court appearances when the media commented on his dishevelled appearance and frizzy hair. Lana's family occupied the front row of the crowded courtroom, where onlookers were standing owing to limited space. Outside the courtroom, Spector's new wife, Rachelle, forty years his junior, distributed Team Spector badges before taking her place in the public gallery.[10]

The prosecution pursued a theory of "implied malice", contending that Spector did not intend to kill Lana but caused her death through reckless behaviour and by taking an extreme risk. Prosecutor Alan Jackson, a youthful-looking veteran with 12 years of experience in the office, declared, "The evidence is going to paint a very, very clear picture of a man, Phil Spector, who turns sinister and deadly in certain circumstances. It is going to paint a picture of a man who put a loaded pistol inside Lana Clarkson's mouth and shot her to death."

Jackson asserted that Lana's murder followed decades of Spector's violent outbursts against women involving firearms: "The evidence will show he has a very rich history of violence against women, a history of violence involving guns."[11] During Jackson's opening statements, a graphic crime scene photograph of Lana was shown to the jury. As the prosecutor outlined his case, Spector squirmed in his seat at the defence table. Occasionally, one of his team members, Linda Kenney-Baden, placed an arm around his shoulders.

Following Jackson's presentation, attorney Bruce Cutler commenced his defence. He accused detectives of prematurely concluding that Lana's death was a murder: "The evidence will show that back on February 3 of '03, before they even had a cause of death, let alone a manner of death, they had murder on their mind."[12] Cutler also voiced doubts about the linguistic abilities of Adrian de Souza, who had quoted Spector as saying he thought he had killed somebody.

Regarding Spector's relationships with women, Cutler portrayed him as a "true romantic of a bygone era". The defence said that

Lana "fired the gun herself", contending that all the evidence would support this claim: "A self-inflicted gunshot wound can be accidental suicide, and that's what it was." Cutler then proceeded to challenge the credibility of various women scheduled to testify about Spector's alleged violent behaviour. Linda Kenney-Baden then took Cutler's place at the podium, informing the jury that gunshot residue had been found on Lana's hands and jacket, while none was discovered on Spector.

Opening arguments concluded, Jackson proceeded to call his first witness: Dorothy Melvin, former manager of American comedian Joan Rivers. In a tense courtroom atmosphere, Melvin disclosed her experiences with Spector during an evening at his Pasadena residence in 1993. Initially, she portrayed Spector in a positive light, describing him as "charming" during their casual dating in the early 1990s. However, her narrative took a dark turn when she revealed waking up on a couch before dawn to find Spector pointing a snub-nosed revolver at her car. Melvin recounted how her screams prompted Spector to turn the gun on her, eventually striking her twice on the head with it.[13]

She disclosed that Spector, who had consumed almost an entire bottle of vodka the previous night, accused her of snooping around his home for items to steal and sell. He then ordered her to undress, but she only took off her jacket. Despite allowing her to leave, Spector threatened her with a shotgun when she reached the end of his driveway and found the gates closed.

Melvin was torn between seeking justice for herself and protecting Joan Rivers from unwanted publicity; after reporting the incident to the police, she decided not to press charges. "I didn't want it to become a *National Enquirer* cover," she explained. Under cross-examination by Roger Rosen, a member of Spector's defence team, Melvin admitted she continued to communicate with Spector via email, mail, and fax after the disturbing incident.[14]

Before the trial resumed next day, the prosecution accused the defence of withholding evidence. Lawyer Sara Caplan, who had earlier worked with Robert Shapiro on Spector's defence, suggested that forensic scientist Dr Henry Lee, hired by the defence, had taken a piece of evidence – possibly an acrylic nail – from the crime scene. She stated that he placed it in a vial, and she had no knowledge of its whereabouts. In his official report, Lee claimed to have recovered only two white threads and some carpet fibre.[15]

Other individuals claimed to have seen Dr Lee picking something up from the floor. Prosecutors accused the defence of concealing evidence that could have shed light on whether Lana was engaged in some sort of a struggle at the time of her death. Ultimately, Judge Fidler agreed that Dr Lee had removed an item from the crime scene and concealed it from the prosecution. Despite this, he decided not to hold Dr Lee in contempt due to conflicting accounts of the incident.[16]

The jury then returned to the courtroom and proceedings continued with Dianne Ogden-Halder, an ex-girlfriend of Spector's. She recounted three instances during the 1980s when he prevented her leaving his home. In the second incident in March 1989, he pressed the barrel of a handgun against her cheek and forehead. She recalled, "He was talking, screaming, like he had been taken over by something. He was demonic."

Ogden-Halder described how he ordered her upstairs and attempted to rape her after rejecting her pleas to leave, saying, "He didn't have to do that; he could have been romantic, but he did it at gunpoint. He wanted to rape me. I don't know why he was doing this." During another confrontation, she asserted that Spector threatened her with a gun, prompting her to escape at high speed in her car. She added that she didn't report the incident because she wanted to shield Spector from adverse publicity.[17]

Next on the witness stand was Stephanie Jennings, a rock music photographer, who testified that Spector had brandished a handgun and prevented her from leaving the Carlyle Hotel after they attended the Rock & Roll Hall of Fame Awards in early 1995. Jennings, who had a casual relationship with Spector in 1994, recounted that during the awards show after-party, she noticed he was "a little drunk" and had become "extremely obnoxious, loud, and insulting". Returning to her hotel room alone, she was disturbed by a knock from Spector's security guard, insisting she visit Spector's suite. When she refused, Spector appeared. When she declined to accompany him to his suite, he slapped and pushed her. He returned shortly afterwards with a gun. "He put a chair against the door and told me I was not going anywhere. I thought I was about to be shot." Despite informing the police, she returned to Philadelphia without pressing charges.[18]

Following Jennings, Melissa Grosvenor took the stand. Having met Spector while a restaurant server, she recounted an incident at his home in the early 1990s. Visiting from New York, she told Spector she was tired and leaving, to which he responded, "What? You want to go?" He left the room and returned minutes later with a handgun in a shoulder holster. Grosvenor told the jury that Spector approached her, holding the gun inches from her face, and declared, "If you leave, I'm going to kill you." Eventually falling asleep in a chair, she awoke the next morning to find Spector acting normally, asking her out to breakfast.[19]

Spector's defence attempted to challenge Grosvenor's testimony, with Rosen suggesting that she hadn't disclosed certain details to detectives in 2004, such as Spector having a gun holster. Grosvenor insisted she was confident she had mentioned this fact. When asked whether Spector had put the gun in her mouth, she initially denied it but then added, "If he had, I would've because I would have done anything he told me." Rosen also compelled Grosvenor to acknowledge a previous conviction for embezzlement in Georgia.[20]

After these unsettling accounts, the focus shifted to the night of Lana's death. Rommie Davis, a high-school friend of Spector's, testified that they had dinner that evening at the Grill on the Alley in Beverly Hills. She expressed concern that Spector, who had previously been teetotal, was drinking and taking medication, and "was not his usual self".[21] Spector drove Davis home around 11:15 p.m. Afterwards, he returned to the city, visiting various nightclubs and consuming more daiquiris and rum while leaving generous tips for the servers.[22]

Around 2 a.m., Spector arrived at the House of Blues accompanied by Kathy Sullivan, a friend and server at the Grill on the Alley. Sullivan testified that they were headed to the club's Foundation Room when Lana Clarkson intercepted them, informing them that they couldn't enter. She hadn't recognized Spector, prompting him to ask, "Don't you know who I am?" Once another club employee intervened and identified Spector, Lana became more accommodating. While Sullivan concurred with Rosen's portrayal of Spector as pleasant and considerate, she recounted an incident when she and another server visited his home, and when they left, he escorted them out with a rifle or shotgun, asserting it was for their protection.[23]

At the House of Blues, Sullivan stayed briefly before Spector's chauffeur drove her home. Spector continued drinking heavily, and Sophia Holguin, another House of Blues server, described him as "very agitated and very fast-speaking, a little slurish".[24] When Lana finished her shift, Spector invited her to join him at his table, and by 2:25 a.m. they left the club in his limousine. Erich Berghammer, general manager of the House of Blues, presented security footage depicting the two of them leaving together. When asked by Rosen if Spector appeared intoxicated – stumbling or falling – Berghammer replied that he did not.

The subsequent – and star – witness for the prosecution was Adriano De Souza, Spector's chauffeur. He said that when he drove Spector and Lana back to Spector's home, she appeared hesitant about coming inside. She remarked to De Souza: "I'm just going for one drink," which prompted Spector to shout, "Don't talk to the driver!"[25] De Souza recounted hearing a gunshot sometime later. Afterwards Spector opened a side door of the house with a gun in his blood-spattered hand. When questioned by Jackson about whether Spector said anything, De Souza answered, "He said 'I think I killed somebody.'" When De Souza asked Spector what had happened, he shrugged. De Souza then looked past Spector and saw Lana's legs sprawled in the foyer.

De Souza returned to the witness stand the next day, and said that after seeing Spector with a gun, he drove off, fearing he could be shot himself. "I didn't know what to do. I tried to escape from that place. He could shoot me." While in the limousine, he placed a 911 call, telling the operator, "I'm afraid to go inside [Spector's mansion]." De Souza, originally from Brazil, additionally told the court that he had learned English and had no problems with any language barrier. Anticipating Spector's defence challenging De Souza's English-language skills, Jackson asked him for details of his English studies in Brazil. De Souza said he had learned English when he was 13. Furthermore, he skilfully imitated Spector's distinctive clipped, nasal voice during his testimony.[26]

Prosecutors then addressed the case's forensic evidence, with Los Angeles coroner Louis Pena, who also performed Lana's autopsy, taking the stand. Pena unequivocally declared the nature of Lana's death as a homicide, citing bruising on her tongue, possibly resulting from the gun being forcibly inserted into her mouth. Pena highlighted additional bruises on Lana's right arm and wrist and described her as an optimistic individual with no prior history of depression or suicide attempts. Pena noted the unusual circumstances of Lana's death, highlighting that she was found in a stranger's home with her purse on one shoulder, suggesting an intent to leave – behaviour inconsistent with suicide.

Pena also revealed crucial details about the crime scene, stating that the gun found beneath Lana's foot had been wiped clean. He pointed out significant bloodstains in the left pocket of Spector's trousers, indicating that the gun had been put there at some stage. The unresolved issue of a missing piece of acrylic fingernail resurfaced, prompting a query from defence attorney Christopher Plourd about the likelihood of breaking a fingernail while firing a gun. Pena responded, "Never heard of it [the fingernail]. Never seen it." Pena informed the court that Lana's hands showed gunshot residue, but he refrained from providing a definitive opinion on whether this meant she was holding the gun when it discharged.

During defence cross-examination conducted by Plourd, Pena conceded that errors were made in evidence collection and handling procedures relating to the case. Specifically, he acknowledged that Lana's body had been improperly moved, resulting in the flow of blood from her mouth impacting the assessment of blood spatter on her dress. Pena also disclosed a significant mishap when a forensic dentist lost a tooth fragment owing to the vial containing it being broken. Despite these admissions, Pena's testimony proved detrimental to the defence. However, his assessment of her state of mind at the time came into question when the defence introduced emails and letters from Lana to friends in which she talked of being "at the end of my rope" and revealed her despondency over her acting career.

Los Angeles County Sheriff's Detective Mike Lillienfeld next showed a bloodstained .38-calibre revolver to the jury, connecting it to a holster and disclosing the discovery of 12 guns in Spector's residence. Like Pena, he observed that the gun had been wiped clean. He also found a bloodstained cloth containing Lana's DNA in a downstairs bathroom.

During cross-examination by defence attorney Bradley Brunon, Lillienfeld faced accusations of evidence contamination owing to the absence of officers wearing gloves, hairnets, or booties. He defended the police's practices, stating that real investigative techniques differed from those seen on television shows like *CSI*: "I don't recall, in 300-plus murders, anyone, except maybe on TV, wearing hairnets to a crime scene." Lillienfeld mentioned detecting "sexual overtones" at the crime scene and finding a Viagra pill in Spector's briefcase. He described a romantically arranged setting in the living room, complete with candles and alcohol.[27]

When Los Angeles County Sheriff's Criminalist, Steve Ranteria, was called by the prosecution, he testified that he found no blood on the wall next to Lana's body or on the carpet. Jackson queried, "Is an explanation for the lack of blood that something was standing between Ms Clarkson and the wall, blocking it?" He replied: "That is one explanation, yes."

Ranteria also provided details of the DNA evidence. He mentioned that DNA possibly belonging to Spector was discovered on Lana's breast, but no DNA was detected beneath her finger-nails. Additionally, genetic material that could have originated from Lana was identified on a portion of Spector's genitals. Ranteria clarified that the gun only contained Lana's DNA but asserted that the absence of Spector's DNA on the gun did not definitively prove he had not handled it. He explained that the presence of other overwhelming DNA could lead to a negative test for specific individuals' DNA.

Forensic identification specialist Donna Brandelli revealed that no fingerprints were found on the gun that killed Lana. This did not surprise Brandelli, who said, "We only get fingerprints off guns eight to ten percent of the time." After his testimony, Judge Fidler ordered former defence lawyer Sara Caplan to be jailed for contempt after she refused to answer questions about Dr Henry Lee's alleged removal of evidence from the crime scene. She cited attorney-client privilege but had earlier testified without the jury present about the incident.[28]

The prosecution's final witness was sheriff's criminologist Lynn Herold, who provided detailed descriptions of Lana's death while additional crime scene photographs were presented. Herold high-lighted that the blood on the gun, on Lana's face and hand was smeared, with three sources of "moving blood" identified as the gun, a bloody cloth, and Spector. When questioned by Jackson about who moved the gun, Herold replied, "That is the inference. I'm assuming no law enforcement personnel moved it." She emphasized that someone had moved Lana's head after her death, as indicated by blood smeared in her hair.

According to Herold, blood spatter typically travels no more than two to three feet from the point where a bullet impacts a person. She believed Spector was standing within two feet of Lana with his arms raised when she was shot, citing blood spatter on the front and back of his white jacket. Herold then drew attention to Spector's bloody trouser pocket, suggesting the blood resulted from placing the gun in his pocket and subsequently taking it out. While the prosecution contended that this demonstrated Spector was standing in front of Lana, holding the gun when she was killed, defence attorney Linda Kenney-Baden proposed that Spector could have been walking or running towards her. Herold acknowledged that this was possible.

The prosecution then rested its case, and the defence called its first expert witness, Dr Vincent DiMaio, who said he believed Lana had taken her own life. He highlighted the gunshot residue and blood on her hands, along with the position of the gun when she was shot, asserting, "She died of a self-inflicted wound. There is no objective scientific evidence that anyone else held the gun." DiMaio addressed the absence of a suicide note, noting that 75 percent of people who take their own lives don't write notes, and added, "She was an actress, was 40 years of age. I'm sorry, that's sex discrimination, but that's the way it is."

Jackson launched a heated cross-examination of DiMaio, accusing him of tailoring his testimony in favour of Spector. Having already received $26,000 from the defence team, DiMaio was asked about potential additional compensation, to which he quipped, "I don't know. The longer you keep talking . . ." Jackson also argued that DiMaio relied too heavily on statistics, emphasizing that the majority of women who take their own lives use poison, with gunshot wounds being only the second most common cause.

At this juncture, Spector's lead attorney, Bruce Cutler, was notably absent, having taken time off to film a new courtroom TV show titled *Jury Duty*, in which he played a judge. Loyola University Law School professor Laurie Levenson remarked, "He is taking celebrity lawyering to a whole new level. It [this trial] seems like just a sideshow."[29]

Nevertheless, the defence proceeded in his absence, calling John Barrons, a playwright, to the stand. He depicted Lana as an ambitious woman for whom career and fame meant "everything". Barrons recounted a conversation shortly before her death when they discussed aging, with Lana reportedly saying, "If you turn 40 in this town and haven't made it, you might as well find a bridge [commit suicide]."

Other friends of Lana testified about her demeanour in the weeks before her death, including Jennifer Hayes-Riedl, who described Lana as having hit rock bottom financially, professionally, and personally. "She was crying her eyes out," she recalled. Another friend, music promoter Punkin "Pie" Irene Elizabeth Laughlin, told the jury that Lana had said to her in January 2003, "I hate this town and I hate the people in it, and I don't want to be here anymore."[30]

Their testimony became the focal point of Spector's defence, suggesting reasons why Lana might have visited Spector's home that night – seeking work to advance her career – and why she might have run out of hope and pulled the trigger.

On the 12th of June, former defence lawyer Sara Caplan reluctantly testified under threat of jail. She claimed to have witnessed the renowned forensic scientist Dr Henry Lee picking up an item roughly one inch in circumference with jagged edges, placing it in a vial, and never seeing it again. While the prosecution suggested it was part of Lana's missing acrylic nail, Caplan insisted it was larger.

Following her testimony, forensic expert Stuart James countered the prosecution's blood evidence, asserting that blood spatter from a gunshot could travel up to six feet. This suggested that Spector, based on the blood on his clothing, could have been too far away from Lana to have shot her. Dr Werner Spitz, a prominent forensic pathologist, also contradicted Dr Louis Pena's testimony by opining that Lana had taken her own life.

There was anticipation that Spector might take the stand, yet after four months of testimony, the defence concluded its case without calling him as a witness. Prior to closing arguments, Bruce Cutler, Spector's lead defence attorney, announced his departure from the case citing "a difference of opinion on strategy" between him and Spector.

In his closing statement, Prosecutor Alan Jackson asserted Spector's guilt, highlighting the accounts of women who claimed he had previously threatened them with firearms. Jackson also reminded the jury of Adriano De Souza's testimony, where Spector allegedly emerged from the house with a gun, confessing, "I think I killed somebody."

During her closing arguments, defence attorney Linda Kenney-Baden noted the scientific evidence she believed exonerated Spector and accused the prosecutors of resorting to theatrics to secure "the first celebrity notch in the government's gun belt". Kenney-Baden argued that Spector was too distant to have fired the weapon, maintaining that Lana had taken her own life. The pivotal question revolved around who the jury believed had pulled the trigger, Lana or Spector. However, after deliberating for 44 hours over 12 days, they were deadlocked ten to two for a conviction. Judge Fidler declared a mistrial due to the hung jury, and prosecutors announced their decision to pursue a retrial.

Spector's retrial commenced on the 20th of October 2008, with the re-presentation of the same evidence before Judge Fidler. Spector, now with a reduced team consisting solely of lawyer

Doron Weinberg, faced prosecution once again led by Alan Jackson. This time, the defence shifted its focus to Adrian De Souza, highlighting eight variations of the phrase "I think I killed someone" uttered by De Souza during conversations with detectives. After 30 hours of deliberation, however, the jury found Spector guilty of the murder of Lana Clarkson. He received a life sentence with a minimum term of 19 years.

Despite multiple appeals, Spector's attempts to overturn his conviction proved unsuccessful. During his years in prison, his physical health declined, evident in his updated mugshots. In 2014, he was transferred from California State Prison in Corcoran to the California Health Care Facility. On the 31st of December 2020, Spector was moved to San Joaquin General Hospital. A month later, he succumbed to complications from COVID-19 on the 26th of January aged 81.[31]

---

[1] Sky News, 30 May 2009 – "Killer Phil Spector Jailed for 19 Years"
[2] *Pasadena Star-News*, 3 February 2003 – "Spector Arrested in Woman's Death"
[3] *Long Beach Press-Telegram*, 12 March 2003 – "Suicide Ruled out in Death at Spector Home"
[4] Associated Press, 4 June 2003 – "Record Producer Phil Spector Tells Magazine That Actress Killed Herself"
[5] *Pasadena Star-News*, 20 November 2003 – "Spector Arraigned"
[6] Enterprise-Record, 2 February 2004 – "Phil Spector Replaces Lawyer, Hires Leslie Abramson to Defend Him"
[7] Agence France-Presse, 28 September 2004 – "Phil Spector Lashed Out at Prosecutors as he's Indicted for Murder"
[8] *Lincoln Journal Star*, 12 February 2007 – "Spector Trial Looks to Be a Spectacle"
[9] *The Guardian*, 20 April 2007 – "Jury Selected in Phil Spector Murder Trial"
[10] *The Daily Telegraph*, 25 April 2007 – "The Plot: Sex, Death and Gunplay"
[11] Agence France-Presse, 25 April 2007 – "Trial of Legendary Music Producer Phil Spector Underway"

[12] The Associated Press News Service, 25 April 2017 – "Opening Statements Begin in Spector Case"

[13] Agence France-Presse, 26 April 2007 – "Spector Brandishing Gun at Ex-Girlfriend, Court Hears"

[14] Associated Press, 26 April 2007 – "Woman Testifies Spector Terrorized Her with Guns During '93 Date"

[15] Associated Press, 3 May 2007 – "Questions in Phil Spector Trial Over Object Found at Crime Scene"

[16] High Point Enterprise, 24 May 2007 – "Forensic Expert in Spector Trial Denies Taking Item from Scene"

[17] Agence France-Presse, 7 May 2007 – "Spector Tried to Rape Me at Gunpoint, Woman Tells Murder Trial"

[18] Agence France-Presse, 9 May 2007 – "Spector Held Me at Gunpoint, Third Woman Tells Murder Trial"

[19] *Pasadena Star-News*, 9 May 2007 – "2 Women Testify to Spector's Threats"

[20] Associated Press, 10 May 2007 – "Spector Defense Seeks to Undermine Woman Who Told of Gun Incident"

[21] Associated Press, 10 May 2007 – "Spector's Fateful Night on the Town is Detailed by Witness"

[22] Creators Syndicate, 10 May 2007 – "Witnesses Tell of Initial Meeting Between Spector and Clarkson"

[23] Associated Press, 14 May 2007 – "Waitress Surprises Spector Trial with Testimony of Gun Incident"

[24] Ca v. Spector

[25] Agence France-Presse, 15 May 2007 – "Spector Told Driver: 'I Think I Killed Somebody'"

[26] Associated Press, 16 May 2007 – "Jury in Spector Murder Trial Hears Chauffer's Frantic Calls for Help"

[27] Associated Press 7 June 2007 – "Lead Investigator in Spector Case Suggests Killing Had 'Sexual Overtones"

[28] *The Mercury News*, 19 June 2007 – "Twist in Spector Trial Puts Focus on Ex-Attorney"

[29] Associated Press, 3 June 2007 – "Spector's Lawyer Absent from Record Producer's Murder Trial"

[30] Creators Syndicate, 16 July 2007 – "Friend Testifies Clarkson Wanted to End It"

[31] *The New York Times*, 17 January 2021 – "Phil Spector, Famed Music Producer and Convicted Murderer, Dies at 81"

The Old Lady Killer

From 2002 until 2006, elderly women in Mexico City were targeted by a serial killer dubbed "La Mataviejitas" or "Old Lady Killer". Witnesses reported the killer as stocky and dressed in women's clothing. Criminologists speculated that the murderer might be a man with a hatred for older women.[1] Given the rarity of female serial killers, police duly drew up a composite sketch of a man and conducted a mass detaining, questioning, and fingerprinting of gender non-conforming sex workers, causing public outrage. However, it soon emerged that the killer was a female wrestler named Juana Barraza.

"I hated ladies because my mother mistreated me, she hit me and always cursed me. One day she gave me away to a grown man and I was abused, that's why I hated ladies. I know that's no excuse, I don't deserve forgiveness."

Juana Barraza

José Joel López González was returning to the one-storey brick apartment that he rented from 81-year-old Ana María Reyes in the working-class neighbourhood of Venustiano Carranza in Mexico City at about 2:30 p.m. on the 26th of January 2006.[2] As José approached the front door, an unfamiliar, broad-framed woman hastily exited and sprinted away down the road. Inside the living room, José found Ana María lifeless, having been asphyxiated with a stethoscope that was still wrapped tightly around her neck.

José promptly alerted two police officers patrolling outside and pointed out the fleeing woman, leading to her arrest. She was 48-year-old Juana Barraza, a former professional wrestler – widely known as The Lady of Silence – and a mother of three. Officer Ismael Alvarado Ruiz searched Barrazo's bag and found a stethoscope, pension forms, and a card identifying her as a social worker.

The police had long suspected that La Mataviejitas gained access to victims' homes by offering them opportunities to sign up for pensions or other social programmes.[3] Barraza was also carrying a figure of Santa Muerte, a popular figure among crime cartels, depicting a saint in skeleton form. The figure is commonly associated with violence, criminality, and the illegal drugs trade.[4] Additionally, Barraza's appearance closely matched the composite sketch and a 3D cast of the killer.

Taken to the police station for questioning, Barraza addressed the assembled media, admitting, "Yes, I did it." She clarified that she was only confessing to the murder of Ana María Reyes and denied being the La Mataviejitas serial killer. Questioned about the number of people she had killed, Barraza replied, "None, this is the first." Subsequently, her fingerprints were taken, and the prosecutor's office revealed that they matched fingerprints found at the crime scenes of at least ten murders and an attempted murder.

When presented with this evidence, Barraza confessed to three additional murders. Mexico City's Attorney General, Bernardo Batiz, commented, "She said it was out of anger. She had a very difficult life. Her mother gave her away when she was little, and the man who took her in had sex with her and she had a daughter."[5]

Juana Barraza was charged with the "qualified homicide" of Ana María, while police continued investigating the string of La Mataviejitas' murders. Qualified homicide involves committing the crime with premeditation, treachery, and advantage, carrying a maximum sentence of 50 years.[6] Judge Enrique Juárez ordered that Barraza undergo a psychiatric examination and be held in solitary at the Santa Martha Women's Social Rehabilitation Center for her own safety.[7]

Barraza's arrest was a media sensation throughout Mexico. Numerous newspapers and television networks swiftly delved into the details of the case. A particular point of interest was Barraza's connection to the exotic world of *Lucha libre*, the distinctive style of Mexican professional wrestling known for its flamboyant action and vibrant costumes, complete with colourful masks.

As a participant in *Lucha libre*, Barraza adopted the persona of The Lady of Silence. Clad in a striking pink and gold leotard, she wore a gold mask shaped like a butterfly that concealed most of her face. Explaining her choice of name, she asserted that it reflected her inherently quiet and isolated nature. Her dedication to the craft was evident in her training at the Star Man Gym in Ciudad

Nezahualcóyotl, where she demonstrated formidable strength by lifting up to 100 kilos. However, in one of her fights, she injured her spine and was told by a doctor she would need to retire from the ring, prompting her to take on a new role as a wrestling promoter.

Shortly after Barraza was arrested, she was paraded before a press conference, positioned beside a 3D cast that had been updated to closely resemble her. The public had anticipated that La Mataviejitas was a man dressed in women's clothes and were surprised when a woman was arrested.[8]

On the 18th of February, the Mexico City Attorney General's Office officially announced Barraza's impending trial for the murder of four women, including María de la Luz González (killed in 2002), Imelda Estrada (killed in 2004), Emma Armenta (killed in 2005), and Ana María de los Reyes (killed in 2006). In addition, the Attorney General's Office revealed that Barraza had been linked to at least twelve murders, with suspicions suggesting her involvement in potentially fifteen more.[9]

By the end of March, Barraza faced additional charges, bringing the total to six more murders. The victims included Natalia Torres Castro and Guillermina León Oropeza (killed in 2003), María Dolores Martínez Benavides and María de los Ángeles Cortés Reynoso (killed in 2004) and María de los Ángeles Repper Hernández and Pérez Moreno (killed in 2005).

Following these developments, Ofelia Utuzuáztegui, the Criminal Proceedings Prosecutor of the Reclusorio Oriente, disclosed that Barraza's psychiatric examination had been concluded. The assessment revealed that she possessed the capacity to comprehend her actions and distinguish between right and wrong.[10] While the Attorney General's Office claimed Barazza admitted to more murders, when she appeared at the 67th Criminal Court, she denied the other murders, but acknowledged she had killed Ana María.

Over the forthcoming year, Barraza was charged with seven

more murders, including the 2003 murders of Colonia Del Valle and Enedina Rizo Ramírez, the 2004 murders of Vera Duplán, Estela Cantoral Trejo, Socorro Enedina Martínez Pajares, and Margarita Arredondo and the 2005 murder of Celia Villaliz Morales.[11] Additionally, she was accused of committing 12 burglaries, not only against her murder victims but also targeting others. According to the Attorney General's Office, Barraza's criminal trajectory began with burglaries, later escalating to murders in order to evade apprehension.

In Mexico's legal system, trials unfold without juries and typically involve minimal public hearings. Instead, a sole judge presides over proceedings, often spanning several years, in which prosecutors and defence attorneys present their cases behind closed doors. Barraza ultimately faced charges for 30 murders and 12 burglaries, with Miguel Ángel Mancera acting as the prosecutor before Judge Enrique Juárez Saavedra.

In the spring of 2008, Barraza confessed to the murder of Ana María, and one count of qualified burglary. She said to the judge, "I hated ladies because my mother mistreated me, she hit me and always cursed me. One day she gave me away to a grown man and I was abused, that's why I hated ladies. I know that's no excuse, I don't deserve forgiveness nor anything."[12] However, she contested all the other charges, which formed the basis of the ongoing proceedings.

One of the psychologists who examined Barraza, Feggy Ostrosky, provided a detailed account of the events leading up to Ana María's murder. On the 26th of January 2006, around 11 a.m., Barraza was loitering near José Jasso Street when she noticed Ana María, who was carrying shopping bags and moving slowly. Seizing her opportunity, Barraza approached Ana María and offered to help her home. Once inside Ana María's apartment, Barraza claimed to provide washing and ironing services. Although Ana María offered her 22 pesos for a dozen clothing items, Barraza deemed it insufficient. According to Barraza, Ana María expressed dissatisfaction. Without uttering a word in response, Barraza took a stethoscope from her bag, approached Ana María from behind, and strangled her to death.

Throughout the protracted trial, the prosecution outlined how Barraza targeted elderly women who were alone in public spaces painting a comprehensive picture of Barraza's methods in exploiting the vulnerability of her victims. At times, she gained their trust and access to their homes by offering pre-paid Sí Vale food cards or by offering to add value to their existing cards. On other occasions, she offered to help carry shopping bags or posed as a cleaner. In some instances, she pretended to be a nurse or social worker, offering free check-ups.

When the elderly women had their backs turned, Barraza would swiftly subdue them and demand information about the location of their valuables. Using a stethoscope she carried for the purpose or any convenient nearby items such as clothing, phone cables, or tights, she proceeded to strangle them to death. Afterwards, Barraza ransacked their homes, seizing whatever valuables and mementos she could find, often focusing on religious ornaments and pictures.

The prosecution proposed that Barraza targeted elderly women in order to release the deep-seated rage she harboured against her alcoholic mother. Among the prosecution's line-up of witnesses were the two arresting officers and the neighbours of certain victims. These neighbours had seen Barraza near the crime scenes during the time of the murders. Additionally, two survivors identified her as their assailant, and five victims of burglaries singled her out in the courtroom. There were also nearly two hundred fingerprints at twelve crime scenes that had come back as a match to Barraza. In addition, thirty items stolen from various victims had been discovered at her home.[13]

Nevertheless, the defence asserted Barraza's innocence. They initially pursued an insanity defence but abandoned it after Barraza was deemed competent and fully aware that her actions were wrong. Barraza contended that her initial statements, including her confession, were made under duress, and she insisted that the fingerprints found at the crime scenes were not hers.

In an effort to substantiate her claims of innocence, the defence presented a few character witnesses. Each one portrayed her as a hardworking single mother dedicated to providing for her three children – a stark contrast to the prosecution's portrayal of her as a merciless killer targeting elderly women.

Her attorneys also emphasized Barraza's troubled life and upbringing. They highlighted that her father had abandoned her on the day of her birth, taking her brother with him. At the age of twelve, Barraza was traded by her mother to a man named José Lugo for three bottles of beer. A year later, Barraza underwent an abortion; at 16, she gave birth to her first son, José Enrique Lugo Barraza.

Barraza never acquired literacy skills, and after parting ways with the man who had "owned" her, she had two more partners, both alcoholics and abusive. She went on to have three more children before tragically losing her eldest son, who was beaten to death during a mugging in 1998 at the age of 24.[14]

On the 31st of March 2008, Juana Barraza, her hair dyed red and clad in a beige blouse and matching trousers, returned to court to face the judge's verdict. She was confined in a cage. Three police officers from the Ministry of Public Security stood guard around it, while another two stood at the courtroom door. The judge ultimately found her guilty of 16 out of the 30 murders, along with 12 counts of burglary. He handed down a staggering sentence of 759 years in prison, with a mandated maximum of 50 years according to Mexican law. This was the lengthiest sentence in Mexico's history. Barraza was also ordered to pay a fine of 100,453 pesos or engage in community service if unable to afford the penalty.[15]

As the sentence was imposed, Barraza showed little emotion, although she quietly uttered, "May God forgive you and not forgive me."[16] She also remarked that since her incarceration, elderly women were still being killed in the city, before adding, "Here (in prison) there are many elderly people who they just should not have, but here they have them, and that is an injustice. What has the Attorney General, the President, done? Nothing, just pull innocent people."[17]

Once Barraza was sent to prison to begin her sentence, Prosecutor Mancera issued a public statement, announcing: "There are a series of very clear indications that implicate Juana Barraza, she is recognized, different people identify her by the same modus operandi: a woman dressed as a nurse who goes with elderly people offering social services and also offers a medical examination."

In July 2008, Barraza spoke with reporters from the newspaper *Reforma* while behind bars at Santa María prison. She disclosed that she had developed diabetes after her trial and vehemently denied involvement in any murders beyond Ana María's. Barraza shared with the reporter that she had taken on work within the prison, cooking and selling tacos to fellow inmates, as a means to financially support her children.[18] According to some reports, she had become known as the "Espantacigüeñas" (slang for abortionist) for helping pregnant inmates to abort by circumventing the security methods at the prison to smuggle in pills and injections.[19]

In 2015, Barraza married another inmate named Miguel Ánge during a mass wedding event organized by the Undersecretariat of the Penitentiary System of the Federal District. However, the marriage didn't last long and a year later, they had separated. Rebeca Peralta, Vice President of the Special Commission on Prisons of the Legislative Assembly said of the separation, "She says that love is over, that men are very unfortunate, and that's all."[20]

Barraza appealed her sentence, but without success. Her conviction marked the end of the investigation into the Mataviejitas killings, leaving over thirty murders unresolved. Before Barraza's arrest, the police had arrested several other people in connection with the murders but released them without charge.

The closure of the case raised suspicions that Barraza might not have acted alone. During her initial arrest, police apprehended another woman, Araceli Tapia Martínez. While Martínez admitted participating in burglaries along with Barraza, she denied any connection to the murders. Martínez was released, leaving lingering questions about the extent of her involvement and potential other accomplices in the unsolved cases.[21] In 2023, the case was immortalized in the Netflix documentary, *The Lady of Silence: The Mataviejitas Case.*

---

[1] *The Guardian*, 27 January 2006 – "Female Wrestler Arrested for Serial Killings of Elderly Women"

[2] Agence France-Presse, 26 January 2006 – "Alleged Murderer of Elderly Women Falls in Mexico"

[3] Associated Press Archive, 26 January 2006 – "Mexico City Detains Two Serial Killers, Including Alleged 'Little Old Lady' Killer"

[4] *El Universal*, 27 July 2023 – "Mataviejitas: They Remove Juana Barraza's Mask on Netflix"

[5] The Associated Press News Service, 27 January 2006 – "Mexican Police Say Anger Spurred Killer"

[6] LATAM, 30 January 2006 – "Judge Orders Trial of Alleged Serial Killer in Mexico"

[7] *Reforma*, 2 February 2006 – "They Threaten to Kill Barraza"

[8] *Milenio*, 26 July 2023 – "Juana Barraza, the Former Fighter Who Went from the Ring to Prison for Killing Women"

[9] *Reforma*, 19 February 2006 – "Barraza May Have 27 Victims"

[10] *Reforma*, 9 March 2006 – "They Allege Barraza's Dementia"

[11] *Reforma*, 11 April 2007 – "They Charge 'Maviejitas' With Four More Murders"

[12] *El Pais*, 1 April 2008 – "Mataviejitas Condemned in Mexico for 16 Deaths"

[13] Associated Press Archive, 31 March 2008 – "Mexico's 'Little Old Lady Killer' Sentenced to 758 Years"

[14] *The Little Old Lady Killer: The Sensationalized Crimes of Mexico's First Female Serial Killer* by Susana Vargas Cervantes

[15] Agence France-Presse, 31 March 2008 – "Mexican Justice Sentences Serial Killer of Elderly Women to 758 Years in Prison"

[16] *The Guardian*, 2 April 2008 – "Little Old Lady Killer Handed 759 Years in a Mexicana Prison"

[17] *Mural*, 1 April 2008 – "'Mataviejitas' Receives 758 Years in Prison"

[18] Reforma, 1 July 2008 – "They Will Operate on Killer"

[19] W Radio, 14 June 2009 – "From 'Mataviejitas to Espantacigüeñas"

[20] *Excelsior*, 27 July 2023- "This is the Life of Juana Barraza in Prison"

[21] *Reforma*,10 February 2006 – "Araceli Gets Freedom"

Trial by Media

In November 2007, American student Amanda Knox was accused of murdering her roommate Meredith Kercher in Italy. The case became a media sensation. Knox's portrayal varied widely, with some outlets depicting her as a cold-blooded murderer and others the innocent victim of a flawed justice system. Ultimately, Knox and her Italian boyfriend, Raffaele Sollecito, stood trial, sparking massive debates about the Italian legal system, media sensationalism, and the treatment of foreigners in the Italian legal process.

———————————

"She is not Amanda the Ripper. She is a little crazy, extravagant. She does the cartwheels in the police station because reality for her is too strong to deal with."

Defence attorney Giulia Bongiorno

———————————

In 2007, Amanda Knox, a 20-year-old American student from the University of Washington, Seattle, decided to spend a year in the picturesque hilltop city of Perugia, Italy, to study at the University for Foreigners. She was pursing an interest in languages and wanted to immerse herself in Italian culture while studying abroad. She moved into the upper apartment at Via della Pergola 7 with three other women, one of whom was 21-year-old British student Meredith Kercher. Knox met Italian Raffaele Sollecito at a classical music concert on the 25th of October 2007, and the two quickly became romantically involved.

On the 1st of November, Italy observes the public holiday known as All Saints' Day, during which Knox and Kercher's Italian housemates were spending time with their families. The following morning, Filomena Romanelli, one of the housemates, awoke at her boyfriend's flat to a call from Knox in which she said that, returning home after spending the night with Sollecito, she had discovered the front door wide open. Despite this unsettling sight, Knox went to take a shower and noticed what looked like bloody footprints in the bathroom. Knox then informed Romanelli that she couldn't find Meredith, whose bedroom door was locked, and that Meredith was not answering her phone. Adding to her concern, Knox found a shattered window in Romanelli's bedroom.

Around the same time, a woman living approximately ten

minutes away heard a phone ringing in her garden. She discovered two mobile phones and promptly contacted the police. They traced the phones back to Meredith and swiftly proceeded to the cottage. Meanwhile, Knox and Sollecito had alerted the police to the situation.

Knox informed the police about the bloody footprints, the shattered window, and Meredith's locked bedroom. Meredith's bedroom door was kicked down, revealing her lifeless body beneath her duvet. She was partially undressed and had deep wounds to her neck. A police source commented, "The weapon could have been a knife or a piece of glass from the broken window."[1] Other than in the bathroom and in Meredith's bedroom, there was no blood, leading police to theorize that the killer or killers had cleaned themselves up before leaving.

Police took Knox's statement and began their investigation but were immediately suspicious. On the floor close to the smashed window, they came across a rock, but they doubted it could have been thrown from the outside. They also learned that the shutters had been left closed, although they could have easily been opened from the outside. They concluded that the break-in had been staged by somebody who knew Meredith, and that her mobile phones had been stolen and then discarded as a ruse.

Forensic experts from Rome arrived, taking control of the situation and preventing the town coroner from examining Meredith's body until midnight, hindering the determination of an accurate time of death. Eventually, Dr Luca Lalli conducted the autopsy, and suggested that bruises to Meredith's face were indicative of somebody putting their hand over her mouth and nose. He also noted some bruises to her genital area, and suggested these were inflicted as somebody attempted to immobilize her during a violent sexual act.

Amanda Knox became a focal point for the police, who found her behaviour peculiar following her housemate's murder.

Witnesses observed her kissing Sollecito near the crime scene, and she allegedly performed cartwheels and the splits while awaiting interrogation. Furthermore, Italian police found it noteworthy that Knox went shopping for a G-string the day after the murder and was overheard promising "wild sex" to Sollecito.[2] During an interview with police, conducted without legal representation, Knox accused Patrick Lumumba, her Congolese employer at the Le Chic bar. Changing her previous story about spending the night in question at Sollecito's flat, she now claimed that Lumumba had been with Meredith in her bedroom when she heard her screaming.

On the 6th of November, Knox, Sollecito, and Lumumba were arrested in connection with Meredith's murder; they all denied any involvement. During a press conference, Interior Minister Giuliano Amato presented the prosecution's theory: "It's an ugly story in which this girl had in her home, friends [who] tried to force her into relations [that] she didn't want."[3] While Knox placed the blame on Lumumba, police believed that all three were involved, and had killed Meredith when she refused to take part in an orgy. Amato revealed that for three hours on the night Meredith was killed, Knox and Sollecito had their mobile phones switched off.

The case quickly unravelled as Lumumba's alibi—working at Le Chic on the night in question—was corroborated by his customers. Lumumba was released without charge. He announced his intention to launch a civil case against Knox, and also accused the Italian police of physical abuse and racist insults during his interrogation. His attorney, Carlo Pacelli, remarked, "As a man, as a father, as a husband, his image has been destroyed."[4]

The media were immediately transfixed by the case, and the perceived physical attractiveness of the individuals involved was a key element. News outlets focused heavily on the "Foxy Knoxy" nickname that Knox had been given as a child, giving it a different connotation emphasizing her appearance. Critics complained that the tabloid tone of reporting could impact the fairness of the trial by influencing public perceptions of Knox.

There were also accusations of flaws in the investigation, and that there was no physical evidence against Knox or Sollecito. King County Superior Court Judge of the State of Washington Mike Heavey accused the Italian authorities of aggressively pursuing Knox to avoid embarrassment. At this point, Knox had penned a statement from jail claiming that she had been struck on the head during interrogation and that she was suffering considerable stress and exhaustion from the authorities' relentless questioning. She mentioned that she had implicated Lumumba because the police had discovered she texted him "See you later" at 8:30 p.m. on the night of Meredith's murder.[5] When questioned about her movements on the night of the crime, she struggled to recall exact times and details, recounting, "I started forgetting everything. My mind was spinning. I felt as if I was going totally blank."

The police investigation continued with Knox and Sollecito behind bars, and forensic experts discovered a crucial lead: a bloody fingerprint on a pillowcase under Meredith's body. It came back as a match to Rudy Guede, a drug dealer known to Italian police. He was arrested in Germany on the 20th of November. Just before his arrest, a Skype conversation with a friend captured Guede stating that Knox was not present during the night of the murder.

Extradited to Italy, Guede was informed that his fingerprints had been found at the crime scene. He alleged that he had been in the cottage that night after meeting Meredith at a Halloween party but said he didn't kill her. He claimed that he saw an Italian man coming out of her bedroom that night, who said to him, "You're a Black man, you will get the blame."[6]

However, DNA testing showed that Guede's DNA matched samples found on Meredith's body and various objects in the cottage. Confronted with this evidence, Guede changed his story and said that he had a sexual encounter with Meredith that night. He then claimed that when he went to the bathroom with an upset stomach, Knox and Sollecito killed Meredith.[7] He suggested that Meredith and Knox had been arguing about money.

On the 11th of July 2008, Knox, Sollecito, and Guede were formally charged with Meredith Kercher's murder. In September, Guede chose to undergo a fast-track trial, which commenced the following month but behind closed doors. Prosecutor Giuliani Mignini asserted that Meredith's murder occurred when she resisted participating in a drug-fuelled sex game with the trio. According to Mignini, "Knox held the knife and stabbed poor Meredith while the others held her down. Sollecito had a knife on him, but he didn't use it. At the same time Guede strangled her and also tried to sexually assault her."[8] Guede's attorney, Nicodemo Gentile, dismissed the prosecution's version of events as "fantasy" and maintained that Knox and Sollecito acted alone.[9]

The DNA and fingerprint evidence against Guede proved compelling, however, leading Judge Paolo Micheli to find him guilty of Meredith's murder after twelve hours of deliberation. Guede was sentenced to the maximum penalty of 30 years in prison. Additionally, Judge Micheli indicted Knox and Sollecito on charges of murder and sexual violence, declaring that they would jointly face trial.

In this legal proceeding, Mignini, a highly regarded magistrate in Perugia, served as the lead prosecutor. Knox was represented by Carlo Dalla Vedova, a lawyer with a meticulous approach, and Luciano Ghirga, who publicly stated that he had developed a father-daughter relationship with her. Sollecito was represented by Giulia Bongiorno, a renowned attorney known for defending royalty, politicians, and star athletes. Bongiorno was retained by Sollecito's affluent family.[10]

In late December, a jury of six was chosen by computer from a random selection of 50 residents in the Perugia region, with four alternates. The case was to be presided over by Judge Giancarlo Massei, who was no stranger to high-profile cases.

In Italy, the judge takes part in deliberations to try and help the jury reach a verdict and court sessions are held only once or twice a week. Furthermore, in Italian trials, defendants are allowed to stand up and make declarations throughout the proceedings. Before the trial began, Meredith's family requested that the trial be closed to the public and media, but this was denied. Judge Massei barred cameras from filming but ruled that the trial would remain open to print journalists, although some sessions would be closed.[11]

Knox was escorted into the fifteenth-century courthouse in Perugia on the 17th of January 2009, dressed in jeans and a grey hooded sweatshirt. She greeted her attorneys with a big smile, but barely acknowledged Sollecito, who was sitting with his legal team. She had earlier told her attorneys, "At last the hour of truth has arrived. I'm not afraid. I hope that the whole truth will come out because I've always been a friend of Meredith's and I didn't kill her." Sollecito also denied any involvement, announcing in court he hardly knew Meredith and had just begun dating Knox. He maintained, "I feel I am the victim of a judicial mistake."

The atmosphere was tense as Mignini launched his opening statements. He asserted that Meredith had been killed in an "erotic game" gone wrong that had been masterminded by Knox. He suggested Knox had persuaded Guede to entice Meredith to take part, telling the jury, "And when Guede failed because of energetic resistance by the victim, the three became incensed and violent. They grabbed Kercher by the neck and tried to strangle her. Sollecito grabbed her violently in the back and on a breast, deforming her bra clasp and then they finished her off with the violent knife stab to the left part of the neck."[12]

It was the prosecution's contention that after Meredith was killed, the three fled from the cottage, with Knox and Sollecito returning later to stage a fake robbery by breaking a window. He singled out the placing of a duvet over Meredith's body as "extremely important from a psychological point of view" and said that it showed a level of pity and respect for the victim: "Amanda, especially as a woman, couldn't bear that naked, torn female cadaver."

Testimony got underway immediately with various witnesses providing accounts of the crime scene. Police Inspector Michele Battistelli, one of the first officers at the scene, informed the court that he hadn't entered Meredith's bedroom, since as a postal police inspector he did not have the authority to do so. However, Meredith's housemate, Filomena Romanelli, said that Battistelli had, in fact, entered the bedroom and may have even touched the duvet.

According to Battistelli, Knox and Sollecito appeared "surprised, but calm" at the crime scene, and said that they "constantly shared affections" as the investigation got underway.[13] He drew attention to the broken bedroom window, and said that the robbery appeared to have been staged as a laptop and camera in clear view hadn't been stolen.[14] Battistelli testified that there was glass on top of clothing in the bedroom, which suggested that the home had been ransacked and the window broken afterwards.

Sollecito's alibi of downloading a movie at the time of Meredith's murder came under scrutiny when Postal Police Chief Filippo Batolozzi revealed that an examination of Sollecito's computer indicated no activity from 9:10 p.m. on the 1st of November to 5:32 a.m. the following morning. While Knox had told police she spent the night at Sollecito's apartment, where they watched a movie, Sollecito couldn't recall whether she had spent all of the night there or just part of it.

Following Batolozzi's testimony, Meredith and Knox's housemate, Filomena Romanelli, took the stand. She told the jury that Knox and Meredith were close initially, but while "they didn't really go separate ways, they developed personal interests that they pursued individually." She described Meredith as someone dedicated to her studies, while she said that Knox was someone with "quite a lot of interests" including music, sports, yoga, and languages." She said that Knox often brought "strangers home" whereas Meredith preferred to keep to herself.[15]

Romanelli recalled the phone call she had with Knox on the morning Meredith's body was discovered. She said she found it odd that Knox had chosen to shower in a bathroom tainted with blood. Returning to the cottage after the call, Romanelli discovered her bedroom had been ransacked, yet none of her possessions, including jewellery, a designer handbag, and sunglasses, were missing. Romanelli vividly recalled Knox reaching out to her a day after the discovery of Meredith's body. During the phone call, Knox expressed concern about their future living arrangements, raising the question of whether they would still be able to live together.[16]

One of Knox's college friends, Robyn Butterworth, was the next prosecution witness. She recounted how another friend had said she hoped Meredith wasn't in too much pain, to which Knox replied, "What do you think? She [obscenity] bled to death." Butterworth said that at that point, she hadn't been told how Meredith had died. She also told the jury she found it strange that Knox wasn't crying: "She had no emotion. Everybody was upset and she didn't seem to show any emotions."[17] Butterworth added that on one occasion Meredith had found a pink vibrator and condoms that belonged to Knox in the shared bathroom in the cottage, which had made her feel uneasy.

The purpose of Butterworth's testimony – as far as the prosecution was concerned – was to show Knox knew details and circumstances of how Meredith had died before anybody else, to highlight her nonchalant demeanour despite the gravity of the circumstances and imply that she was sexually active. Following Butterworth's testimony, Knox asked if she could address the court. She stood up and defiantly said: "I am innocent, and I have faith this will all work out." The examination of Knox's attitude continued as six more friends testified about her casual behaviour in the aftermath of Meredith's murder, while housemate Laura Mezzetti informed the court that she noticed a scratch on Knox's neck on the 2nd of November.

The scrutiny of Knox's conduct continued, with Domenico Giacinto Profazio, a former head of the Perugia detective squad, recounting that Knox sat on Sollecito's lap at the police station, and at other times did cartwheels and the splits. Profazio confirmed that Knox and Sollecito's mobile phones were turned off around 8:30 p.m. on the night of the murder, rendering their subsequent whereabouts untraceable. Profazio also stated that, while Knox initially denied being in the cottage when Meredith was killed, she later broke down and admitted to being there and accused Lumumba of killing Meredith. However, she had later reverted to her first statement – that she was at Sollecito's flat at the time of the murder.

The prosecution then turned its attention to the forensic evidence it claimed implicated Knox and Sollecito. Monica Napoleoni, head of the homicide squad in Perugia, testified that forensic experts discovered a woman's shoeprint on a pillow beneath Meredith's body. According to Napoleoni, the print ranged in size from 36 to 38, and Knox wore a size 37, although she acknowledged that a matching shoe had not been found. During a break, Knox's team dismissed Napoleoni's testimony and accused the police of contaminating the crime scene. The officers who conducted the examination had not followed forensic guidelines, as they did not change gloves each time they moved an object, a claim corroborated by Profazio.[18]

Napoleoni also revealed that a bloodied bra clasp belonging to Meredith had Sollecito's DNA on it. Under cross-examination by Bongiorno, it was suggested that an "error" had been made by not immediately securing the evidence when it was found. Napoleoni disclosed that the bra clasp was not removed until six weeks later. Bongiorno observed, "Before you can start talking about DNA traces on that bra clasp, you have to make sure that the evidence in question was properly handled – and in this case, it was not."[19]

When police officer Daniele Moscatelli took the stand, he informed the jury that Sollecito had a knife in his pocket when questioned at the police station. Moscatelli recounted that Sollecito appeared "quite confused and nervous" during questioning, stating that he was a "fan of arms and knives". Sollecito stood up in court and announced that the police had denied his request to call his father and a lawyer during questioning. Knox also commented on her treatment during questioning, alleging that officers called her "a stupid liar" and slapped her.[20]

The prosecution said that this knife wasn't the murder weapon. Instead, they pointed to one found in Sollecito's kitchen. It was a common kitchen knife picked out from the drawer because it looked clean. It had Knox's DNA on the handle, and the prosecution claimed it had both Knox's and Meredith's DNA on the blade. However, it was noted that the DNA traces were not blood (it was not disclosed what the DNA traces were). Forensic police biologist Patrizia Stefanoni testified that blood or genetic material that tested positive for both Knox and Meredith was identified in three different areas of the cottage. Knox's attorneys argued that the findings were unsurprising, given that they lived together.[21] Under cross-examination, it was revealed that multiple samples were taken using the same cotton swab, opening up the possibility of cross-contamination.

The prosecution then called Lorenzo Rinaldi, who directed the identification section of the crime scene squad. He testified that a footprint in the bathroom and the corridor appeared to belong to Sollecito. Following his testimony, Sollecito stood up once more and declared, "Those prints of bare feet are absolutely not mine. My consultants will testify and explain why."[22] Rinaldi further said that another footprint found on the bathmat could possibly be Guede's or Knox's, while all the bloody footprints found in Meredith's bedroom were compatible with a pair of size 11 Nike Outbreak 2 shoes that belonged to Guede.[23]

Midway through the trial, on the 16th of March, Lumumba was awarded 8,000 euros in damages by the Italian state. Testimony continued, featuring grocer Marco Quintavalle, whose account contradicted Knox's narrative. She had told police that she woke up mid-morning the day after Meredith was killed and returned from Sollecito's apartment to the cottage. According to Quintavalle, Knox was in his grocery store near Sollecito's apartment at 7:45 a.m. He said he had seen Knox at the store a few times before with Sollecito, a frequent customer. Defence attorneys questioned the reliability of the witness, with Vedova asking how tall Sollecito was, and what colour his eyes were. Quintavalle gave an indication of his height, but said he wasn't sure about the colour of his eyes.[24]

The focus of testimony then shifted back to the night of the murder, with two women who lived near the cottage testifying that they heard a scream on the night of Meredith's murder. Mara Capezzali, who lived across a parking lot from the house, testified that at about 11:30 p.m., she awoke, went to the bathroom, and heard a woman screaming. She recollected, "It was not a normal scream. It made my skin crawl." Shortly afterwards, she said she heard at least two people running in opposite directions almost simultaneously. A second witness, Antonella Monacchia, recounted waking up sometime after 10 p.m. to the sounds of a heated argument between a man and a woman speaking Italian. This confrontation was followed by a woman's piercing scream.

The next prosecution witness, Albanian agricultural worker Hekuran Kokomani, testified occasionally in Albanian through a translator. He claimed that on the night of Meredith's murder, while driving, he encountered what he initially thought was a large black trash bag in front of the cottage. He later identified the "bag" as Knox and Sollecito, pointing them out in court. Kokomani's testimony was confusing; he mumbled about punching Sollecito and being threatened by Knox with a knife, saying she uttered, "Come here and I'll show you." Kokomani's credibility was questioned owing to his arrest a month earlier on drug charges. He also claimed to have seen Knox and Sollecito with an unidentified "American uncle" of Knox's in the summer of 2007, prompting Knox to express disbelief, shaking her head, as she hadn't met Sollecito at that time.[25]

A crucial prosecution witness, medical examiner Dr Vincenza Liviero, asserted that Meredith was assaulted by more than one person, citing evidence of sexual violence. Liviero highlighted numerous bruises and wounds on Meredith's body, inflicted by a knife, hands, and suffocation. She opined that a lone attacker would have needed three or four hands to cause such injuries, suggesting Meredith was restrained, sexually assaulted, and then fatally stabbed. Supporting this diagnosis, gynaecologist Mauro Marchionni informed the court that, based on his experience, the wounds observed were inconsistent with consensual sex, indicating a sexual assault. Due to the graphic nature of the testimony, including photographs of Meredith's body, the proceedings were conducted privately in chambers.[26]

On the 12th of June, the defence began presenting its case. Amanda Knox took the stand, confidently professing her innocence in fluent Italian. She accused the police of coercing false statements from her and forcing her into a fabricated narrative. Knox claimed that on the night of Meredith's murder, she and Sollecito were at his home, where they smoked marijuana, engaged in consensual activities, and watched a movie. When presented with a photograph showing a red mark on her neck in the days following Meredith's murder, she explained it as a "hickey" from Sollecito.[27] In contrast to earlier testimony, Knox emphasized the closeness of her relationship with Meredith, stating, "I confided in her, I would often ask her for advice." She attributed her behaviour in the aftermath of Meredith's murder to the effects of "shock".[28]

There was speculation regarding whether Sollecito would testify, but he ultimately refrained from doing so, following his attorneys' advice. They believed it was in his best interests to maintain the focus on Knox. The defence then called forensic scientist Dr Francesco Introna to dispute earlier prosecution testimony. He said that no more than a single attacker could have assaulted Meredith on the night of her murder and that her stab wounds had been caused by a shorter knife than the one found in Sollecito's kitchen. Introna declared that the bedroom where Meredith was killed was far too small, and that it would have been "physically impossible" for three people to have attacked her.[29]

The defence also questioned the credibility of the two neighbours who reported hearing a woman scream on the night of Meredith's murder, presenting Pasqualino Colette as a witness. He said that he was parked near the cottage between 10:30 p.m. and 11 p.m. because his car had broken down. Colette stated that his attention was not drawn to anything specific during that timeframe, and he did not hear any screaming or arguing.[30]

After Colette's testimony, the trial briefly halted when it was revealed that lead prosecutor Giuliano Mignini was under investigation for misconduct in another case, that of serial killer Pietro Pacciani, the "Monster of Florence". Mignini was charged with misconduct, accused of providing inappropriate assistance to Police Chief Giuttari by offering criminal analysis that should have been formally requested and compensated for by the police.[31] Eventually, he was acquitted of the allegations.

Testimony resumed the following week, featuring Carlo Torre, a noted professor of criminal science in Turin, Italy, and genetic specialist Sarah Gino. During a dramatic trial day, they challenged the prosecution's case. Torre and Gino both asserted that the knife found in Sollecito's apartment could not have been the murder weapon. Torre testified: "It is not just difficult, it is completely impossible that a knife like this would make these two wounds. The murder weapon is a survival knife, a 'Rambo' knife, not this one."

Gino raised concerns about the DNA testing on the knife, stating it was not conducted properly, and the biological material on the blade was so minimal that it could not undergo double-testing, a standard protocol for admissible DNA. She further noted that only Meredith and Guede's DNA were discovered in her bedroom, despite the prosecution entering into evidence a bra clasp that contained Sollecito's DNA.[32]

Dr Adriana Tagliabracci challenged the DNA findings on the bra clasp, suggesting the possibility of later contamination. He remarked, "DNA has no wings, but it can fly," indicating that the genetic material might have been transported onto the clasp through dust. He pointed out that the clasp was collected 47 days after the murder and found in a location more than one metre away from its initial observation.

After Dr Tagliabracci's testimony, the court adjourned for a two-month summer recess. Upon resuming in September, Knox and Sollecito's attorneys sought to have the murder indictments dismissed, but Judge Massei rejected the request, determining that the trial should proceed. Dr Tagliabracci continued his testimony, focusing on the DNA allegedly found on the knife. Like Gino, he emphasized that DNA traces on the blade were so minimal that any result would be subject to debate.[33]

The trial then revisited the crime scene footprints, with forensic expert Francesco Vinci disputing the findings of the prosecution's experts. Vinci asserted that the footprints attributed to Sollecito did not match his footprints, pointing out dissimilarities in the shape of the toes and the balls of the feet. He presented visual comparisons, telling the jury, "Differences, one by one, can be seen." According to Vinci, the bloody footprints were "compatible" with the foot of the third defendant, Rudy Guede, who was already serving a 30-year prison sentence.[34]

The final witness in the trial, neurologist Carlo Caltagirone, suggested that stress might have impacted Knox's memory during her interrogation. He proposed that Knox's "confession" to being at the scene and hearing Meredith scream could be attributed to "false flashbacks" induced by the significant stress she had experienced after prolonged questioning.

As the trial concluded, Rudy Guede appealed his 30-year sentence. He testified that he was at the cottage on the night of the murder and overheard Knox and Meredith arguing about money just minutes before the fatal incident. Guede claimed he was in the bathroom when he heard Meredith scream, and entering the bedroom, saw an unidentified man and the "silhouette" of Knox fleeing. While Guede's testimony wasn't admissible in Knox and Sollecito's trial, the judge and jury were aware of his statements as they were made in open court with no reporting restrictions.[35] Guede's sentence was later reduced to 16 years.

Summing up the case on the 20th of November, prosecutor Mignini portrayed Knox as the driving force behind the murder. He alleged that she "harboured hatred" for Meredith and orchestrated a drug-fuelled sexual assault that escalated into "an unstoppable crescendo of violence", with Guede holding Meredith down while Sollecito and Knox inflicted the fatal stab wounds to her neck. Mignini announced his intention to seek the maximum sentence against Knox, which in Italy is life in prison. He questioned, "Is she really a she-devil, focusing on sex, drugs, and alcohol?"

The defence delivered its closing arguments, with Luca Maori, one of Sollecito's attorneys, asserting that their client was incapable of participating in the murder. Maori said that the trial had already convicted Rudy Guede, who had no ties to Knox or Sollecito. Sollecito's attorney Bongiorno questioned Sollecito's guilt by highlighting his actions, such as raising the alarm and waiting for investigators at the crime scene, asking, "Would a killer do that?"[36] She referred to her client as a submissive young man who did whatever Knox told him to do, before stating, "She is not Amanda the Ripper. She is a little crazy, extravagant. She does the cartwheels in the police station because reality for her is too strong to deal with."

In his summation, Vedova argued that Knox had been caught in a "tsunami" that led to her arrest, urging the jury to clear her of all charges owing to the prosecution's flawed case. He emphasized the lack of conclusive evidence and questioned the reliability of the DNA presented. Vedova also pointed out the absence of proof that Knox, Sollecito, and Guede had conspired to attack Meredith.[37]

At the conclusion of the trial, the jury had been presented with a stark contrast in the cases presented by the defence and prosecution. A critical point of contention was the murder weapon, as well as conflicting views of the DNA evidence. After some twelve hours of deliberation, Judge Giancarlo Massei pronounced the verdict in a subdued tone: guilty. In a subsequent news conference, Meredith Kercher's brother, Lyle, expressed satisfaction with the decision but emphasized the solemnity of the moment, speaking on behalf of his family: "We are pleased with the decision, but this is not the time for celebration; it's not a moment of triumph. We got here because our sister was brutally murdered."[38]

Amanda Knox received a 26-year prison sentence, while Raffaele Sollecito was sentenced to 25 years, leading to strongly divergent opinions in Italy and in the US. Italian commentators perceived the convictions as a triumph, while many American commentators considered the verdicts a serious miscarriage of justice. A typical response came from forensic DNA expert Greg Hampikian, Director of the Idaho Innocence Project, who criticized the DNA analysis, highlighting the minimal traces found on the knife and raising concerns about forensic reliability and contamination possibilities.

Both Knox and Sollecito appealed, initiating a new trial in November 2010. This phase brought forth a series of legal challenges aimed at debunking the prosecution's case. The defence teams contested the reliability of the evidence, particularly the DNA analysis, which had been pivotal in the initial convictions. A court-ordered review of the DNA evidence occurred at this time, involving independent experts who re-examined the forensic findings. The defence presented alternative interpretations, challenging the prosecution's narrative and emphasizing the need for a thorough re-evaluation of the evidence.

On the 3rd of October 2011, in a dramatic turn of events, the appeals court in Perugia overturned Amanda Knox and Raffaele Sollecito's convictions for the murder of Meredith Kercher. The court cited serious flaws in the investigation and the prosecution's case, including concerns about the reliability of the DNA evidence and the overall handling of the forensic analysis. Knox, who had spent four years in an Italian prison, was released, and she returned to the US, while Sollecito returned to his home in Italy.

However, the legal saga did not conclude with the acquittals. In March 2013, the Supreme Court of Cassation, Italy's highest court, set aside these acquittals and ordered a new trial for Knox and Sollecito. The court criticized the appeal court's handling of the evidence and highlighted the need for a comprehensive case review. Knox and Sollecito were found guilty once more; however, following another appeal in March 2015, they were definitively acquitted.

Following their release, Knox and Sollecito's lives took separate paths. Knox returned to Seattle, Washington, and became an advocate for the wrongfully convicted. She wrote a memoir, *Waiting to Be Heard*, and contributed articles, sharing her experiences and insights. In October 2023, she was convicted of defamation for wrongfully accusing Patrick Lumumba of the murder. She appealed the conviction, and a retrial was ordered.

Sollecito remained in Italy, where he faced challenges re-establishing a normal life. Despite being finally acquitted, Sollecito continued to face media scrutiny and wrote a book, *Honor Bound*, to share his perspective on the controversial case.

---

[1] *The Sunday Times*, 4 November 2007 – "Student Killer Leaves Bloody Footprint Clue"

[2] *The Age*, 5 October 2011 – "Acquitted Knox in the Eye of Media Storm"

[3] *The Guardian*, 7 November 2007 – "Flatmate and Friends Held by Italian Police Over Murder of British Student"

[4] *Seattle Post-Intelligencer*, 12 January 2009 – "Stage Is Set for Knox Trial"

[5] *The Sun Herald*, 14 June 2009 – "Murder Accused Tells of Police Pressure"

[6] Evening Standard, 4 December 2007 – "Meredith Suspect Can Identify Her Real Killer"

[7] *The Guardian*, 23 November 2007 – "Suspect's DNA Found in Meredith Murder Inquiry"

[8] *The Daily Telegraph*, 19 October 2008 – "Knox Stabbed Meredith in Throat, Court Told"

[9] *The Guardian*, 26 October 2008 – "Kercher Accused Blames Others"

[10] *Seattle Examiner*, 12 January 2009 – "Meet the Players in the Amanda Knox Trial"

[11] *Coalinga Record*, 16 January 2009 – "Trial Opens for US Suspect in Italy Slaying"

[12] *The Sunday Times*, 18 January 2009 – "Meredith was 'Softened Up for Fatal Sex Game'"

[13] The Associated Press News Service, 6 February, 2009 – "Italian Defendant Denies Killing British Student"

[14] *Evening Standard*, 6 February 2009 – "I Find it Hard to Kill a Fly, Suspect Tells Kercher Trial"

[15] Associated Press Archive, 7 February 2009 – "Roommate Testifies in Trial of US Student in Italy"

[16] *The Express*, 8 February 2009 – "Meredith and Foxy's Rift Over Her Lovers"

[17] *The Yorkshire Post*, 13 February 2009 – "Meredith's Killer Joked After Murder"

[18] *The Guardian*, 27 February 2009 – "Knox Admitted Being in the House when Kercher was Murdered, Court is Told"

[19] *The Scotsman*, 1 March 2009 – "Murder Suspect DNA on Bra"

[20] Associated Press Archive, 13 March 2009 – "Italian Suspect Had Knife at Police Station"

[21] *Seattle Post-Intelligencer*, 22 May 2009 – "Expert Says Knox's DNA on Murder Weapon"

[22] Associated Press Archive, 9 May 2009 – "Expert Says Print Matched Italian in Student Death"

[23] *Seattle Post-Intelligencer*, 9 May 2009 – "Expert Says Footprints Belong to Knox, Ex-Boyfriend"

[24] The Associated Press News Service, 21 March 2009 – "Witness Contradicts Accused in Italy Murder Trial"

[25] The Associated Press News Service, 28 March 2009 – "US Suspect Brandished Knife"

[26] *The Express*, 5 April 2009 – "Meredith Was Held Down in 'Horrific Rape'"

[27] Agence France-Presse, 12 June 2009 – "US Student Alleges Police Coercion in Italian Sex-Murder Case"

[28] Associated Press Archive, 12 June 2009 – "American Student Testifies at Italian Murder Trial"

[29] The Associated Press News Service, 20 July 2009 – "Coroner Testifies at Italian Trial"

[30] The Associated Press News Service, 23 June 2009 – "Kercher Trial: Witness Heard No Screams"

[31] *The Daily Beast*, 1 July 2009 – "The Other Murders That Could Save Her"

[32] *The Daily Beast*, 7 July 2009 – "Knox Defence Has Its Day"

[33] Associated Press Archive, 14 September 2009 – "Knox Defence Witness in Italy Doubts DNA Evidence"

[34] Associated Press Archive, 18 September 2009 – "Expert: Bloody Footprint Not Italy Defendant's"

[35] *The Times*, 19 November 2009 – "Kercher Case Appeal Hearing"

[36] Agence France-Presse, 30 November 2009 – "Knox Lawyer Make Closing Case at Sex Murder Trial"

[37] Associated Press Archive, 1 December 2009 – "Knox's Defence in Italy: Not Enough Evidence"

[38] *The Sunday Times*, 6 December 2009 – "Lust and Lies Snare Foxy"

Self-defence or Murder?

The Castle Doctrine is a legal principle in the US that generally permits individuals to use force, including deadly force, to protect their homes from intruders. In 2012, in Little Falls, Minnesota, Byron David Smith was arrested after fatally shooting two teenage intruders, an incident he had captured on audio recording. The subsequent trial sparked charged discussions on self-defence laws and the permissible use of lethal force for home protection.

———————

"He became frightened – scared to live in his own home.

That is what the heart of this case is all about."

Defence Attorney Steve Meshbesher

———————

Byron David Smith was a 64-year-old man who lived alone in a secluded area north of Little Falls, Minnesota. During 2012, he experienced a series of burglaries, although he reported only one of them to police – on the 27th of October that year. (Smith later said he didn't report the other burglaries because he didn't feel that they were "significant enough."[1]) Among the stolen items were a shotgun, rifle, thousands of dollars in cash, a watch that belonged to his late father, and jewellery.

The theft of both valuable and sentimental possessions eroded Smith's sense of security, and despite a police investigation, the burglars remained at large. In response to the break-ins, Smith took measures to safeguard his property. This included the installation of surveillance cameras at the front and back of his home and an audio recording system designed to capture and document sounds within the house.

On the 22nd of November 2012, at approximately 12:35 p.m., cousins 18-year-old Haile Kifer and 17-year-old Nicholas Brady were captured on Smith's surveillance cameras. With their faces partially concealed by hoods, they peered through windows and checked for unlocked doors. Smith was in the basement when he heard a window break upstairs, followed by footsteps overhead.

Arming himself with a Mini-14 semiautomatic rifle and a .22-calibre revolver, Smith positioned himself in a chair at the bottom of the basement stairs, waiting. Approximately seven minutes later, Nicholas Brady descended the stairs. As soon as his body became visible, Smith shot him in the chest. Nicholas fell to the bottom of the staircase and Smith shot him again, in the face. Smith dragged Brady's body onto a tarp, pulled him to his workshop, returned to his chair, and reloaded his rifle.

About eight minutes later, Haile Kifer appeared and began descending the basement steps. As her torso came into view, Smith shot her once in the hip. She tumbled to the bottom of the stairs, and Smith attempted another shot, but his rifle jammed. Picking up his revolver, he shot her multiple times in the chest. Moving her body to the workshop, Smith realized she was still alive and, to "end her suffering", he shot her "under the chin up into the cranium".

Because it was Thanksgiving, Smith opted not to "trouble" the police, leaving the bodies in the workshop for the remainder of the day and night. The next afternoon, he reached out to his neighbour, William Anderson, seeking a lawyer recommendation before requesting Anderson contact the police. When two officers arrived, Smith greeted them with clothes and shoes stained in blood. He pointed out the smashed window, explaining the multiple break-ins he had experienced. Smith then insisted on showing the officers something important and led them to the basement.[2]

The officers immediately noticed spent rifle cartridges and bloodstains on the wall, carpet, and steps. Following Smith to the workshop, they discovered Haile Kifer and Nicholas Brady's bodies lying on blood-soaked tarps. Smith was arrested, and during his interview with detectives at the police station, he admitted that neither Kifer nor Brady was armed but maintained he had feared that they could have been, and that he felt his life was in danger. He stated, "I figured they're willing to use guns if they steal guns, and I decided that I've got a choice of either shooting or being shot at."

Under Minnesota law, homeowners are permitted to use deadly force on an intruder if a reasonable person would fear danger or harm. However, Morrison County Sheriff Michel Wetzel publicly announced that Smith's actions went beyond the bounds of self-defence. Morrison County Attorney Brian Middendorf agreed, commenting, "Mr Smith intentionally killed two teenagers in his home in a manner that goes well beyond self-defence."

Not everyone in the community shared this view. Smith's friend, John Lange, offered a different perspective, saying, "Just imagine that you lived alone. That would really get to you. That's what people need to understand. A person should be able to defend their home."[3] Another friend, William Anderson, suggested that if the police had done their job in October when investigating the previous burglary at Smith's property, Haile and Nicholas might still be alive.

On the 26th of November, in Morrison County District Court, Smith faced charges of two counts of second-degree murder without premeditation. He was held on $2 million bail, with the prosecution arguing that he could be a flight risk, considering his extensive travel history while working as a security officer for the US State Department. The judge said that Smith could post $1 million bail if he agreed to surrender his passport and weapons, committing not to leave the state.[4]

News of the shooting elicited strong emotions on social media, sparking a divisive debate. Some argued that Smith had crossed a line by repeatedly shooting Haile and Nicholas, while others contended that his actions were justified, placing blame on the teenagers for their own deaths. In response to the public discourse, Sheriff Metzel addressed the controversy, stating to the Associated Press, "If people [had] all of the facts, they would not be quite so divided in their opinions."[5]

On the 18th of December, Smith returned to court for a bail hearing, where Assistant County Attorney Todd Kosovich urged

Judge Douglas Anderson to double or triple the sum. Kosovich asserted that Smith had deliberately waited for the teenagers, citing audio recordings in which Smith sneered, "You're dying" to Kifer after wounding her but before delivering the final shot to her head. He also said the audio recording had captured Smith telling Nicholas, "You're dead," and referring to Haile as a "bitch" as she lay dying. Kosovich argued, "The state will show that this was an ambush, and a murder," highlighting Smith's actions such as unscrewing basement lightbulbs, leaving only the one above the stairs, and preparing a tarp on the ground for moving the bodies.

Kosovich highlighted the seven-minute gap on the sound recording between the noise of Haile Kifer and Nicholas Brady smashing the window and Smith firing the first shot. He suggested that in those seven minutes, Smith had an opportunity to call the police. In response, Smith's older brother, Bruce, laughed out loud in the courtroom. The prosecutor also quoted Smith's disturbing description of Kifer's murder to detectives during his interview: "She gave out the death twitch; it works the same as in a beaver or deer." This remark prompted gasps in the courtroom, with someone in Kifer's family whispering, "Oh, my God."[6]

In an attempt to secure a lower bail, Smith's attorney, Steve Meshbesher, portrayed him as a Little Falls native who had retired after 16 years with the Department of Homeland Security in a computer job. Meshbesher drew attention to Smith's proactive approach to the 27th of October burglary, mentioning that he had written a memo to the sheriff's office, seeking assistance and guidance. Describing his client as a concerned and good citizen, Meshbesher argued for understanding and a fair evaluation of the circumstances.

Judge Anderson ruled that Smith could secure his release from jail by posting either $50,000 in cash or a $500,000 bond, provided he met certain conditions, including surrendering his passport. Later that afternoon, Smith posted the $50,000 cash bail and was released from jail; he moved in with his neighbours. The decision caught Haile Kifer and Nicholas Brady's families off guard, and they publicly said that the teenagers might have deserved legal consequences for breaking into Smith's home but not to the extent of losing their lives.

The Minnesota County Attorneys Association, representing the Morrison County Attorney's Office, reached out to Washington County Attorney Pete Orput, and asked him to assume the role of lead prosecutor. The Morrison County Attorney's Office sought extra assistance due to the exceptional circumstance of having to handle nine homicide-related cases simultaneously. Orput, who had been serving as Washington County Attorney since 2011 expressed confidence that the Smith case was suitable for presentation to a jury.[7]

In April 2013, Smith faced new charges, finding himself accused of two counts of first-degree, premeditated murder. A grand jury had dedicated two days to reviewing evidence and hearing testimony in the state's case against Smith. Under Minnesota law, a premeditated murder case necessitated a grand jury to issue a first-degree murder indictment, carrying a sentence of life in prison without the possibility of parole.

Smith's attorney announced plans to mount a defence grounded on an individual's right to protect their home. They intended to invoke the "Castle Doctrine", a legal concept originating from the 17th-century British jurist Sir Edward Coke. In his work *The Institutes of the Lawes of England*, Coke asserted that "an Englishman's home is his castle" and that individuals have the legal right to exclude others from their homes. This principle accompanied colonists to the New World, evolving over the years and merging with American frontier individualism and the prevalent gun culture. The notion of protecting one's home and property became deeply ingrained in US legal tradition, eventually evolving into the "Stand Your Ground" laws, which were operative in twenty-six states at the time.

On the 30th of August, Smith's team argued that there was insufficient evidence for the first-degree murder charges and requested their dismissal. Judge Anderson granted them until November to submit written arguments, after which he would decide.[8] Judge Anderson subsequently declared that the first-degree murder charges against Smith would proceed. He determined that the grand jurors had followed proper procedures in establishing probable cause.[9]

The following month, Smith's attorney sought a review of the judge's decision from the State Court of Appeal. The request was denied. In the early new year, Smith entered a plea of not guilty to the two murders, setting the stage for a murder trial to commence in April.[10] Before the trial, Judge Anderson excluded evidence about the teenagers' histories, including court documents that showed that Nicholas Brady had previously broken into Smith's home and garage.

By the 22nd of April, a jury comprising 12 individuals selected from a pool of 140 potential jurors was finalized, and opening statements prepared. The judge noted the widespread publicity surrounding the case and announced that proceedings would take place in the courtroom of Morrison County to accommodate a larger audience.

Entering the courtroom dressed in a grey suit, Smith appeared sombre as he took his seat next to his legal team. Assistant State Prosecutor Kurt Wartner, presenting the prosecution's opening statement, pointed out that, following the shootings, Smith had not immediately called the police. Wartner contended that Smith's actions were deliberate, asserting that he patiently waited for Kifer and Brady to enter his home, positioned in a chair in the basement. He declared, "He was down there waiting for them, and he shot and killed them."[11]

Wartner asserted that Smith's actions constituted first-degree murder, emphasizing that he had fatally shot Brady and Kifer

Career criminal and murder suspect Richard Allen Davis is arraigned for drunken driving, Mendocino, California, 2 December 1993.

Polly Klaas, aged 12, abducted and murdered by Richard Allen Davis.

Marc Klaas, Polly's father, complained about the length of Davis's murder trial.

A photo of victim Lana Clarkson presented by the prosecution, 28 June 2007.

Music producer Phil Spector and his attorney Roger Rosen leaving court, 19 March 2007.

Detective Mark Lillienfeld displays one of Spector's many guns during the trial.

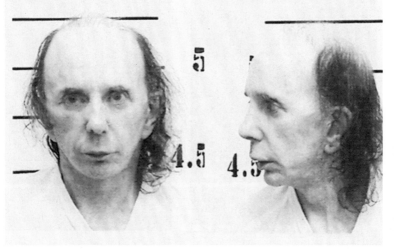

An official photo of Spector released following his murder conviction, 10 June 2009.

The Old Lady Killer

Juana Barraza, accused of murdering 10 elderly women, is presented to the press, Mexico City, 25 January 2005.

Trial by Media

Amanda Knox arrives for the final day of her trial, 1 November 2007.

Knox's then boyfriend, Raffaele Sollecito, 20 November 2009.

A photo of murder victim Meredith Kercher displayed at her funeral.

Extradited from Germany, Rudy Guede is met by police at Rome's Fiumicino airport, 6 December 2007.

Police examine the balcony of the villa where Kercher was killed.

Self-defence or Murder?

Jay and Jennifer Kifer, the parents of Haile Kifer, who was killed while breaking into Byron David Smith's home on Thanksgiving Day 2012.

A warning sign to deter potential intruders from entering Smith's property, November 2012.

Byron David Smith, soon to be convicted of the premeditated murder of two teenagers, at his trial hearing.

Extremist Anders Breivik strikes a pose at his trial for mass murder, 16 April 2021.

The crater left by the bomb Breivik detonated near government buildings in Oslo, resulting in eight people losing their lives.

A memorial to the 69 victims of Breivik's murderous rampage on Utøya Island.

Son Versus Father

Blood-spatter expert Rod Englert analyzes blood patterns found on Uta von Schwedler's clothing.

John Brickman Wall, Matheson Court House, Salt Lake City, 30 April 2013.

Satisfied by the jury's verdict, Pelle Wall leaves court after his father's conviction for murdering his mother.

A Tragic Mistake or Homicide?

Oscar Pistorius with girlfriend Reeva Steenkamp at a party, Tashas restaurant, Johannesburg, 26 January 2012.

His conviction upgraded to murder, Pistorius is mobbed by the press as he leaves court, 14 June 2016.

What police found in the house

1 & 2 Balconies

3 One cartridge in the passage way, three in the bathroom

4 Oakley cabinet with sunglasses. Found two packets of "testosterone", needles and injections

5 Taurus 9mm pistol

6 Two mobile phones

7 Cricket bat

8 Four bullet holes in the toilet door and one in the wall

9 Slippers, overnight bag and a gun holster

.38 Special bullets found in the bedroom safe

Another two phones

Balconies

Bathroom 2

Second bedroom

Wardrobes

Sliding doors

Main bedroom

Main bedroom entrance

To stairs and outside

Informal lounge

Shower

Wardrobes

Wardrobes

Toilet

Bathroom entrance

Representation based on the floor plan presented in court

Two dogs in the surrounding yard

Graphic: RUDI LOUW, Graphic24

The state case

Hilton Botha, investigating officer, testifies:

■ Gunshots look like they were fired downwards
■ No emergency numbers were dialled from mobile phones confiscated by police
■ Witness for the state who heard arguing, lives 600 m from the Pistorius house
■ Police confiscated two packets of testosterone
■ Pistorius did not lay any complaints with police regarding death threats
■ Pistorius knew Steenkamp was in the bathroom and murdered her

The defence case

Adv. Barry Roux SC submits:

■ Pistorius fired shots without wearing his prosthetic legs
■ Pistorius called Netcare911
■ Pistorius and Reeva Steenkamp were deeply in love; they were sleeping and Steenkamp went to the toilet while Pistorius was on the balcony
■ It is a legal herbal substance used by many sports persons, not steroids
■ Pistorius received death threats and was a victim of crime, he went to see the Hawks about this
■ Pistorius thought Steenkamp was in bed and that there was an intruder in the bathroom

A graphic shows the floorplan of Pistorius's house, along with evidence relating to the crime presented in court.

Pistorius demonstrates to the court his limited mobility without his prosthetic legs, 15 June 2016.

Caught on Camera

Protesters demonstrate in downtown Minneapolis on the first day of Chauvin's trial for killing George Floyd, 29 March 2021.

An official photograph of former police officer Derek Chauvin taken shortly after his conviction for murder.

Folllowing Chauvin's conviction, demonstrators display posters of Black victims of police brutality Trayvon Martin and George Floyd.

A live news feed on a mobile phone shows the moment of Chauvin's conviction, 20 April 2021.

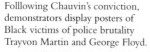

multiple times, even after the teenagers were clearly disabled by previous gunshots. He added that on the day of the shooting, Smith had moved his pickup truck down the street. The prosecution contended that this was a deliberate strategy to attract burglars, while Smith argued that he was merely cleaning out the garage and wanted to prevent vandalism to his vehicle.

In his opening statement, defence attorney Steven Meshbesher claimed that the time lapse between the shootings and the call to the police was indicative of Smith's fear, not guilt. Pacing back and forth, Meshbesher addressed the jury, stating, "He [Smith] is not criminally responsible for the deaths. He is not a murderer." Describing the events surrounding the case as a tragic loss of life, Meshbesher acknowledged, "Nobody, including my client, is happy to be here today. Frankly, I wish no one had to be here today, but here we are." He argued that Smith's actions fell within the bounds of the law, and that understanding Smith's background was crucial for the jury to comprehend his actions. Meshbesher outlined how, throughout 2012, Smith's home had been subjected to twelve break-ins, making it impossible for Smith to feel secure in his own home. He said that Smith had cooperated with detectives because he had nothing to hide and accused the prosecution of attempting to portray Smith as a cold-blooded killer. "He became frightened – scared to live in his own home. That is what the heart of this case is all about."

The prosecution called Brady and Kifer's parents, who recounted the harrowing moment of identifying their dead children at the medical examiner's office. The defence had the opportunity to cross-examine them, but chose not to do so.

The prosecution next played an audio recording of a conversation between Deputy Investigator Jeremy Luberts and Smith on the afternoon of his arrest. When asked why he thought he was being arrested, Smith responded, "Because there were bodies in the basement," adding, "And that's a good reason." Additional recordings captured Smith expressing to Luberts and to Sheriff's Deputy David Sherping his frustration with the repeated break-ins, highlighting the fear he lived with knowing that someone had consistently invaded his home and stolen various items, including firearms. Smith asserted to the officers, "Whoever it was breaking into my home – it was too much. I was no longer going to live in fear."[12]

At the police station, Smith engaged in a polite conversation with detectives about the burglaries, and this recording was also presented to the jury. He likened the string of burglaries to a pack of well-fed dogs that kept returning to the same feed pile. While acknowledging that he fired more shots than necessary, Smith explained that he feared there might be more people outside waiting to come inside and they could all gang up on him.

According to Smith, upon realizing that Kifer was female, he initially thought she might be one of his female neighbours, Ashley Williams, whom he had suspected of earlier burglaries. He anticipated her father coming to his house that night in search of her, preparing for a potential confrontation. Smith cited this as one of the main reasons for delaying a call to 911, coupled with not wanting to disturb the police on Thanksgiving. He explained, "The first couple of hours, I was just shaking. Gradually, I shifted into worrying about another accomplice."

The prosecution introduced a pivotal piece of evidence: Smith's own audio recording. They played a 29-minute excerpt from the six-hour recording, capturing the fatal shooting of Kifer and Brady. The courtroom fell silent as the recording unfolded, commencing with the sound of shattering glass and footsteps from upstairs. After a pause, the recording continued with the audible descent of Nicholas Brady down the basement stairs. A sudden gunshot rang out, followed by Brady's cry of pain and a second gunshot. The recording captured Nicholas tumbling down the stairs directly into Smith's path. Another loud pop echoed, after which Smith could be heard declaring in a sinister tone, "You're dead."

Following the gunshots, came sounds of Smith walking around, breathing heavily, and moving objects. In his interview with detectives, Smith admitted to dragging Brady's body onto a tarp and then moving it to the workshop in the basement. Approximately eleven minutes later, additional footsteps were audible at the top of the stairs, accompanied by Haile Kifer softly calling out, "Nick?" Moments later, gunshots resonated through the courtroom, followed by the sound of Kifer falling down the stairs.

Smith could be heard apologizing, saying, "Oh, sorry about that." According to Smith's interview with detectives, this apology was a reference to his gun jamming. Haile exclaimed, "Oh, my God," and began to scream. Smith retorted, "You're dying, bitch," as he opened fire with his revolver. Once Haile fell silent, Smith sneered, "Bitch." The recording captured more sounds of movement, followed by another solitary gunshot.

After Brady and Kifer met their demise, Smith whispered, "Of course, I'm safe now," referring to them as "vermin" and deeming them "social mistakes and social problems." He characterized the act as "cleaning up a mess" and went on to belittle Kifer, suggesting she thought she was "a real pro" at burglaries, adding, "It's all fun, cool, entertaining and highly profitable until someone kills you." Smith was concerned that if he hadn't taken drastic action, the teenagers might have served a short jail sentence and then sought revenge, stating, "I cannot live a life like that."

As the chilling half-hour audio recording played, Smith sat silently, hands folded. In contrast, the victims' friends and family audibly cried, and one juror wiped a tear from her eye. The prosecution then called Chad Museus, a senior special agent with the Minnesota Bureau of Criminal Apprehension. Museus described finding a working landline phone near the bodies of Brady and Kifer during his investigation the day after the shootings. Additionally, the teenagers had cell phones in their pockets, and Meseus testified that Kifer had exchanged text messages with a friend in the hours before the shootings, referring to herself and Brady as a "team". Museus interpreted this term to mean a "team for burglaries".

Nate Pearlson, a forensic scientist from the BCS lab, testified about the evidence collection at the crime scene. He had observed a rug and two pieces of carpet that seemed "out of place" at the bottom of the stairs. Once they were removed, bloodstains were revealed on the floor, with one of the more saturated stains appearing to contain brain matter. Screens in the courtroom revealed a red chair standing against the wall facing the stairs; next to it were a jug of water and snack bars. The tape recorder that had captured the incident was on a nearby shelf. Pearlson noted that light bulbs were missing from the three main fixtures in the basement. They were found near the red chair.

The jury was shown a photograph of Brady and Kifer's bodies partially wrapped in a camouflage tarp, having been moved from the bottom of the stairs to Smith's workroom. Pearlson determined that two bullet holes in the hood of Kifer's sweatshirt were likely made at distances of about 6 inches and 12 inches, while another found on her right sleeve was made from around 12 inches away. He was less distance specific about the shots fired at Nicholas.[13]

Dr Kelly Mills, a pathologist from the Ramsey County Medical Examiner's Office, offered further insights into the deaths of Kifer and Brady. She said that the initial gunshots did not result in their immediate deaths; instead, both victims were shot multiple times. Brady sustained three gunshot wounds, including one to the abdomen and the back of his left shoulder. While these two shots caused severe internal injuries that would have been fatal given enough time, they wouldn't have immediately incapacitated him. It was the final shot, which travelled through his right hand into his temple, that proved fatal. Kifer was shot a total of six times, including two close-range shots to the head. The shot that ultimately caused her death was the fifth one, a close-range shot behind her left ear that struck her brainstem.[14]

During cross-examination by Meshbesher, Dr Mills acknowledged that before the fatal shots, both Kifer and Brady could have been capable of movement and could have been perceived as threats by Smith. Meshbesher suggested that either of them could have reached for a weapon if they had had one, although both teenagers were unarmed. Dr Mills also testified that Brady had tested negative for drugs and alcohol, while Kifer had a cough medicine ingredient – dextromethorphan – in her system at a level that could have caused intoxication and possibly hallucinations.

After the prosecution rested, the defence summoned Morrison County Sheriff's Deputy Jamie Luberts to the witness stand. Luberts testified about the 27th of October burglary at Smith's home, revealing that when Smith reported it, he had mentioned earlier burglaries that were not officially reported. When Luberts responded to the October burglary, he discovered that the bottom panel of the basement walkout door had been kicked out. Smith showed him areas that had been ransacked, including the dresser in his bedroom. Luberts informed the jury that he didn't collect fingerprints from the door handles but found a fingerprint on the nightstand, though it wasn't of sufficient quality for a clear print.[15]

The purpose of Lubert's testimony was to illustrate that Smith had been living in fear for his life following the series of burglaries. The defence presented three character witnesses, starting with Smith's older brother Bruce, who attested to his brother's reputation for honesty in the community. Bruce stated, "He's highly regarded by everyone that has known this family." He also highlighted his brother's role in training three generations of Eagle Scouts. The other two character witnesses were Smith's nextdoor neighbours, Kathleen Lange and her 16-year-old son, Dylan Lange, who both described Smith as honest and a good neighbour.[16]

Following Smith's decision to waive his right to testify, the defence rested its case, setting the stage for closing arguments. Taking the podium first, Pete Orput confidently asserted that

Smith had intended to kill, making a deliberate choice with each trigger pull. He questioned whether fear truly motivated Smith or if there were other factors at play. Orput suggested that Smith moving his truck to create the appearance of an empty home indicated premeditation. He concluded by urging the jury, "Now it is your case. You know what happened. You know what his state of mind was. I'm asking you now to bring back just verdicts."[17]

When Meshbesher addressed the jury, he framed the case as one about courage. Meshbesher argued that Brady and Kifer, as they scouted Smith's home, had intruded into a space meant for safety. He portrayed Smith as a victim and said that homes are where people seek refuge. Meshbesher pointed out that Brady and Kifer would still be alive if they hadn't chosen to break into Smith's home, telling the jury, "Had they run away, yeah, that might be murder, but he never left his house. They came into his house."[18]

After the closing arguments, the judge instructed the jury that the state bore the burden of proving beyond a reasonable doubt that Smith did not use reasonable force. The jury had the option to acquit Smith or convict him of first-degree murder, the lesser charge of second-degree murder, or both.

The jury deliberated for a mere three hours before delivering their verdict. Byron David Smith was found guilty on two counts of second-degree murder and two counts of first-degree premeditated murder. As the verdict echoed in the courtroom, Smith displayed no emotion, while audible sobs came from Brady's and Kifer's mothers in the public gallery. A juror later remarked: "That audio recording of the actual killings and the audio recording of Mr Smith's interview immediately after his arrest pretty much convinced me that we were dealing with a deranged individual."[19]

Smith was automatically sentenced to life in prison without parole, yet Meshbesher announced his intention to appeal. Following the verdicts, family members were permitted to address the court. Brady's grandmother, Bonnie Schaeffel, described Smith as a "sour, angry old recluse who felt he was above the law". While expressing regret for the burglary of Smith's home, she said that Haile Kifer and Nicholas Brady deserved the chance to grow up and learn from their mistake. Kifer's aunt, Laurie Skipper, delivered a statement written by her parents: "Byron Smith made a conscious choice to shoot and kill our beautiful daughter, Haile. The feelings of helplessness are overwhelming."[20]

In the aftermath of the convictions, arguments surrounding Smith's degree of culpability persisted, dividing the local community. Some supported the conviction; others believed that Smith should have been acquitted.

Following the trial, Smith was mandated to pay restitution totalling approximately $21,000 to Brady and Kifer's families.[21] Undeterred, Smith initiated an appeal with the Minnesota Supreme Court, contending that the judge had denied him a fair trial by disallowing testimony regarding Brady and Kifer's criminal records. On the 9th of March 2016, the Minnesota Supreme Court upheld his conviction and sentence.[22]

In November 2018, Smith's legal team pursued a federal appeal, reiterating the argument that the jury should have been privy to evidence suggesting Brady's prior break-in, as disclosed by one of his friends. However, this appeal was deemed irrelevant, given Smith's ignorance of Brady being the previous burglar. In November 2020, Smith's attorneys mounted a final appeal, meeting a similar denial.[23] Byron David Smith remains incarcerated at Oak Park Heights Prison.

---

[1] *St. Paul Pioneer Press*, 28 November 2012 – "Suspect Told Police of Three Other Break-Ins"
[2] *St. Paul Pioneer Press*, 9 December 2012 – "Little Falls: Teens' Break-in Seen on Surveillance, Their Deaths Heard on Tape"
[3] *St. Paul Pioneer Press*, 25 November 2012 – "Little Falls Man Describes Finishing Teenagers with Shots to Heads"

[4] Minnesota Public Radio, 27 November 2012 – "Little Falls Shooter a Retired US State Dept. Security Engineer"

[5] Associated Press State Wire, 28 November 2012 – "Killing of 2. Minn. Teens Sparks Controversy"

[6] *Star Tribune*, 18 December 2012 – "Little Falls Defendant Getes Bail Lowered"

[7] *St. Paul Pioner Press*, 30 December 2012 – "Little Falls Break-In Homicide Case to Be Prosecuted by Washington County Attorney"

[8] Associated Press State Wire, 30 August 2013 – "Little Falls Man Wants Murder Charges Dismissed"

[9] Minnesota Public Radio, 25 November 2013 – "Judge Denies Motion to Dismiss Charges in Little Falls Shooting"

[10] *St. Paul Pioneer Press*, 23 January 2014 – "Little Falls Homeowner Pleads Not Guilty in Teen Intruder's Shooting Deaths"

[11] *SC Times*, 21 April 2014 – "Smith Thought Neighbor Had Burglarized Home Previously"

[12] *Brainderd Dispatch*, 21 April 2014 – "Opening Arguments Set the Stage for Byron Smith Murder Trial"

[13] *St. Paul Pioneer Press*, 22 April 2014 – " 'You're Dead,' Little Falls Homeowner Said After Shooting Teen Intruder"

[14] *Twin Cities Pioneer Press*, 23 April 2014 – "Little Fall Teens Were Not Fatally Wounded Initially, M.E. Testifies"

[15] *Morrison County Record*, 24 April 2014 – "Prosecution Rests After Jury Sees Graphic Autopsy Photos"

[16] CBS News, 28 April 2014 – "Defense Rests for Minn. Man Who Killed Two Teen Burglars"

[17] WJON 29 April 2014 – "Breaking – Court to Announce Jury's Verdict in Byron Smith Murder Trial"

[18] KARE 11 29 April 2014 – "Jury Begins Deliberating Byron Smith Murder Case"

[19] Huffington Post, 2 May 2014 – "Court Releases Recording of Byron Smith Gunning Down Teens"

[20] NBC News, 30 April 2014 – "Minnesota Homeowner Byron Smith Convicted of Premeditated Murder"

[21] *St. Paul Pioneer Press*, 19 November 2014 – "Little Falls Homeowner Must Pay $21k to Slain Teens' Families"

[22] Minnesota Public Radio, 9 March, 2016 – "Minnesota Man Who Killed Teens in his Home Denied New Trial"

[23] *Star Tribune*, 31 August 2018 – "Man Who Killed Two Teens Will Appeal"

Massacre of the Innocents

Norway is known as one of the safest countries in the world, with a low crime rate even in big cities. But in July 2011, a bomb exploded outside the prime minister's office in Oslo, shattering the nation's peace and setting in motion an afternoon of terror. By the end of the day, 77 people would be dead, most of them teenagers at a camp held by the AUF, the youth wing of the ruling Norwegian Labour Party, on Utøya Island. A man named Anders Behring Breivik was arrested. What followed was Norway's most harrowing criminal trial since the prosecution of Nazis after World War II.

"Breivik made an error when he decided to spare me, seen from his perspective. Now I really understand how fragile our society is. I see how much it is worth and the importance of politics. I will continue with politics, and the Labour Party remains closer to my heart."

Adrian Pracon

Norway's capital, Oslo, was quieter than usual on the 22nd of July 2011. It was a wet Friday during the summer holidays, and that afternoon, Anders Behring Breivik, a 32-year-old Christian fundamentalist harbouring anti-Islamic sentiments, embarked on a mission he had methodically crafted over five years. His preparations included personal training, donning backpacks filled with rocks, membership of an Oslo shooting club, and the purchase of firearms and ammunition. [1] Drawing inspiration from the infamous Red Army Faction's Andreas Baader, he constructed a bomb.

After leaving his mother's flat in Oslo's West End, Breivik climbed into his VW Crafter van, and put on a black compression top with plastic police insignia on the sleeves and a bulletproof vest. The back of the van contained a 950-kilo bomb Breivik had assembled containing ANFO (ammonium nitrate-fuel oil). At 3:13 p.m., Breivik parked the van in the government quarter of the city outside a tower block; the Prime Minister's office was on the top floor.

Nine minutes after Breivik left the van, the bomb detonated. Despite most workers being on holiday and Prime Minister Jens Stöltenberg working remotely, the toll was severe – eight individuals lost their lives, and nine others sustained serious injuries.[2] The devastating explosion left a large crater in the road, wrecked the façade of the targeted building, and inflicted damage on several neighbouring structures.

Shortly thereafter, word of the bomb blast reached Utøya Island, some 40 kilometres northwest of Oslo, where around 600 young people were enjoying their third day of camp run by the youth wing of the ruling centre-left Labor Party. Each year, the island played host to the summer camp, and hundreds of teenagers as young as 14 flocked there from all over Norway. One camper later recalled: "We comforted each other with the knowledge that at least we were safe on the island."[3] But they were wrong.

After leaving the van, Breivik walked to Hammersborg Square where he had parked his Fiat car. He then drove out of the capital and boarded the ferry, MS *Thorbjørn*, at Utøykaia in Tyrifjorden. Equipped with two guns and employing a phony police badge and service certificate, he identified himself as a police officer conducting a routine security check following the Oslo bomb. Breivik arrived on Utøya Island at 5:17 p.m. and walked up to the white-painted main house on its east side. Four minutes later, he shot and killed his first victims – Monica Bøsei, the general manager of activities on the island, and Trond Berntsen, a hired guard. He then opened fire at random.

By 6:30 p.m., the death toll numbered 69 individuals, aged from 14 to 51. Phone calls from the island flooded emergency lines, but in the confusion, some callers were told not to jam the telephone line if their call wasn't related to the Oslo attack; crucial information had not been shared between departments, causing delays. During the mass shooting, Breivik even phoned police twice himself and gave them his full name, identifying himself as a commander in the Norwegian resistance movement against the Islamization of Europe and Norway. He also told them: "Mission accomplished."[4] At about 6:35 p.m., a police anti-terror unit arrived on the island in small boats as the unit's sole helicopter was not ready for immediate deployment. Breivik was arrested without resistance and confessed to the two attacks.

At first, many assumed that the terrorist attacks had been

perpetrated by Islamic fundamentalists, and the public was stunned to learn that this was not the case. Two days later, Prime Minister Jens Stoltenberg captured the sombre national mood: "Our response is more democracy, more openness and more humanity. If one man can create that much hate, you can only imagine how much love we as a togetherness can create."[5]

Following Breivik's arrest, it was revealed that he had written a 1,500-page manifesto before the attacks, denouncing multiculturalism and Muslim immigration. He disclosed that he had been contemplating a "martyrdom operation" at least since autumn 2009. The revelation that Breivik had attempted to send his manifesto to 8,000 people on his email list (only 1,000 were successful before a spam filter intervened) added another layer of astonishment to a nation proud of its societal openness.

Breivik hired Geir Lippestad, who had once defended neo-Nazi Ole Nicolai Kvisler, as his attorney. On the 24th of July, Lippestad announced to the media: "[Brievik] admitted responsibility. He feels that it was cruel to have to carry out these acts but that, in his head, it was necessary."[6] Lippestad also said that Breivik had two wishes for his first court appearance: that the hearing be public, and that he be allowed to wear a military uniform.[7] His requests were denied, and the following day, he appeared in court and was remanded in custody for eight weeks, the first four of which would be in solitary confinement with a ban on all communication with the outside world.[8]

Breivik initially claimed there were "more cells" in "our organization". Detectives investigated but found no evidence that anybody else was involved. Breivik was charged with the premeditated murder of 77 people, as well as violating paragraph 147a of the Norwegian code – "destabilizing or destroying basic foundations of society" and "creating serious fear in the population" – both acts of terrorism.[9] These charges carried a maximum penalty of 21 years in prison, but sentences could be prolonged indefinitely for inmates deemed to still pose a danger to society.

The day after Breivik's first court appearance, Lippestad announced, "This whole case indicates that he is insane," setting in motion extensive psychiatric examinations of Breivik in August.[10] In Norway, an insanity defence necessitates that the defendant be in a state of psychosis during the commission of the crime. After meeting Breivik 13 times, psychiatrists Synne Sørheim and Torgeir Husby concluded that he suffered from paranoid schizophrenia, rendering him criminally insane. They connected his "deviant statements" about immigration to his immersion in an anti-Islamic movement, drawing parallels between his state of mind and that of a brainwashed cult member.[11]

If the court were to accept the psychiatrists' findings, Breivik would receive treatment in a psychiatric facility instead of being sentenced to prison. Opposition from the victims' families and the general public prompted the court to appoint two new psychiatrists, Terje Tørrissen and Agnar Aspaas, who deemed Breivik legally sane.

Breivik's trial commenced on the 15th of April 2022. He entered the 200-seat courtroom, built specifically for the trial, seemingly composed and wearing a dark suit. Once unhandcuffed, Breivik flashed a closed-fist salute, before shaking hands with prosecutors and court officials, common practice in a Norwegian court. He then declared: "I don't recognize Norwegian courts because you get your mandate from the Norwegian political parties who support multiculturalism." The trial was presided over by five judges, including Judge Wenche Elizabeth Arntzen. Breivik said he didn't recognize her authority, because she was a friend of the sister of former Norwegian Prime Minister and Labour Party leader Gro Harlem Brundtland.

Breivik's face registered no emotion as Prosecutor Inga Bejer Engh read out his indictment, detailing charges of terrorism and premeditated murder, along with a description of each victim's death. Most had met the same fate, succumbing to gunshot wounds to the backs of their heads as they ran for their lives. The horrific details reduced many survivors and family members to tears.

The prosecutor then explored Breivik's life, highlighting various failed business ventures and a year-long hiatus during which he apparently immersed himself in playing the video game *World of Warcraft*. Engh also presented a 12-minute YouTube video posted by Breivik before the massacre. The video featured a sequence of photographs and sketches of Islamists set to soft music, and as it played, Breivik appeared visibly emotional. The video concluded with the chilling sentence: "Islam will again be banished from Europe!" When the prosecutor had concluded his opening statement, Breivik admitted killing 77 people but pleaded not guilty, claiming he had acted out of "necessity".[12]

The trial's central issue was Breivik's mental state at the time of the murders. In an unusual move, the defence sought to prove that Breivik was sane. Concerns arose that Breivik might exploit the trial to propagate his extremist views, leading to the installation of thick glass partitions to separate him from the victims' families and friends in the public gallery. Before proceedings resumed the next day, one of the five judges, Thomas Indreboe, was removed from the trial due to his online call immediately after the massacre for Breivik to receive the death penalty. He was replaced by Judge Anne Elisabeth Wisloeff.[13]

The trial's first witness was Breivik himself, who was granted the opportunity to present a statement he had composed. He characterized the massacre as a "preventative" strike aimed at safeguarding ethnic Norwegians and averting a potential European culture clash with Muslims. Referring to Christians as a "persecuted minority", Breivik urged the court to release him. He declared, "Yes, I would have done it again," asserting that spending his life behind bars or sacrificing himself for his people would be "the highest honour".

Breivik proceeded to explain why he specifically targeted Utøya

Island. He drew parallels between the Labour Party's youth wing and the Hitler Youth, dismissing the teenagers on the island as "naïve and indoctrinated". In the public gallery, survivors and victims' relatives shook their heads in utter disbelief. Breivik then delved into Islamophobic and anti-immigration ideologies, prompting Chief Judge Wench Elizabeth Arntzen to interject, requesting him to temper his rhetoric. He retorted, "If I can't lay out the framework of my defence, then there's no point in me explaining myself."

Though allocated only thirty minutes to address the court, Breivik had extended this to approximately one hour and fifteen minutes – nearly the same amount of time he spent carrying out his shooting spree on Utøya Island.[14] Concluding his statement, he proclaimed his actions as "the first drops of water heralding the coming storm. Rivers of blood will run through the cities of Europe".[15] He then proceeded to spend five days on the witness stand elaborating his motives for the massacre.

Breivik disclosed that he had believed he only had a slim chance of escaping Oslo alive after detonating the bomb, anticipating a confrontation with police. "I estimated the chances of survival as less than five percent," he remarked. Despite his expectations, no one intervened, enabling him to drive to Tyrifjorden and board the ferry to Utøya Island.

Breivik claimed he had planned a more extensive killing spree, involving three car bombs and additional shootings at various targets across Oslo, including the Labour Party headquarters, the *Aftenposten* newspaper, and City Hall. He had also envisioned driving to the Socialist Left Party headquarters to "execute as many people as possible". Another plan involved the beheading of former Prime Minister Gro Harlem Brundtland, with the intention of posting a video of her execution online.

As Breivik started discussing target-shooting techniques, a disturbing smile appeared on his face, prompting Prosecutor Svein Holden to issue a reprimand. Breivik then revealed that, in preparation for the massacre, he had taken testosterone and ingested anabolic steroids on the day of the attacks.[16] He also admitted studying the 1993 bombing of the World Trade Center in New York and Timothy McVeigh's 1995 Oklahoma City attack. Despite differing goals, he also referred to the Islamist group Al-Qaeda as "the most successful revolutionary movement in the world" and advocated it as an inspiration for far-right militants.

The primary aim of Breivik's defence strategy was to avoid an insanity ruling, a verdict that could undermine his political assertions. Throughout his testimony, he claimed affiliation with a clandestine anti-Muslim militia called the Knights Templar, which he said he had founded in London in 2002 with three other individuals. When pressed to disclose the identities of the other participants, he refused, citing a memory lapse regarding the crucial meeting. Prosecutors expressed scepticism about the existence of the alleged militia.[17] Breivik responded that they hadn't sufficiently investigated it.

Breivik's testimony shifted to the day of the massacre, but before giving details, he issued a warning to those uncomfortable with the "gruesome" account, suggesting they could leave. No one chose to leave the courtroom. Breivik proceeded to recount his arrival at Utøya Island, revealing his initial hesitation about carrying out the plan. After briefly deliberating whether or not to proceed with the shootings, Breivik calmly related approaching a café building teeming with people, where he killed 11 victims.

Despite claiming not to recall every detail of his shooting spree on the island, Breivik provided vivid descriptions, including the methodical shooting of four or five people in a group, targeting their heads. A faint sneer crossed his face as he remarked: "I think many [were] screaming and begging for their lives." Breivik added that some victims were so frozen in fear that they couldn't run, and that others pretended to be dead which prompted him to fire indiscriminately at them. He recalled yelling: "'You will die today,

Marxists."[18] Breivik was anxious to prove he was sane and said that the "plot" to portray him as insane was part of a "racist" plot to discredit his anti-Muslim ideology. According to Breivik, he would never have been given a psychiatric evaluation if he had been a "bearded jihadist". He said that "to a political activist, the worst thing that can happen is to end up in a mental hospital", explaining "that would delegitimize everything you stand for".[19]

After Breivik left the witness stand, multiple individuals testified regarding the bomb in Oslo. Security guard Tor Inge Kristoggersen vividly described the scene as resembling a "war zone". Police operations leader Thor Langli recounted receiving initial reports indicating two suspects and the potential threat of two additional bombs. The first report mentioned a "non-Nordic" suspect leaving the scene, while the second identified a "Nordic-looking" suspect, leading Langli to believe there were multiple perpetrators. However, learning about the shooting on Utøya Island, Langli revised his assessment, concluding that both the bomb and the shooting were the actions of a single individual. Turning his attention to Breivik, he remarked, "I could not imagine there being two people with so many crazy ideas."[20]

Ole Morten Stoerseth, a police official tasked with identifying the blast victims, told the court: "More than 100 body parts were found in the government district." Pictures of the injuries were not shown in court, but were distributed to the judges, prosecutors, and defence attorneys.

Testimony also shed light on how the victims on Utøya Island were killed. Coroner Torleiv Ole Rognum said that the average age of the victims on the island was eighteen. He went on to illustrate how Breivik was armed with a Ruger Mini-14 Ranch rifle equipped with a bayonet, a pistol and more than 1,000 rounds of ammunition. Additionally, Breivik carried a gas mask, a tourniquet, a flashlight, and three chocolate bars. The word "Mjolnir", representing the hammer of the Norse god Thor, was etched onto the pistol in Norse runes, while "Gungnir", the name of the Norse god-king Odin's magical spear, was inscribed in marker pen on the rifle.[21]

In an attempt to humanize each individual case, the attorneys representing the victims shared poignant pictures of their lives and read aloud heartfelt descriptions provided by their families, occasioning audible sobs in the courtroom. Rognum testified that most of the 69 victims on the island had died "instantly" but when asked if any had suffered before they died, he responded, "In some cases, the injuries resulted in massive bleeding and they might have lived a short while, but when you [lose] a lot of blood you lose consciousness."[22]

The trial's focus then pivoted back to Breivik's mental state during the massacre. The second report, declaring him sane, still awaited approval from the Norwegian Board of Forensic Medicine, which requested additional information. Breivik returned to court determined to establish his sanity. He vehemently contested the initial examination, denouncing it as containing "more than two hundred lies" and deeming the diagnosis "the ultimate humiliation". According to him, the two psychiatrists were "emotionally affected" by the massacre, rendering them incompetent to assess someone responsible for political violence.[23]

Following Breivik's testimony, survivors from Utøya Island shared their accounts. Jon Olson, captain of MS *Thorbjørn*, recounted how he initially mistook Breivik for a police officer when he boarded the ferry. He vividly described the "angst and full panic" that ensued as Breivik opened fire after the ferry docked. Olson's wife, Monica Boesei, was one of the first victims. Olson struggled to recollect whether he had witnessed Breivik shooting her, stating, "I don't remember if I saw him shooting Monica, but I think I did."[24]

In a resolute tone, survivor Tonje Brenna recounted hearing Breivik's exuberant shouts amid the chaos as bodies fell around her while she sought refuge in a cliff crevice. "I am absolutely sure that I heard cries of joy. If I had to spell it out, it would be WOO-HOO. Obviously cries of joy." Breivik, seated just metres away, displayed no emotion.[25] Subsequently, he proposed dropping his defence in exchange for the opportunity to question survivors. The judge dismissed his request, leading Breivik to argue that the decision was "ideologically" motivated.

Several survivors followed Brenna to the witness stand, vividly recounting the day that forever altered their lives and the enduring injuries they would carry. Bjoern Ihler described shielding two boys with his body as gunshots drew nearer. Frida Holm Skoglund, addressing Breivik, declared, "We won, he lost," while Ylva Helene Schwenke labelled him a "cowardly little man, really". Adrian Pracon, who had been shot in the shoulder, defiantly stated, "Breivik made an error when he decided to spare me, seen from his perspective. Now I really understand how fragile our society is. I see how much it is worth and the importance of politics. I will continue with politics, and the Labour Party remains closer to my heart."

On the 11th of May, proceedings were disrupted when a man in the courtroom threw a shoe at Breivik, inadvertently hitting his defense attorney. The man, Hayder Mustafa Qasim, the older brother of one of Breivik's victims, Karar Mustafa Quasim, exclaimed, "Go to hell!" before being escorted out. Later he remarked, "I had to send the killer a message from all those whose lives he has destroyed."[26]

Witnesses, identified as former friends of Breivik, expressed concerns about his mental state prior to the murders. Requesting anonymity, they said that he might have been grappling with deep depression or struggling with his sexual orientation, speculating that he may have been gay but unable to accept it. During this period, Breivik had cut off social ties and moved back in with his mother. One friend disclosed that Breivik had undergone a nose job, purportedly to achieve a more "Aryan" appearance, and frequently wore make-up. Another friend recounted Breivik's obsession with immigration post-2006 (perhaps the year Breivik became bankrupt), noting that political discussions with him inevitably revolved around this topic.[27]

Returning to the witness stand on the 4th of June, Breivik explored childhood incidents that he claimed had shaped his anti-Muslim sentiments. He recounted an incident at age seven involving a Turkish diplomat, a friend of his father, who allegedly destroyed his bicycle because Breivik had offended him. Breivik listed several other occurrences, including slaps, fights, attempted thefts, and three alleged rape cases, either involving him or people he knew. In every case, the girls he claimed had been victims of sexual assault denied his accounts during police interviews. Breivik asserted that, initially, he had sought to bring about change in Norway by democratic means but growing frustration with the lack of progress by 2006 led him to develop plans for the 22nd of July massacre.[28]

Following Breivik's testimony, several Norwegian far-right extremists took the stand to support his assertions that Norway was in a supposed "war" against Islam. The objective was to demonstrate that individuals sharing Breivik's views could hold these beliefs without being considered mentally ill.[29]

As the trial neared its conclusion, contrasting psychological perspectives were presented. Erik Johannesen, who extensively interviewed Breivik, likened the encounter to meeting Hannibal Lecter from the film *Silence of the Lambs* and asserted that Breivik's radical views stemmed from extremist ideologies rather than mental illness. He expressed scepticism about therapy or medication effectively treating Breivik. Another psychologist, Einar Kringlen, rejected the notion of Breivik being insane, pointing out that "evil cannot always be explained by illness".[30] Ulrik Frederik Malt suggested Breivik might have Aspergers Syndrome or Tourette Syndrome but said that he exhibited no signs of psychosis.

Torgeir Husby and Synne Sørheim stood by their diagnosis, however, asserting that Breivik was psychotic and, therefore, not criminally responsible for his actions. Sørheim testified, "He thinks he's going to save us all from our losing fight in the battle between good and evil. In combat, he thinks he has responsibility and a mission consistent with deciding who has the right to live or die." Both psychologists maintained that Breivik genuinely believed he was the commander of The Knights Templar, although the existence of this group could not be substantiated.

Following the psychiatrists' testimony, Prosecutor Svein Holden presented his closing arguments. Holden contended that Breivik's sanity had not been definitively proven and proposed that he be mandated to undergo psychiatric treatment. In the event that the judges deemed him sane, Holden asserted that he would request the country's maximum penalty – 21 years in prison, extendable as needed. Breivik, visibly angered by Holden's statement, abruptly stood up and made a salute with his right hand before being escorted from the court.[31]

In his closing arguments, defence attorney Geir Lippestad advocated for Breivik to be declared legally sane, arguing that his actions were rooted in extremism rather than psychotic delusions or an uncontrollable impulse for violence. When Breivik was granted a final statement, over thirty people left the courtroom, with Christian Bjelland, the support group chair for survivors and families, stating, "He has a right to talk. We have no duty to listen."[32] Breivik asserted to the remaining attendees, "The July 22 attacks were preventative attacks in defence of my ethnic group, and I can therefore not acknowledge guilt." He claimed to be acting on behalf of "my people, my religion, and my country" before requesting acquittal.

While the judges deliberated, a government-appointed commission released its report on the attacks. The findings indicated that the police and domestic intelligence services could have taken measures to prevent or interrupt the massacre. The report highlighted lapses, including incomplete construction of physical barriers approved in 2010 and a lack of strict enforcement of parking bans near government buildings. It also revealed police response delays attributed to communication system flaws and other operational errors.[33]

On the 24th of August, the five judges delivered a unanimous verdict, declaring Anders Behring Breivik sane – an outcome consistent with the preference of the far-right extremist himself. Breivik smiled on hearing the verdict and announced his decision not to appeal. He received the maximum allowable sentence of 21 years, with the potential for indefinite extension, referred to as "preventive detention". The verdict and the seemingly lenient sentence triggered a public debate about Norway's legal system. While some saw the decision as a demonstration of Norway's commitment to legal principles, others criticized what they perceived as insufficient justice given the gravity of Breivik's crimes.

Breivik is currently serving his sentence in Ringerike Prison, near Tyrifjorden, where he enjoys relatively comfortable conditions, including a personal kitchen, exercise room, and TV lounge. He even keeps two budgies, having requested permission to have a pet. Despite these favourable living conditions, Breivik has filed two lawsuits against the state, alleging violations of his human rights regarding his sentence and prison conditions.[34] Breivik also applied for parole in 2022, but this was rejected as he was still deemed a threat to society.

---

[1] *The Guardian*, 24 August 2012 – "Anders Behring Breivik Spent Years Training and Plotting for Massacre"

[2] *Afterposten*, 22 July 2021 – "Such Was the Day of Terror, 22 July, 2011"

[3] *Spiegel International*, 25 July 2011 – "A Chronology of the Twin Attacks"

[4] Sky News, 3 August 2011 – "'Mission Accomplished': Breivik Call to Cops"

[5] *Irish Times*, 19 July 2021 – "Ten Years on, Norway Still Deals with Wounds from Breivik Massacre"

[6] Agence France-Presse, 24 July 2011 – "Norway Carnage Suspect Admits Responsibility"

[7] Agence France-Presse, 24 July 2011 – "Norway Killer Wants to Wear Uniform at Court"

[8] Agence France-Presse, 25 July 2011 – "Norway Massacre Suspect Remanded in Custody"

[9] Oslo District Court: Ruling on Holding Anders Behring Breivik in Custody"

[10] *Bergens Tidende*, 26 July 2011 – "Breivik Is Insane"

[11] GlobalPost, 15 January 2012 – " Breivik Psychiatric Report Published by Norway Tabloid"

[12] Associated Press, 15 April 2012 – "Breivik Admits Massacre But Pleads Not Guilty"

[13] Agence France-Presse, 17 April 2012 – "Norwegian Killer Says He Would Do It All Again"

[14] Agence France-Presse, 17 April 2012 – "Breivik Met by Smirks and Scoldings on the Stand"

[15] The Standard, 16 February 2015 – "One of Us: The Story of Anders Breivik and the Massacre in Norway"

[16] Agence France-Presse, 19 April 2012 – "Breivik Says Initial Plan Was Three Bombs"

[17] *The Australian*, 19 April 2012 – "Breivik Starts to Crack on Milia"

[18] *The Toronto Star,* 21 April 2012 – "Breivik Details Victims' Reactions"

[19] Associated Press, 24 April 2012 – "Breivik: Insane Diagnosis Based on 'Fabrications'"

[20] Associated Press, 24 April 2012 – "Witnesses Recall Chaos After Breivik Attack"

[21] *Rutland Herald*, 4 May 2012 – "Witnesses Describe Island Massacre in Norway Trial"

[22] *Observer-Dispatch*, 5 May 2012 – "Norway Victims Died Instantly, Medical Examiner Testifies"

[23] Agence France-Presse, 25 April 2012 – "Breivik Accuses Experts of Lies as He Pleads for his Sanity"

[24] *The Independent*, 4 May 2012 – "'Breivik Told Us He Was a Policeman,' Say Witnesses"

[25] Agence France-Presse, 9 May 2012 – "Breivik Shouted with Joy During Utoeya Massacre"

[26] *The Buffalo News*, 12 May 2012 – "Victim's Vin Throws Shoe at Norway Killer"

[27] *The Sydney Morning Herald*, 30 May 2012 – "Friends Suspected Breivik Was Depressed About Being Gay"

[28] Agence France-Presse, 4 July 2012 – "Breivik Says Childhood Incidents Shaped his Views on Muslims"

[29] Associated Press, 5 June, 2012 – "Far-Right Extremists Testify in Breivik Trial"

[30] Agence France-Presse, 11 June 2012 – "Talk with Breivik 'Like Meeting Hannibal'"

[31] Agence France-Presse, 21 June 2012 – "Prosecutors Want Breivik Sent to Closed Psychiatric Unit"

[32] Agence France-Presse, 22 June 2012 – "Norway Killer Breivik Demands Acquittal as Trial Ends"

[33] NOI Rapport fra 22. Juli-kommisjonen

[34] *Afterposten*, 19 December 2023 – "This is How the Mass Murderer Anders Behring Breivik is Serving Time in Prison"

Son Versus Father

In 2011, Dr John Brickman Wall found himself at the centre of a legal saga when his ex-wife, Uta von Schwedler, was found dead in the bathtub at her Salt Lake City home. At first it was thought that Uta had taken her own life. However, the narrative shifted dramatically when the couple's teenage son, Pelle, emerged as a determined force seeking justice. Convinced that his father was involved in his mother's death, Pelle spearheaded efforts to bring his own father to trial.

———————

"You add up the different pieces — the death, his behaviour beforehand and afterwards, as well as his general feelings or emotions towards my mother — I think it was a pretty clear analysis of the situation."

Pelle Wall

———————

During the 27th of September 2011, Nils Abramson was becoming increasingly concerned that his girlfriend of one year, Uta von Schwedler, was not responding to his text messages. Uta, a 49-year-old German-born mother of four, was a respected biologist and HIV researcher at the University of Utah. That night, at about 7:45 p.m., Abramson drove over to Uta's home on Harrison Avenue in Sugar House, Salt Lake City, Utah.

When he pulled up outside, he noticed that the empty garbage can and the daily newspaper were still in the driveway and only the bathroom light illuminated the otherwise dark house. Abramson entered and went upstairs. As he passed Uta's open bedroom door, he observed signs of a struggle. Items were scattered on the floor, a lamp lay on the bed, and there were what looked like bloodstains on one corner of the duvet.[1]

The sound of running water led Abramson to the bathroom. There he came upon a shocking sight: Uta's semi-nude body was submerged in the bathtub. A photo album, featuring pictures of Uta's youngest daughter, floated by her feet. Abramson later said, "I grabbed her thinking maybe she just fell down . . . But she was stiff, so I [knew] she had been dead for a while."[2] After lifting Uta out of the bath, Abramson spotted a paring knife that had been lying underneath her body. He also saw blood on the sink and shower.

Police and paramedics soon responded to Abramson's 911 call and Uta was pronounced dead. The medical examiner determined that her death resulted from a combination of an overdose of the powerful tranquilizer Xanax and drowning, although he couldn't say whether her death was a suicide or a homicide. He placed the time of her demise as between 2:30 and 5:00 that morning.

Despite discovering sharp-force injuries on Uta's left wrist and leg, the medical examiner believed they were inconsistent with typical self-inflicted wounds in suicide cases and looked more indicative of defensive injuries. During the autopsy, hematomas on the left side of Uta's neck were noted, posing the possibility of either fall-related blunt-force injury or a blow during an assault.

Owing to these inconclusive findings, an investigation was launched. Abramson spoke with detectives and asserted that, far from being suicidal, she had a positive outlook on life. He also drew attention to the album found in the bathtub with Uta, and said that the possession of it, and others Uta had made, were a "bone of contention in her divorce".

In 2006, Uta and her paediatrician husband, Dr John Brickman Wall, had become involved in a contentious divorce and custody dispute marked by mutual accusations of abuse. Throughout the divorce proceedings, Wall had withheld the albums chronicling their children's lives, prompting legal action from Uta, who eventually regained possession of them. Wall had primary custody of their four children – Pelle, 18, Malkie, 16, Liam, 12, and Ilona, 11 – but about a week before Uta's death, she had filed a motion requesting an evaluation for a change in custody so that she could spend more time with them.[3]

Questioned by detectives, Wall's account of the night Uta died revealed inconsistencies. He initially claimed to have been asleep, but his responses grew increasingly vague or conveniently forgetful when pressed for specifics about his whereabouts. Detectives noticed scratches on his forearms and internal bleeding in one eye, which he attributed to an incident involving his dog. Since Uta's death had not been classified as a murder, and there was no direct evidence against Wall, he was released without charge. He seemed surprised, commenting to detectives, "So I'm not going to jail? But I'm a monster."

In February, Salt Lake City Police Chief Chris Burbank indicated that the case remained open, and said efforts were ongoing to determine whether Uta's death was suicide or homicide. After his interview with detectives, Wall had hired attorney Fred Metos, who commented in the media that he had advised his client to stop speaking to detectives and maintained that he was not involved in Uta's death in any way.

By this juncture, the conviction that Wall was responsible for Uta's death had firmly taken root in the mind of their 18-year-old son, Pelle. He told detectives that his father was absent from home on the morning of the 27th of September, and that when he showed up, he had scratches to his eye and forearms. Pelle said that his father told him the same thing he had told the police: that their dog had accidentally scratched him as he slept on the porch, somewhere Pelle said his father had never slept before. Pelle also informed detectives that his father had made suspicious comments to him and his siblings about his mother's death, including, "What if I did it and I don't remember?" and "I loved Uta – I couldn't have done that to her, right?"

As Pelle's suspicions mounted, he moved out of his father's home and moved in with the family of his best friend, Jessica Oglesby. In April, he filed a petition in Salt Lake City's Third District Court requesting that his three younger siblings be removed from his father's home as well. In the document, Pelle voiced fears for their well-being, and said that they were "suffering physical, emotional, or developmental injury or damage" under his father's care. Pelle painted a disturbing picture, accusing his father of neglecting to provide sufficient food, resulting in his siblings hoarding food in their backpacks. Above all, Pelle's petition expressed a profound fear that they were living with a potential murderer, placing their lives in jeopardy.[4]

Pelle wasn't alone in harbouring suspicions about Wall. Abramson and Uta's sister, Almut von Schwedler, also had reservations. Despite police investigation hitting a standstill, this trio – led by Pelle – urged detectives to press on, prompting the issue of a search warrant for Wall's car. Though the search yielded no immediate red flags, it revealed that the vehicle had recently been cleaned. In May, the Third District Juvenile Court intervened and removed Pelle's siblings from their father's care; however, the two youngest were returned to him the following month.

In the aftermath of Pelle's petition, Wall retaliated by suing his son for possession of the albums put together by Uta, which Pelle had sent to relatives in Germany. Pelle filed a counterclaim using the inheritance money his mother had left him. This asserted that his father had administered a lethal dose of Xanax to his mother before drowning her in the bathtub. The lawsuit sought monetary damages for the four children and also punitive damages and legal fees.

On the 25th of April 2013, John Wall was arrested and charged with first-degree murder; bail was set at $1.5 million. Salt Lake County District Attorney Sam Gill announced that no single piece of evidence had cracked the case; rather, it was the cumulative effect of various factors that had emboldened prosecutors to press charges. These included the discovery of DNA beneath Uta's fingernails that couldn't be conclusively ruled out as Wall's, the revelation that Uta had died partly owing to a non-prescribed Xanax overdose, and Wall's inability to account for his whereabouts on the night of her death.[5]

Pelle's attorney, Margaret Olson, hailed the arrest as long-awaited for those seeking justice for Uta. Pelle remarked on the development, "You add up the different pieces – the death, his behaviour beforehand and afterwards, as well as his general feelings or emotions towards my mother – I think it was a pretty clear analysis of the situation." Pelle's two youngest siblings were once more removed from their father's home to temporarily live with him, with a view to making a permanent arrangement under the care of another relative in the near future.

The preliminary hearing to determine whether there was enough evidence for Wall to stand trial began on the 1st of October. Over the next two days, multiple witnesses testified, and Third District Judge Robin Reese ruled that there was sufficient evidence. Wall's subsequent court appearance on the 21st of October saw him enter a plea of not guilty to murder. His trial was scheduled for February 2015.[6]

Amidst the legal proceedings, Pelle took an active role advocating for legislative change in Utah. He spearheaded efforts to empower juvenile district court judges to temporarily remove children from a parent's home if that parent was a suspect in the other parent's death. Pelle's advocacy bore fruit when, on the 22nd of March 2014, Utah Governor Gary Herbert signed the measure into law. Reflecting on this legislative victory, Pelle commented, "I think it has really tremendous potential to save a lot of lives. I know it would've been an immediate relief for me and my family."[7]

Jury selection began in the Scott M. Matheson Courthouse in Salt Lake City on the 17th of February and after two days a jury comprising six men and six women was selected. As Wall entered the courtroom the next morning, flanked by his defence team, Pelle took a moment to address the gathered media outside: "This trial is something we have long been awaiting. I think we're all a little nervous but also excited about the prospect of closure. No matter what the outcome of the trial, I will never forget who this is really about, I will never forget her playfulness or curiosity, her passion for protecting and enjoying the outdoors and, certainly, her outspoken mind." He then stepped inside and took his place in the front row of the public gallery.

Shortly after 9 a.m., Prosecutor Anna Rossi laid out the prosecution's case. Rossi asserted that Wall had taken Uta's life amid an increasingly acrimonious custody battle, exacerbated by his feelings of depression and resentment. She highlighted the presence of Xanax in Uta's system, informing the jury that she lacked a prescription for the medication, while Wall had obtained a large supply, allegedly for his mother, in the months preceding Uta's death. Addressing the bloodstains on the duvet, Rossi stated, "Uta was not alone when those bloodstains were placed in her bedroom. There is only one person who did this to Uta, who had the means and the motive."[8]

In his opening statements, defence attorney Fred Metos challenged the prosecution's narrative, asserting, "It's clear the death was not a homicide. It was either a suicide or an accident." He said that there was an absence of evidence indicating a forced injection of Xanax, suggesting that Uta might have voluntarily ingested the drug and subsequently moved around the bedroom after self-inflicting injuries. Addressing the jurors directly, Metos claimed, "This is one of the most highly prescribed drugs in this country. People trade it back and forth, give it to friends." Additionally, he introduced another person of interest, Uta's boyfriend, Nils Abramson, insinuating that Abramson sounded "cold" in his 911 call after discovering Uta's lifeless body.

Abramson, the first witness to testify, recounted the events of the 26th of September 2011. He said that Uta was "frustrated" after she tried to talk to Wall about taking the children on a trip to California when he picked them up from her home. Abramson said Wall refused to speak to her, and just drove off with the children.[9] Abramson then took the jury through the moment he found Uta in the bathtub, telling them that he knew that she was dead because she was completely stiff. As he testified, the jury was presented with photographic evidence showing Uta's body and bloodstains in the bathroom, on her clothing, and on the bedding.[10]

The 911 call made by Abramson was played, capturing his somewhat anxious yet composed tone of voice. He informed the operator, "She's drowned. She's dead. I don't know what happened. She's in the bathtub." When asked if he believed she was "beyond help" Abramson affirmed, "Yes, she's dead." Drawing on his past experience as an EMT (Emergency Medical Technician), Abramson assured the operator that he knew "what dead looks like". Abramson shed light on the significance of the album found in the bathtub with Uta. He explained she had meticulously crafted these albums with the family's memories throughout the years, and said that during the divorce, Uta and Wall had fought over who got to keep them.

While the defence insinuated that Abramson's demeanour appeared unusually composed when he found Uta's body, the first firefighter on the scene, Mike Alleman, countered this perception, testifying that Abramson was visibly "shaken". Once Abramson stepped down from the witness stand, the prosecution called on Carolyn Reed, whose son played soccer with one of Uta's son's. She recounted an encounter at a soccer match on the afternoon of the 26th of September 2011, and said Uta seemed to be in a "great mood" and had exhibited no signs of depression.[11]

Uta's boss, Joshua Schiffman, recalled a meeting with Uta the day before her death, discussing a significant breakthrough she had achieved in understanding the genetics of childhood leukaemia. Schiffman stated, "This was a big discovery. This was a big day for our lab that Uta had figured this out."[12] The purpose of his testimony was to show that Uta had big things happening in her life, making it extremely unlikely that she had killed herself.

Uta's sister, Almut von Schwedler, took the stand next day. Almut discussed her sister's "agitated" state of mind post-divorce from Wall and revealed that Uta had briefly experimented with an anti-depressant in 2007 but stopped after a couple of days because she didn't like how it made her feel. Almut said that she had no knowledge of her sister taking Xanax, and that when they cleaned out her house days after her death, they found no bottles or prescriptions for drugs.[13]

The prosecution further countered the defence's insinuation that Uta was suicidal by calling Dr Jennifer Bell, Uta's physician for a decade. Dr Bell attested that throughout their long patient-doctor relationship, Uta had never exhibited severe depression or suicidal tendencies. During Uta's divorce, Dr Bell prescribed a sleeping aid and an anti-depressant, but Uta stopped taking the latter after just four days due to side effects. Prosecutor Matthew Janzen queried: "Did she ever indicate to you that she had been diagnosed for severe depression?" Bell responded that she had not.[14]

Dr Richard Blackman, Uta's physician since 2009, echoed Bell's statements, affirming that Uta had never displayed severe depression or expressed suicidal thoughts during their interactions. Dr Blackman recalled, "There was always something she was looking forward to, travel, or camping. She expressed sadness at times, but I never heard hopelessness." Both physicians stressed that they had never prescribed Xanax to Uta.

Wall looked on intently from the defence table as blood spatter analyst Rod Englert testified about his findings at the crime scene. He displayed Uta's green-and-blue duvet and pointed out the blood spatters on it. He believed that Uta had been attacked, and the crime scene staged to look like a suicide. He meticulously detailed the various blood-spatter patterns on items such as Uta's tank top, the duvet, a sheet, and a rug, reinforcing the narrative of a staged crime scene. "This is consistent with a violent struggle," he concluded.

Regarding the cuts on Uta's wrist and leg, Englert claimed they were indicative of an attempt to shield herself from an assailant wielding a knife.[15] In his extensive experience, such injuries were inconsistent with suicides or accidents. During cross-examination by Metos, who proposed that Uta may have self-inflicted the injuries, Englert conceded that he hadn't precisely reconstructed the attack but maintained that the cuts did not appear self-inflicted. He highlighted the absence of blood on walls or light switches, suggesting Uta hadn't touched any surfaces, as he would expect in cases of suicide or accident.

After Englert's testimony, the prosecution called medical examiner Erik Christensen to discuss Uta's autopsy. He detailed how the initial appearance of suicide shifted when the nature of her wounds, and the Xanax in her system hinted at homicide. He acknowledged the difficulty of forcibly injecting Xanax owing to it not being available in liquid form but couldn't rule this out. While Christensen declared drowning as the cause of death, he refrained from definitively characterizing Uta's death as homicide or suicide.[16] Christensen said that what confused him the most was that no pill fragments were found in Uta's stomach and that he had found no needle marks to indicate she had been injected. He posed a hypothetical question: "She just happened to take this and happened to be killed the same night? That doesn't really make sense."[17]

Forensic pathologist Scott Denton was then called by the prosecution. Denton contended that Xanax could be finely ground, dissolved, and administered via injection. Despite the absence of a clear injection site on Uta's body, Denton highlighted a shallow wrist wound surrounded by a bruise, suggesting it might conceal an injection point. When cross-examined by Metos, Denton admitted that the wrist was an unusual place to inject a drug.

Denton also highlighted an internal injury to Uta's neck, which could have come from somebody restraining her, and a bruise on her lip, which could have been the result of somebody shoving a cup against her mouth to force her to drink. Denton posited his belief that Uta had been injected with Xanax, and also forced to swallow some of the medication. He agreed with Christensen's findings of drowning, but said he believed the manner of death was a homicide.[18]

Following this, Scott Scriven, a police crime lab technician, presented his findings. He had conducted a thorough examination of Uta's residence and found no indications of forced entry. Valuable items such as a laptop, cash, and a mobile phone were undisturbed, leading him to rule out the possibility of a burglary gone wrong.

Melissa Bean, an attorney who had represented Uta in family law matters for an extensive period of time, was the next prosecution witness. Bean's testimony shed light on the protracted disputes between Uta and Wall, spanning years and encompassing contentious matters related to their children, financial concerns, and the coveted albums crafted by Uta. Bean recounted that in the months before Uta's death, she had been seeking a custody re-evaluation. She recollected, "The parties did not get along well."[19]

On the 25th of February, the prosecution explored Wall's potential motive for killing Uta. A key witness was Klaus Fiebig, a longstanding childhood friend of Wall. He described Uta and Wall's relationship as heated and said that fights were increasingly ugly on both sides. Fiebig recalled a conversation he had with Wall several months before Uta died. "At the end he said something peculiar: 'Would it be bad if Uta wasn't here anymore?'" Fiebig added, "She didn't plan to move away." After Uta's death, Fiebig spoke with Wall again. "He was still fixated on explaining to me all the bad things that Uta had done, and that's sort of where this whole thing eroded, in my mind."

Following Fiebig's testimony, Kathy Newman, Wall's former office manager, recounted peculiar events on the day Uta's body was discovered. She noted that Wall arrived at work with a bloodied eyeball and scratches on his face. When questioned about the cause, Wall attributed the injuries to sleeping on the porch, claiming that his dog had become startled and inadvertently stepped on him. Newman remarked, "I remember looking and thinking that just seemed strange to me."

Christina Gardner-Smith, Wall's former medical assistant, disclosed that Wall had expressed a desire for his "ex-wife to disappear" and had even joked about hiring a hitman.[20] As Gardner-Smith concluded her testimony, the prosecution proceeded to call their next witness: Malkie Wall, Uta and Wall's 19-year-old daughter, who had been living with her father at the time of her mother's death. Malkie faced the court in a composed yet resolute manner. She recounted an exchange with her father in the aftermath of Uta's death, where he questioned his own culpability and pondered aloud, as he had earlier to the police, "Am I a monster? I could be a monster."[21]

On the morning of the 27th of September 2011, Malkie recalled waking up at about 6 a.m. to find her father missing from home. She couldn't reach him by text or phone call, and eventually walked to the train station and went to school. (According to the prosecution, that morning, Wall had the interior of his car shampooed and had told car-wash employee, Anthony Izarras, to pay special attention to light pink drip stains behind the driver's seat. When Izarras testified, he said he found this request strange, because the car was otherwise clean.)

Malkie further described how, later that day, detectives summoned her father to the police station for questioning. Returning three hours later, her father broke down, and revealed that the police suspected him of her mother's murder. Wall subsequently had a breakdown and was taken to a mental health facility where he stayed for several days while the children went to live with relatives. According to Wall's legal team, the detectives who interviewed him had been so aggressive that they had made him question his own sanity.

The trial then pivoted back to the presence of Xanax in Uta's body with testimony from Lynn Hooper, an investigator with the Utah Division of Occupational and Professional Licensing. Hooper revealed that Wall had written a prescription for a large amount of

Xanax for his mother in May 2011. Wall personally picked up the prescription at a Murray pharmacy. However, no patient records in Utah were found for Wall's mother, who lived in California.[22]

On the trial's seventh day, the courtroom hushed as film of the original police interrogation between Wall and Detective Mark Hardin was presented. In the grainy footage, Detective Hardin pressed Wall for information on his whereabouts on the crucial night, emphatically stating, "The reason why you don't want to remember is because you killed her. You took her life! Yes, you did!" The detective repeatedly questioned Wall about whether he had killed Uta. Wall claimed he couldn't remember if he had killed Uta or where he was on the night of her death. "I hope I would be self-aware enough to know that that's happening," he said. At one point, Wall attributed his confusion and lack of memory to the antidepressants he was taking.[23]

Wall had undergone several interrogations, and his story changed after male DNA was discovered underneath Uta's finger-nails. While initially claiming the last time he saw Uta was when he picked up the children the night before she was killed, he later claimed that he had found Uta in his garage later that night. Wall alleged that she had broken in and that she had done this before in the past. According to Wall, Uta struck him in the face and then fled the garage. When pressed for more details, Wall suggested Uta may have entered the garage to retrieve an old bag of coffee he believed she had laced with drugs, causing his girlfriend to miscarry twice.

The trial reached a pivotal juncture with the highly anticipated testimony of Pelle, Uta and Wall's eldest son. Pelle, a key figure in the movement to have his father arrested for his mother's murder, asserted that his mother had been in good spirits the night before. However, when his father picked him and his siblings up the next day, "He didn't look at her, he looked straight ahead and rolled up the window and pulled out."[24]

Pelle revealed that a few months later, his father aggressively tried to convince him that his mother's death was suicide, even forcing him to read her autopsy report. The next day, Pelle moved out of his father's house, and initiated legal proceedings to have his siblings removed from his care. According to Pelle, his father had hated his mother for some time, and often berated her in front of him and his siblings. Throughout his testimony, Pelle directly faced the jury, avoiding eye contact with his father.

The prosecution then began presenting the DNA evidence. Analyst Emily Jeskie said that DNA discovered in Uta's bedroom could have come from Wall. The DNA was discovered on the duvet and pillowcase and was a match to one of the family. When Metos cross-examined Jeskie, he argued the DNA could have come from one or more of the couple's four children, and that it could have been transferred in a washing machine. Jeskie also testified that male DNA was found beneath Uta's fingernails, but there wasn't sufficient to say whether it might have belonged to Wall.[25]

When the prosecution rested its case, the defence requested that Judge James Blanch dismiss the charge against Wall. They argued that the DNA evidence was weak and the theory of Wall injecting Uta with Xanax was unreliable. The judge disagreed. The defence promptly called forensic expert Judy Melinek. She suggested that Uta's death looked more like an accident or suicide than a homicide, commenting, "Nobody is going to allow another person to stab them, slice them, all in line."[26] She also questioned the prosecution's timeline, contending that more water-related wrinkling on Uta's hands and feet should have been present if she had been in the bathtub overnight, suggesting Uta died in the afternoon before the discovery, not overnight.

Sgt Justin Hudson, a detective involved in the initial investigation testified that he doubted Uta was defending herself against an assailant, stating, "When I typically see a stabbing, it's because someone wants to kill someone. They're not trying to be nice about it. So, they're stabbing, they're slicing the neck, trying to get the stomach, trying to get whatever they can. And they're pretty deep cuts." Anna Zannin, a bloodstain expert, concurred, expressing her belief that the blood patterns on Uta's duvet did not indicate a clear struggle: "There's some sort of movement, but it's not spread over an enormous area."[27]

The defence enlisted the services of private investigator Richard Montanez, who said that Xanax could be illegally purchased online without a prescription. He further suggested that gift cards, obtainable without revealing personal details, could be used to make such online purchases, but said he had never tried to purchase the drugs to see if they were legitimate since that would be illegal. Prosecutor Matthew Janzen raised concerns about the legitimacy of these websites, questioning whether they could be fraudulent. Additionally, Janzen highlighted that Montanez's investigation occurred years after Uta's death, lacked insight into her online purchasing history, and was purely speculative.[28]

The defence concluded its case, opting not to call Wall. Throughout the trial, a stark contrast emerged between the prosecution and defence's narratives surrounding Uta's death. According to the latter, Uta, driven by depression, had taken her own life by a Xanax overdose and drowning. The prosecution suggested that her death was the result of foul play by her ex-husband amidst a tumultuous divorce and custody battle. The onus now fell on the jury to decide which narrative to believe.

Before the jury embarked on its deliberations, however, both sides presented compelling closing arguments. Prosecutor Nicholas D'Alesandro stated, "It defies logic to think she was having a great day, a great week, a great discovery, she went home and suddenly killed herself." He said that Wall was in an angry downward spiral and had focused his hate on his ex-wife as she sought more time with their four children. "He just couldn't stop talking about how much he hated her." He asserted that Wall's profession as a doctor could have helped him orchestrate the murder and crime scene and contended that overwhelming circumstantial evidence pointed to his guilt.

For the defence, attorney Fred Metos highlighted the atypical combination of elements involved in the alleged murder – knife, drugs, and drowning. He argued that suicides more commonly encompass such elements whereas murders do not. Metos underscored the case's circumstantial nature, reminding the jury that neighbours didn't hear any sounds of a struggle, and the inconclusive DNA findings at the crime scene. He also posited that Uta's wounds would have been more severe if she had faced a knife-wielding assailant.[29]

After a day of deliberation, the jury found John Wall guilty of the murder of Uta von Schwedler. Gasps, both of surprise and relief, filled the courtroom, prompting Wall to lower his head in disbelief. Outside the court, Pelle addressed reporters, expressing gratitude to the Salt Lake City police for their thorough investigation and stating, "We have spent the last three-and-a-half years seeking justice. Justice has prevailed. Now it is time to heal."[30]

On the 8th of July, John Wall was sentenced to 15-to-life in prison. A rueful smile showed on Pelle's face as he exchanged handshakes and hugs with family and friends, marking the end of a prolonged legal battle for justice for his mother. During the sentencing, Pelle had urged Judge James Blanch to ensure his father faced a lifetime behind bars.

Outside the court, Pelle didn't mince his words. Alluding to his father he commented, "He's convinced himself of an alternate reality. It's super disrespectful to true victims." He recalled his mother as an esteemed researcher, driven, self-confident, and remarkably colourful. Despite their enduring grief, he and his siblings would continue to draw life lessons from the wonderful woman they dearly missed.[31]

---

[1] *The Salt Lake Tribune*, 15 February 2012 – "Salt Lake Police Still Investigating Woman's 'Suspicious' Death"

[2] FOX – 13 KSTU, 3 May 2012 – "Boyfriend Believes U of U Researcher's Death a Homicide"

[3] State v. Wall

[4] Associated Press, 2 May 2012 – "Son Says He Fears Father After Mom Dies in Utah"

[5] Associated Press, 25 April 2013 – "Salt Lake City Doctor Charged with Killing Ex-Wife"

[6] Associated Press, 3 October 2013 – "SLC Paediatrician Ordered to Stand Trial on Murder"

[7] Associated Press, 22 March 2014 – "Utah Law Aims to Protect Kids After Parent's Death"

[8] Associated Press, 18 February 2015 – "Opening Statements Given in Utah Doctor's Murder Trial"

[9] The Salt Lake Tribune, 18 February 2015 – "Prosecutor to Utah Jury: John Wall 'Absolutely' Murdered Ex-Wife"

[10] FOX – 13 KSTU, 18 February 2015 – "Couple's Son Spoke Out Against Father in Doctor's Murder Trial"

[11] *The Deseret News*, 19 February 2015 – "Murder or Suicide? Trial Begins for Doctor"

[12] Associated Press, 20 February 2015 – "Expert at Doctor's Trial: Blood Spatter Indicates Struggle"

[13] FOX – 13 KSTU, 19 February 2015 – "Blood Spatter Expert, Deceased's Sister Testify on Day Two of John Wall Murder Trial"

[14] FOX – 13 KSTU, 24 February 2015 – "John Wall's Ex-Wife Showed no Signs of Depression"

[15] Associated Press, 19 February 2015 – "Expert at Doctor's Trial: Blood Spatter Indicates Struggle"

[16] Associated Press, 23 February 2015 – "Examiner: Autopsy Found Ex-Wife of Utah Doctor Had Wounds"

[17] Associated Press, 23 February 2015 – "Examiner: Autopsy Found Doctor's Ex-Wife Had Fatal Drug Dose"

[18] *The Salt Lake Tribune*, 23 February 2015 – "Utah Medical Examiner Says Xanax in Alleged Murder Victim's System is 'Confounding'"

[19] *The Salt Lake Tribune*, 24 February 2015 – "Utah Woman's Doctors Testify She Was not Suicidal Prior to Death"

[20] FOX – 13 KSTU, 25 February 2015 – "Friend of John Wall, His Former Employees Testify in Murder Trial"

[21] Associated Press, 26 February 2015 – "Daughter: Doctor Accused of Murder Asked if He Was Monster"

[22] *The Salt Lake Tribune*, 26 February 2015 – "Utah Murder Trial: Daughter Testifies"

[23] FOX – 13 KSTU, 2 March 2015 – "Interrogation Tapes Heard on Day 7 of John Wall Trial"

[24] FOX – 13 KSTU, 4 March 2015 – "Son of John Wall Testifies in Murder Trial, Describes Mother's Mood on Night Before her Death"

[25] Associated Press, 4 March 2015 – "Analyst Says Doctor Could Have Left DNA in Ex-Wife's Room"

[26] Associated Press, 9 March 2015 – "Defense Expert: Utah Doctor's Ex-Wife Likely Wasn't Murdered"

[27] FOX – 13 KSTU, 9 March 2015 – "Not Enough Evidence to Prove Ex-Wife's Death was a Homicide"

[28] *The Salt Lake Tribune*, 5 March 2015 – "Prosecution Rests Its Case Against Utah Man Accused of Killing His Ex-Wife"

[29] Associated Press, 12 March 2015 – "Deliberations Begin in Utah Doctor's Murder Trial"

[30] FOX – 13 KSTU, 12 March 2015 – "Jury Finds John Wall Guilty of Murdering His Ex-Wife"

[31] Associated Press, 8 July 2015 – "Utah Doctor Sentenced to 15 Years to Life in Ex-Wife's Death"

A Tragic Mistake or Homicide?

Oscar Pistorius was celebrated as the "Blade Runner" for his remarkable achievements in overcoming double amputation to secure Paralympic gold. His inspirational story won the admiration of millions all over the world. However, esteem turned to horrified shock at the news that he had shot his girlfriend, Reeva Steenkamp. At first it was assumed her death had to be a terrible accident. But as his trial unfolded, it became apparent that the shooting could have been a deliberate act of murder . . .

———————

"I can only convey to the court what I heard that evening.
I cannot comprehend how I could distinctly hear a woman scream,
but Mr Pistorius could not."

Michelle Burger

———————

Around 3 a.m. on Valentine's Day 2013, Michelle Burger was awoken by screams coming from a home in the gated community of Silver Woods Country Estate, Pretoria, South Africa. "It was very traumatic. You could hear it was bloodcurdling screams," she recalled. Moments later, she heard what sounded like gunshots.[1] Burger was sure they had come from her neighbour Oscar Pistorius's house, so she had her husband, Charl Johnson, call the complex's security guard, Pieter Baba, and ask him to check.

Baba contacted Pistorius, who assured him, "Security, everything is fine." However, in a subsequent call, Pistorius seemed distressed and unable to communicate clearly. Arriving at Pistorius's home, Baba was shocked to see the world-famous athlete descending the stairs, cradling Reeva Steenkamp in his arms, her hair matted with blood. Reluctant to enter, Baba was directed by Pistorius to call the police and an ambulance while he attempted mouth-to-mouth resuscitation.[2]

One of the first responders, Detective Hilton Botha, encountered a chaotic scene. Reeva had suffered three gunshot wounds and lay at the foot of the staircase. Neighbour Dr Johan Stipp was attempting a jaw-lift manoeuvre to open her airways. Detective Botha recounted, "And then she stopped breathing." Reeva had sustained bullet wounds to her head, hip, and elbow, with the bullet on the right side of her head fracturing her skull and penetrating her brain.

Pistorius explained to detectives that during the early morning hours, he had woken up and gone outside onto the bedroom balcony to fetch a fan. On that particular night, Reeva was staying over. As he closed the sliding doors and curtains, he heard a noise coming from the bathroom. The bathroom lacked bars across the windows, leading Pistorius to believe that an intruder had entered through the window. Pistorius told detectives that he had received death threats in the past and experienced break-ins at his residence, adding that he habitually slept with a pistol beneath his bed.

Reacting to the perceived threat, Pistorius stated that he grabbed his gun and approached the bathroom on his stumps, as there was no time to put on his prosthetics. He recounted, "On my way to the bathroom, I screamed words to the effect for him/them to get out of my house and for Reeva to phone the police. It was pitch dark in the bedroom, and I thought Reeva was in bed." Entering the bathroom, he noticed an open window. (An open window is visible in crime scene photographs, but it is not known how it came to be open or who opened it.) The door to the adjoining small toilet cubicle was shut.

Pistorius described raising his gun and firing shots at the toilet door while urging Reeva to call the police but received no answer. Only then did he realize that Reeva might be inside the cubicle. Panicked, he hurried back to the bed, finding it empty. Pistorius tried to open the locked toilet door, ultimately resorting to breaking it down with his cricket bat.[3]

It seemed a tragically familiar scenario in a country grappling with one of the highest rates of homicides and violent crime, where many people kept firearms at home for protection. However, the police began to grow sceptical of Pistorius's account when they interviewed neighbours who reported hearing screams before the shooting. An unnamed neighbour mentioned "talking that sounded like non-stop fighting from two to three in the morning".[4] Detectives also found aspects of the crime scene puzzling, questioning why an intruder would lock themselves in the toilet cubicle and why Pistorius didn't check whether Reeva was okay before indiscriminately firing shots through the door.

Pistorius was arrested at his home and buried his face in the hood of his jacket as he was escorted to Pretoria's Boschkop police station. Later that day, Courtroom C in the Pretoria Magistrate's Court brimmed with reporters, photographers, and videographers, witnessing Pistorius being formally charged with Reeva Steenkamp's murder. As the charge was announced, Pistorius broke down in loud sobs, prompting Chief Magistrate Demond Nair to console him. His father, Henke, and brother, Carl, voiced their sympathy from the public gallery."[5]

Pistorius's arrest sent shockwaves through a nation that had hailed him a hero, triumphing over adversity to excel in elite sports. Born without fibula bones due to a congenital defect, Pistorius had undergone leg amputation before he was one year old. He had made history as the first double amputee to compete in the London 2012 Olympics, participating in the 400 metres and 4 x 400-metres relay. Overcoming legal hurdles with the International Association of Athletics Federations regarding his prosthetic blades, Pistorius earned the right to compete in traditional competitions.[6]

Despite facing a grave charge, Pistorius garnered widespread support from fans who believed his assertion that he had mistaken Reeva for an intruder. The entire Pistorius family stood firmly behind him, expressing their commitment to doing "whatever needs to be done" to help clear his name.[7]

On the 19th of February, Pistorius returned to court where the murder charge was upgraded to a category six: premeditated murder. Prosecutor Gerrie Nel shared speculation that during an argument, Reeva had locked herself in the toilet, following which Pistorius armed himself, put on his prosthetic legs and intentionally killed her. Barry Roux, a prominent Senior Counsel and Pistorius's lead defence attorney, contested the prosecution's theory, stating, "We submit it's not even a murder. There's no concession that it's murder."[8] The elevated charges posed challenges for Pistorius in securing bail, given the stringent requirements for those facing a category six offense in South Africa.[9]

The bail hearing commenced the following day, featuring Detective Botha's testimony, which proved to be somewhat perplexing. He miscalculated the distances from which Reeva was shot and admitted that the forensics team had left behind one of the fired bullets that was later found in the toilet. Detective Botha mentioned a neighbour who claimed to have heard an argument between 2 a.m. and 3 a.m. on the night of Reeva's death but conceded, under cross-examination, that this neighbour lived 600 metres away. Later, he mentioned the discovery of syringes and steroids in Pistorius's home, only to be corrected by Prosecutor Nel, who clarified that the substances were actually testosterone.[10]

After Detective Botha's testimony, it came to light that he was facing seven counts of attempted murder for a 2011 incident in which he and other officers had fired at a commuter minibus while investigating the murder of Denise Stratford. Incorrectly believing the minibus was involved, Detective Botha and the officers allegedly did not see the passengers at the time and were not initially charged. However, prosecutors later decided to file charges. Allegedly unbeknownst to Prosecutor Nel and police authorities, once this information became public, South African Police Commissioner Riah Phiyega removed Detective Botha from the investigation. Detective Vinesh Moonoo, who had spent the past 27 years working his way up the ranks to become head of the detective service, replaced him.[11]

Pistorius was granted bail on the 22nd of February. Chief Magistrate Nair set bail at 1 million rand, almost unprecedented in a South African court, but Pistorius paid it in two instalments.

Despite granting bail, Nair expressed scepticism about Pistorius's claim that he mistook Reeva for an intruder, questioning, "Why would he venture further into danger?"[12] Shortly after his release, Hilton Botha resigned from the police force while Pistorius appealed his bail conditions, specifically the restriction on travelling outside South Africa. Judge Bert Bam approved the appeal, granting him permission to leave the country if he wished to participate in international events.[13]

In August, he returned to court to be formally charged with premeditated murder by a grand jury, a charge that carried a mandatory sentence of life imprisonment with a minimum of 25 years if convicted. He was additionally charged with reckless endangerment, the firing of a gun in a built-up area or a public place, and of negligent damage to property relating to two separate incidents. In September 2010, he fired a gun from the open sunroof of a car while travelling near Modderfontein. He had also discharged his Glock 27 in a restaurant on Melrose Arch, Johannesburg, in January 2013. According to the indictment, "the shot narrowly missed his friends and hit the floor of the restaurant."[14]

Pistorius's murder trial was set for the 3rd of March 2014. According to South Africa's legal system, Pistorius's culpability or innocence would be determined by a single individual: Thokozile Matilda Masipa, an esteemed High Court Judge. Breaking barriers in 1988, she had become the second Black woman to attain a position on the bench during the apartheid era. Before pursuing law at the University of South Africa, Judge Masipa had a background in social work and journalism.[15] She appointed two assessors, Janette Henzen du Toit and Themba Mazibuko, to assist her. MultiChoice, South Africa's top cable provider, announced a "pop-up" channel that would provide "round-the-clock" coverage of the "blockbuster" trial.

Pistorius looked nervous as he entered the North Gauteng High Court dressed in a black suit and tie. Inside the packed, wood-panelled courtroom, Reeva's family was already seated in the public gallery, anxiously awaiting the opening day. As proceedings got underway, three discreet cameras, mounted in the two front corners and the back of the courtroom, broadcast live around much of the world. Pistorius took his place in the dock, as his defence attorney, Kenny Oldwage, read aloud from a statement Pistorius had written. He referred to Reeva's death as a "tragic accident" and admitted to killing her but denied murderous intent. "This allegation is denied in the strongest terms. We were in a loving relationship," he said. The prosecution, on the other hand, said they would prove premeditated murder, and show that Pistorius killed Reeva following an argument.

The prosecution began by setting the scene of the shooting with their first witness, Michelle Burger. From her home some 177 metres from Pistorius's home, she said she heard what sounded like a man and woman arguing, followed by a woman screaming. "She screamed terrible and yelled for help."[16] Following the screams, Burger claimed to have heard four shots, one distinct and the others closely grouped. Subsequently, a woman screamed, and a man's voice shouted for help. Burger's account directly contradicted Pistorius's narrative. He had told detectives that he believed Reeva was asleep and hadn't mentioned hearing any screams.

During cross-examination, defence attorney Barry Roux raised discrepancies in Burger's testimony, pointing out that her husband had informed detectives he had heard five or six shots.[17] When Roux enquired whether she considered Pistorius untruthful, Burger responded, "I can only convey to the court what I heard that evening. I cannot comprehend how I could distinctly hear a woman scream, but Mr Pistorius could not." Roux proposed an alternative scenario to Burger, suggesting that she had heard Pistorius screaming, not a woman, and that the sounds she interpreted as gunshots were, in fact, Pistorius breaking down the door with a cricket bat. Despite Roux's suggestions, Burger remained steadfast in her assertion that she had heard a woman screaming and gunshots. When Burger's husband, Charl Johnson, testified, he corroborated what his wife had heard, although he still maintained he had heard five or six shots.

Roux continued in his attempts to undermine their testimony, specifically addressing their assertion of hearing a woman screaming after the gunshots. He asserted that Reeva could not have screamed owing to her lack of cognitive function caused by brain damage. The next witness, Estelle van der Merwe, who lived approximately 100 metres from Pistorius's house, testified that she was awakened at 1:56 a.m. that morning by a couple arguing. Later, she claimed to have heard four noises, potentially gunshots, leaving her paralyzed with fear.[18] During cross-examination, Roux cited a series of "scream" tests conducted in the neighbourhood, arguing that it was impossible for her to have heard an argument from her home.

The prosecution sought to raise questions about Pistorius's character by calling his friend, Kevin Lerena, to testify about a previous incident in January 2013. Lerena said that they were at a Johannesburg restaurant when another friend, Darren Fresco, passed his gun to Pistorius under the table. Within moments, a shot went off, piercing the floor. Lerena recalled Pistorius apologizing and asking if everyone was okay. Before restaurant management approached the table, Pistorius requested that Fresco take responsibility, stating, "There's too much media hype around me." The truth about the shooting only became public knowledge after Reeva's tragic death.[19]

Samantha Taylor, a former girlfriend of Pistorius, next took the stand. She recounted Pistorius carrying a gun with him "all the time" during their relationship. Taylor described an incident in September 2012 when Pistorius fired a gun out of a car's sunroof after they were stopped by a police officer for speeding. Another episode involved being followed by an unidentified car, prompting Pistorius to jump out of their vehicle with his gun, holding it to the driver's window before speeding away. Taylor, at one point during her testimony, broke down in tears as she revealed that Pistorius had cheated on her with Reeva.[20]

She refuted the defence's suggestion that the screams neighbours heard could have been Pistorius, stating that she had heard him scream "a few times" when angry, and he always sounded like a man. Taylor also mentioned an occasion when Pistorius woke her up and retrieved his gun, fearing an intruder. Prosecutor Nel interjected, pointing out, "But he woke you up."

Testimony then shifted to the night of the shooting, with Dr Johan Stipp, a neighbour and radiologist, recalling waking up to three loud bangs resembling gunshots. He heard what sounded like a woman screaming three or four times, followed by a man calling for help. Afterwards, he heard three more bangs that resembled shots. Dr Stipp described walking to Pistorius's house and seeing Reeva on the floor at the bottom of the stairs, with Pistorius crouched beside her attempting to open her mouth with his fingers. When Pistorius became aware of Dr Stipp's presence, he confessed, "I shot her. I thought she was a burglar." Despite Dr Stipp's efforts to save Reeva, she had no pulse. He recalled Pistorius expressing extreme distress, pledging to dedicate his life to her and God if she survived. As Dr Stipp spoke, Pistorius covered his ears and rocked back and forth.

Security guard Pieter Baba was already present at the scene when Dr Stipp arrived. In his testimony, Baba recounted Pistorius assuring him that everything was "fine" when he called him at 3:21 a.m., just four minutes after the sound of gunshots. Shortly after this initial call, Pistorius called back, now in tears, before the line went silent. Baba and another security guard arrived at Pistorius's home, followed by Johan Stander, a manager of the housing estate. The police and an ambulance were then called. Cross-examining, Roux suggested that Pistorius may have actually stated, "I'm fine," during the phone call, but Baba insisted that Pistorius had said, "Security, everything is fine." Roux also proposed that Pistorius initiated the first call to Baba, but Baba insisted it was the other way around.

Professor Gert Saayman followed Baba to the stand, where he elaborated on his findings from Reeva's autopsy. He revealed that Reeva had been struck by Black Talon bullets designed to expand on impact, inflicting severe damage. The fatal head shot from Pistorius's 9mm pistol likely resulted in instant death, causing severe brain damage and multiple fractures to her skull. Prof. Saayman's testimony painted a dark picture of Reeva's last moments inside the locked toilet cubicle. As the pathologist recounted these details, Pistorius was visibly affected; he hunched over, retched, and vomited into a nearby bucket. Additionally, Prof. Saayman noted that, based on the contents in Reeva's stomach, she had likely consumed a meal no more than two hours before her death – a detail conflicting with Pistorius's previous assertion that they were both in bed by 10 p.m.[21]

Police Colonel Gerhard Vermeulen showed the court the bullet-riddled toilet door and the cricket bat that Pistorius had used to break it down. In a demonstration, he illustrated how the bat was used to strike the door and subsequently utilized to wedge a gap between a panel and the inner frame. Vermeulen pointed out, based on height measurements, that Pistorius was not wearing his prosthetic legs during the bat-striking incident, contradicting Pistorius's provided account. According to Pistorius, after realizing that Reeva was in the toilet, he had put on his prosthetic legs and attempted to kick down the door before resorting to the cricket bat.[22]

Vermeulen faced rigorous cross-examination by Roux, who asserted that the crime scene had been compromised. Roux maintained that the toilet door had not been handled with due care, and pointed out that footprints resembling police boots were visible in photos of the door but had since been erased. Roux also insisted

Pistorius was wearing his prosthetic legs when he hit the door, as he had claimed, and said the bat marks were lower because he swung with a "bent back".

Colonel Giliam van Rensburg presented stark photographs of Pistorius's blood-spattered home. The images showed a pistol on a grey towel next to an iPhone in the bathroom. Nel drew attention to a dented silver panel in the bathroom and a hole in the bedroom door, suggesting a more extensive confrontation. In the course of the photo presentation, a distressing image of Reeva briefly emerged, prompting gasps in the courtroom and causing Pistorius to vomit once again. Another photograph revealed Pistorius standing shirtless in his garage with bloodstained prosthetic legs. Roux argued that this suggested he had worn them while breaking down the locked door to the toilet.[23]

Sean Rens, manager of the International Firearm Training Academy in Walkersville town opened the third week of testimony. Rens informed the judge that Pistorius had "a great love and enthusiasm" for guns. In a conversation months before Reeva's death, Pistorius allegedly shared with Rens an incident where he drew his gun and went into "combat mode" after mistaking the noise of the tumble dryer for an intruder. Rens also noted that Pistorius's firearms competency test indicated awareness that firing at an unseen target was illegal.

Once he stepped down, more photographs were presented by Warrant Officer Bennie van Staden, who had extensively documented the crime scene. Roux questioned him about differences in the photographs of the 9mm pistol and the bat, highlighting their displacement between the images. Van Staden acknowledged, "It seems like that." The aim of the cross-examination was to suggest mishandling of the scene, with crucial evidence possibly being moved.[24] Testimony then shifted to the trajectory of the bullets fired at Reeva, with Captain Christiaan Mangena using metal rods and a laser beam to show the trajectory. He concluded that the bullets were fired in a slightly downward trajectory, and that Pistorius was standing more than 2 metres away.[25]

Mangena's analysis indicated that Reeva was positioned in the toilet cubicle, facing the closed door when she was struck in the right hip by the first of four hollow-point bullets fired by Pistorius. Subsequently, she fell back, receiving shots to the right arm and head as she crossed her arms over her head in a defensive gesture. Mangena noted that a fourth bullet, likely the second one fired, had missed Reeva and ricocheted off a wall inside the cubicle. He expressed his opinion that Pistorius was likely not wearing his prosthetic legs when he discharged the shots, aligning with the defence's stance. Mangena's assertion that there was enough time between the first and final shots for Reeva to scream presented a challenge to Pistorius's version of events.

To further challenge Pistorius's account, the prosecution introduced text messages exchanged between him and Reeva. Just three weeks before her tragic death, Reeva had stated: "I'm scared of you sometimes and how you snap at me. You have picked on me incessantly. You do everything to throw tantrums." These messages revealed a pattern of criticism from Pistorius, illustrated by another one of Reeva's texts: "I get snapped at and told my accent and my voice are annoying. Stop chewing gum. Do this, don't do that." As the messages were presented, Pistorius shook and sobbed.[26]

The defence countered this evidence with a selection of other text messages, emphasizing that these messages represented only a small fraction of the approximately 1,700 extracted. Roux highlighted that numerous messages between Reeva and Pistorius were affectionate. Roux also presented CCTV footage of Reeva and Pistorius kissing at a convenience store on the 4th of February 2013. Nel rebuffed this by asserting that the couple's moments of affection were brief compared to their frequent arguments.

The prosecution concluded its case on the 25th of March, and the defence commenced theirs on the 7th of April, following a brief break owing to one of the court assessors falling ill. Roux's first witness was former pathologist Jan Botha. His testimony aimed to cast doubt on the earlier testimony of Professor Gert Saayman, who claimed that Reeva had eaten approximately two hours before her death. Botha argued that determining the time of death through gastric emptying is speculative and referred to it as a "highly controversial and inexact science."[27]

After stepping down, Pistorius took the witness stand, visibly upset, and began his testimony by apologizing to Reeva's family. His jaw trembled as he said, "I was trying to protect Reeva. I want people to know that she was loved when she went to bed that night." Pistorius revealed he had terrible nightmares and sometimes woke up smelling blood since the killing. He informed the courtroom that, since the shooting, he had been taking sleeping pills and antidepressants. He recalled a night when fear overwhelmed him, leading him to crawl into a cupboard.

Pistorius then recounted his upbringing, describing a childhood with an often-absent father and a mother with security fears who frequently called the police at night. He also spoke about the vulnerability he felt without his prosthetic legs, stating, "I don't have balance on my stumps." Pistorius stressed that, despite occasional troubles in their relationship, he and Reeva always resolved them, and said they loved one another and planned for a life together.

He then recalled the night of the incident, describing how he heard a noise from inside the toilet. "Before I knew it, I'd fired four shots at the door," he admitted. Pistorius detailed repeatedly shouting for Reeva to call the police before realizing she was inside the toilet cubicle. "I don't think I've ever screamed like that [before]." He remembered putting on his prosthetics to try kicking down the door before grabbing his cricket bat. He sobbed while recalling, "I sat over Reeva. She wasn't breathing."[28] At one point, Pistorius removed his prosthetic legs to demonstrate how he stood by the toilet door when firing, admitting he had made a "mistake" by shooting Reeva.

Pistorius faced intense cross-examination from Nel, who demanded, "You made a mistake? You killed a person, that's what you did! You shot and killed her. Won't you take responsibility for that?" Nel presented a photograph displaying Reeva's head turned to the side, her blonde hair matted in blood, and a mass of tissue on the back and upper parts of her skull. Pistorius turned away, refusing to look at the photograph and telling the prosecutor, "I don't have to look at a picture. I was there."

Nel proceeded to play a video of Pistorius firing a gun at a watermelon at a shooting range, commenting, "You know the same happened to Reeva's head. It exploded."[29] Nel then questioned the nature of Pistorius and Reeva's relationship, pointing out that the words "I love you" never appeared in any of their text conversations. Pistorius pushed back, telling the prosecutor, "I never got the opportunity to tell Reeva I loved her." He broke down in tears while reading aloud the Valentine's Day card Reeva had written for him: "I think today's a good day to tell you that I love you."

According to Nel, the only "reasonable explanation" for Reeva standing behind the cubicle door and facing it was because she and Pistorius were arguing through the door. He pointed out that Reeva's jeans were on the floor while the rest of her clothes were packed neatly in her overnight bag, suggesting she was planning to leave. Pistorius vehemently denied this. Nel also questioned why Pistorius had not privately apologized to Reeva's family, instead opting to do so in public in court. Pistorius explained that he had wanted to apologize earlier but was informed that the family wasn't ready. In the public gallery, Reeva's mother, June, sat stone-faced and stared directly at Pistorius. Nel then raised the question of why, when Pistorius moved down the corridor leading to the bathroom allegedly screaming for Reeva to call the police, she didn't make a sound. Pistorius responded, "I don't know."[30]

The next defence witness was forensics expert Roger Dixon, formerly of the University of Pretoria. He contradicted various pieces of prosecution evidence, and said that in his opinion Reeva was shot in the hip and arm when her arm was extended out, possibly in the process of opening the door. Dixon additionally testified that he took part in audio tests for the defence that showed sounds of gunshots and a cricket bat hitting a door were similar and could be confused. It was the defence's theory that Pistorius's neighbours had heard sounds of him hitting the door with the bat, not the gunshots, and that the screams were uttered by Pistorius, not Reeva. When cross-examined by Nel, Dixon was forced to admit that he had no expertise in light and sound measurement, ballistics, or blood-spatter evidence. In addition, he had not attended Reeva Steenkamp's postmortem. Dixon inadvertently described himself as a "layman" and Nel accused him of "irresponsibility" for making inferences in areas in which he was not an expert.

After Dixon's testimony, the trial recessed until the 5th of May to prevent scheduling conflicts with other cases.

When proceedings resumed, the defence presented two witnesses to bolster their narrative that Pistorius was emotionally distressed after shooting Reeva. Johan Stander and his daughter, Carice Viljoen, arrived at Pistorius's home shortly after the incident, both attesting that Pistorius was in anguish, praying, and attempting to aid Reeva's breathing. Viljoen recounted Pistorius repeatedly urging Reeva, exclaiming, "Stay with me, my love, stay with me." Stander expressed his belief that the shooting was accidental. "I saw the truth there that morning, I saw it, and I feel it."[31]

Contrary to earlier neighbours' testimonies, Pistorius's nextdoor neighbour, Michael Nhlengethwa, claimed he was awakened by a loud bang on the night of Reeva's death, followed by a man's high-pitched screams. His wife, Eontle, and another neighbour, Ricca

Motshwane, also asserted they did not hear a woman screaming that night but instead heard a man screaming. Nel suggested that the Nhlengethwas might have slept through the argument, the woman's screams, and the gunshots, only to wake up to Pistorius breaking down the toilet door with a cricket bat and calling for help.

The subsequent witness was Yvette van Schalkwyk, a social worker and probation officer. She recounted visiting Pistorius in a police cell the day after the shooting. "I saw a heartbroken man. He cried 80 percent of the time. He talked to me about what they planned for the future, his future with her." She clarified that her decision to testify was prompted by her dismay at suggestions that Pistorius might be feigning grief to influence the judge in his favour.

Following her testimony, the defence called Thomas Wolmarans, a seasoned ballistic expert. Wolmarans, with decades of experience, testified that he discovered a bullet fragment in Pistorius's toilet bowl and handed it to the police, who had overlooked it during their initial crime scene investigation. Although he concurred with most of Captain Christiaan Mangena's earlier testimony regarding the bullets' trajectory, he argued that Reeva wasn't standing facing the door; instead, he posited that the splinters around the bullet wound to her right arm suggested she was reaching forward, as if attempting to open the door.[32]

Psychiatrist Dr Merryll Vorster told the court that she believed that Pistorius had an anxiety disorder that might have played a role in the fatal shooting. Describing him as a mistrustful and guarded person with many features of anxiety, she suggested that this, combined with his disability, could have led him to react differently from other people when he fired four shots through the locked door. Her testimony prompted the prosecution to request Pistorius undergo a month-long evaluation at a psychiatric hospital, a request approved by Judge Thokozile Masipa, leading to a temporary halt in the trial.

Returning to court on the 29th of June, Pistorius was deemed sane. The psychiatric assessment concluded that he did not suffer from a mental illness or defect that would have influenced his actions on the night Reeva was killed. The defence then called engineer Ivan Lin as its next witness, who proposed that the neighbours testifying for the prosecution lived too far away to have heard anything that night, especially an argument. Pistorius's agent, Pet van Zyl, followed as a character witness, stating that Pistorius was preoccupied with fears for his personal security. Van Zyl added that less than a week before Reeva's death, Pistorius had been planning an overseas trip with her. Sports physician Wayne Derman testified afterwards, asserting that Pistorius acted on a "fight or flight" impulse when confronting what he believed was an intruder, as his disability prevented him from fleeing.

Closing arguments commenced with Gerrie Nel outlining the prosecution's case that Pistorius had intentionally killed Reeva. Referring to Pistorius as a "deceitful witness", Nel argued that even if Judge Masipa accepted Pistorius didn't know that Reeva was behind the door, he should still be convicted because he shot with the intention to kill whoever was there. In his closing arguments, defence attorney Barry Roux questioned the police handling of the case and maintained that Pistorius's disability made him vulnerable and anxious about crime.

The verdict was delivered on the 11th of September, with Judge Thokozile Matilda Masipa finding Pistorius not guilty of murder but guilty of the lesser charge of culpable homicide, akin to manslaughter. The judge concluded that the prosecution had not proven beyond a reasonable doubt that the killing of Reeva was premeditated.

The following month saw Pistorius sentenced to a maximum of five years, part of which could be served under correctional supervision. On the 21st of August 2015, the prison case management committee recommended Pistorius be released under correctional supervision, having served a sixth of his sentence. He was ultimately released on the 19th of October.

The legal saga continued as the case underwent an appeal process. In December 2015, the South African Supreme Court of Appeal overturned the original verdict, replacing it with a conviction of murder. Subsequently, in July 2016, Pistorius received a sentence of six years in prison. However, the state deemed this insufficient and appealed for a longer sentence. In the following year, the sentence was increased to 13 years and five months. Finally, on the 5th of January 2024, after serving nine years, Oscar Pistorius was released on parole.

---

[1] *The Guardian*, 3 March 2014 – "Oscar Pistorius's Neighbour: 'I Knew Something Terrible Was Happening'"

[2] ABC News, 7 March 2014 – "Oscar Pistorius Trial: Security Guard Says Athlete Told Him 'Everything is Fine'"

[3] *The Guardian*, 19 February 2013 – "Oscar Pistorius Defence Statement"

[4] Agence France-Presse, 20 February2013 – "Pistorius 'Fought Non-Stop' With Girlfriend on Night of Killing"

[5] Associated Press, 15 February 2013 – "Weeping Pistorius Faces Premeditated Murder Charge"

[6] AllAfrica, 14 February 2013 – "Oscar Pistorius Shock News"

[7] *The Daily Telegraph*, 17 February 2013 – "Oscar Pistorius Murder Charge"

[8] Agence France-Presse, 19 February 2013 – "Pistorius Says 'No Intention' to Kill Girlfriend"

[9] *San Francisco Examiner*, 19 February 2013 – "'She Died in my Arms': Oscar Pistorius' Bail Hearing Affidavit"

[10] Associated Press, 20 February 2013 – "Police Offer Confused Testimony in Pistorius Case"

[11] *The American News*, 21 February 2013 – "South Africa Replaces Lead Detective in Pistorius Inquiry"

[12] Associated Press, 22 February 2013 – "Oscar Pistorius Gets Bail as Murder Trial Looms"

[13] *The Times*, 29 March 2013 – "Pistorius Can Travel Abroad to Compete, Judge Rules"

[14] S v. Pistorius

[15] *The Daily Telegraph*, 19 January 2014 – "Judge Announced Ahead of March Murder Trial"

[16] Agence France-Presse, 3 March 2014 – "Pistorius Pleads Not Guilty as Witness Describes 'Terrible Screams'"

[17] Agence France-Presse, 3 March 2014 – "Pistorius Pleads Not Guilty as Witness Tells of 'Bloodcurdling Screams'"

[18] *The Times*, 5 March 2014 – "Second Witness in Pistorius Trial Tells of Row Before Shots"

[19] *St. Paul Pioneer Press*, 4 March 2014 – "Boxer Recounts Gunshot at Restaurant"

[20] Associated Press, 7 March 2014 – "Pistorius: Former Girlfriend Testifies on Gunplay"

[21] Associated Press, 10 March, 2014 – "Pistorius Vomits During Graphic Testimony"

[22] Agence France-Presse, 12 March 2014 – "Pistorius Court Shown Damaged Bat, Door from Death Scene"

[23] *Evening Standard*, 13 March 2014 – "Picture of Reeva Steenkamp's Dead Body Mistakenly Shown to Court"

[24] Associated Press, 18 March, 2014 – "Defense Alleges Police Error"

[25] *The Daily Telegraph*, 18 March 2014 – "Oscar Pistorius Trial Hears Athlete Fired Gun from a Distance"

[26] *The Atlanta Journal-Constitution* 24 March, 2014 – "Text Messages Show Jealous, Critical Pistorius"

[27] Agence France-Presse, 7 April 2014 – "Pistorius Defence Calls Expert as First Witness"

[28] Agence France-Presse, 8 April 2014 – "Overwrought Pistorius Describes Shooting Girlfriend"

[29] Associated Press, 9 April 2014 – "Pistorius Refuses to Look at Photo of Dead Lover"

[30] *The Paper for Today*, 12 April 2014 – "Prosecutor Asks Pistorius: 'Why Didn't Reeva Scream?'"

[31] Associated Press, 5 May 2014 – "Pistorius Neighbour Says Shooting Accidental"

[32] *The Daily Telegraph*, 9 May 2014 – "Expert Witness Tells Oscar Pistorius Trial: 'We Will Never Know What Happened Behind That Door'"

Caught on Camera

On the 25th of May 2020, Minneapolis police officer Derek Chauvin was caught on video kneeling on the neck of George Floyd, a Black man, for over nine minutes during an arrest. Despite Floyd's repeated pleas that he couldn't breathe, Chauvin refused to take his knee off his neck. Floyd's death sparked worldwide protests and discussions about systemic racism and police brutality. Chauvin's trial served as a litmus test for the US justice system's ability to hold law enforcement accountable for excessive use of force, particularly against people of colour.

———————————

"Today starts a landmark trial that will be a referendum on how far America has come in its quest for equality and justice for all."

Civil Rights Lawyer Ben Crump

———————————

Minnesota had recently transitioned from its stay-at-home order during the COVID-19 pandemic to the "stay safe Minnesota" order. On the evening of the 25th of May 2020, just before 8 p.m., 46-year-old George Floyd entered the Cup Foods grocery store at the intersection of 28th Street and Chicago Avenue in South Minneapolis.

George Floyd's life had been marked by turbulence, including eight jail terms between 1997 and 2005 for various offences, such as drug possession, theft, and trespass. In 2007, he faced charges of aggravated robbery with a deadly weapon. This incident involved Floyd and five men entering an apartment, where he held a pistol to a woman's stomach during a robbery. Subsequently, he was arrested in 2009 and sentenced to five years in prison, being paroled in 2013 as he approached 40 years of age.

This significant event served as a catalyst for Floyd's transformation. On his release, his friend Travis Cains remarked: "He came home with his head on right." Embracing change, Floyd became actively involved in Resurrection Houston, a Christian church and ministry. Here, he dedicated himself to mentoring young boys, aiming to break a perceived cycle of violence. In a video, Floyd passionately implored, "I've got my shortcomings and my flaws. But, man, the shootings that's going on, I don't care what 'hood' you're from. Put them guns down."[1]

In 2014, Floyd made a pivotal decision to leave Houston for Minnesota to rebuild his life and provide for his five children. He obtained a security job at a Salvation Army shelter and later trained to become a truck driver while working as a club bouncer. Unfortunately, the pandemic forced the closure of his workplace.

On that fateful day in May 2020, Christopher Martin was serving customers in the Cup Foods grocery store when Floyd paid for cigarettes with a $20 bill. Martin believed the note was counterfeit and when Floyd refused to return to the store, he informed the store manager who asked another employee to call the police. (Whether the note was in fact counterfeit is unclear.) Four officers responded: Derek Chauvin, Tou Thao, J. Alexander Keung, and Thomas Lane. They found Floyd sitting in a SUV outside the store with a man and a woman, forcibly removed him from the vehicle and handcuffed him.

Nearby, a woman named Darnella Frazier began recording the incident on her phone. Floyd was hurled to the ground as Chauvin knelt on his neck. Over the next nine minutes, Floyd repeatedly uttered distressing phrases such as: "I can't breathe"; "My stomach hurts"; and "My neck hurts"; while also calling out for his "Mama". Onlookers pleaded with Chauvin to release the pressure on Floyd's neck and put him in the police car. Only when Floyd's body became limp did Chauvin finally lift his knee from his neck. Floyd was transported on a stretcher to the Hennepin County Medical Center emergency room. He was declared dead at 9:25 p.m.

The shocking video capturing George Floyd's death went viral after Darnella posted it on her Facebook page. The video ignited widespread protests, initially in Minneapolis, then extending to other states; eventually it created a global outcry. Floyd's death swiftly became a powerful symbol, representing broader issues of racial injustice, inequality, and police misconduct that disproportionately impacted Black communities. Streets filled with people rallying against police brutality. George Floyd's haunting last words, "I can't breathe", became a powerful slogan demanding justice and the arrest of the four police officers involved.

It rapidly emerged in the media that during his 19-year career in the police, Chauvin had opened fire on two suspects, and had almost twenty complaints and two letters of reprimand filed against him.[2] Over several nights, protestors congregated around Chauvin's home, marking the road with messages such as "A murderer lives here". In the city, some protests escalated into violence, with some participants looting stores and setting fires, resulting in night-time curfews running from 8 p.m. until 6 a.m. A call to defund and abolish the police gained momentum, resonating with the global clamour for change. Memorial services for George Floyd were held worldwide, underscoring the widespread impact of his tragic death on the collective consciousness.[3]

The FBI along with Minnesota state authorities launched an investigation and the four officers involved were fired from the department. Minneapolis Mayor Jacob Frey called for them to be arrested, asking in a press conference, "Why is the man who killed George Floyd not in jail?"[4]

On the 1st of June, the Hennepin County Medical Examiner's office announced that George had "experienced cardiopulmonary arrest while being restrained by law-enforcement officer(s)" and listed his cause of death as "cardiopulmonary arrest complicating law enforcement subdual, restraint and neck compression". They also noted that Floyd tested positive for coronavirus, suffered from heart disease and hypertension, and listed fentanyl intoxication and recent methamphetamine use, but did not list these under cause of death and recorded his death as a homicide.

Chauvin was arrested and charged with second-degree murder, third-degree murder, and second-degree manslaughter. Hennepin County Attorney Mike Freeman announced, "This is by far the fastest we've ever charged a police officer."[5] Notably, this marked the first instance in Minnesota's history where a white police officer faced arrest and charges for the murder of a Black citizen. Chauvin's bail was set at $1.25 million, with Minnesota Attorney General Keith Ellison assuming control of the case after Minnesota Governor Tim Walz expressed a lack of confidence in the Hennepin County prosecutor. The other three officers involved were also arrested and charged with aiding and abetting second-degree murder. Each of them faced a bail amount of $1 million.

On the 29th of June, Judge Peter Cahill scheduled the trial date for the four defendants for the 8th of March 2021. Prosecutors, as indicated in court documents, expressed their intention to pursue severe sentences for the four if found guilty. The document stated: "George Floyd, the victim, was particularly vulnerable because officers had already handcuffed him behind his back and then placed him chest down on the pavement, and Mr Floyd clearly and repeatedly told the officers he could not breathe."[6]

In July, George Floyd's family initiated a lawsuit against the city of Minneapolis and the four police officers. The lawsuit alleged that the officers violated Floyd's rights and asserted that the city allowed a culture of excessive force, racism, and impunity to persist within its police force. The family sought compensatory and special damages, the specific amount to be determined by a jury.[7]

Over the next couple of months, Chauvin and the other three defendants were released from jail after posting their bonds. In the new year, Judge Cahill announced that Chauvin's trial would be separate from the other three defendants, citing limited courtroom space due to COVID-19 restrictions.[8] By now, The City of Minneapolis had reached a settlement with the Floyd family for $27 million, the largest pre-trial settlement in a civil rights wrongful death case in US history.

Jury selection commenced in early March, with the case presided over by the widely respected Judge Cahill, known for his no-nonsense and impartial approach. The courtroom featured experienced attorneys on both sides, with Attorney General Keith

Ellison leading the prosecution – Minnesota's first African American attorney general – and Eric Nelson, known for representing numerous police officers throughout his career, heading the defence. Due to pandemic restrictions on attendance, it was decided that the entire trial would be televised.[9] This decision to broadcast the trial at a time when so many people all over the world were forced to stay at home with little to do but watch TV and stare at computer screens, fuelled the deep intensity of reaction generated by this case – as compared to others with similar facts and circumstances. While jury selection continued, hundreds of protestors outside the Hennepin County Government Center chanted, "No justice, no peace!" Speakers passionately appealed to the jurors to "do the right thing", while others displayed banners with the plea, "Justice for George Floyd."[10]

By the 23rd of March, a jury comprising six white women, three Black men, three white men, two mixed-race women, and one Black woman was selected. Opening statements were scheduled to commence on the 29th. Outside the heavily guarded courtroom, Ben Crump, a civil rights lawyer and attorney for the Floyd family, declared, "Today starts a landmark trial that will be a referendum on how far America has come in its quest for equality and justice for all." Crump and the Floyd family then took the knee for the same amount of time that Chauvin had knelt on Floyd's neck.[11]

Prosecutor Jerry Blackwell was the first to address the court, asserting that Chauvin had disregarded police procedures and persisted in pressing Floyd's motionless body to the ground until paramedics intervened, stating, "Nine minutes and 20 seconds is how long that went on." He then showed the video depicting Chauvin pressing his knee on Floyd's neck until he lost consciousness. The courtroom fell eerily silent as Floyd's moans and gasps echoed around it, with bystanders imploring the officer to get off. Floyd reiterated twenty-seven times that he couldn't breathe.

The prosecutor emphasized to the jury that the trial was not an indictment of all police officers but specifically focused on Chauvin. "There are any number of things that this case is not about, maybe an infinite number of things the case isn't about. But one of those things that this case is not about: all police, all policing. Police officers have difficult jobs. They sometimes have to make split-second life-and-death decisions."[12] However, he also asserted that this case wasn't about split-second decision-making.

In response, defence attorney Eric Nelson stated, "Derek Chauvin did exactly what he had been trained to do over his 19-year career." Nelson urged the jurors to set aside political and social considerations surrounding Floyd's death and maintained that he had been resisting arrest as the crowd around the officers grew larger and more hostile. Nelson contested that Chauvin was to blame, highlighting the absence of clear signs of asphyxiation and pointing out the presence of fentanyl and methamphetamine in Floyd's system. He suggested that Floyd's drug use, coupled with his heart disease and blood pressure issues ultimately led to his death from a heart rhythm disturbance.

The atmosphere in court was tense as the first witness, 911 dispatcher Jena Scurry, approached the stand. Scurry recounted witnessing Floyd's arrest unfold through a video feed from city security cameras. She described the struggles of the three officers who attempted to place Floyd into a squad car before he was forced to the ground. Scurry admitted that initially she thought the video had frozen, shocked by the prolonged duration of Officer Chauvin's knee on Floyd's neck. "My instincts were telling me something [was] wrong, something [was] not right. I don't know, but something was not right. It was an extended period of time." Scurry said she became so concerned that she took the unusual step of calling a police sergeant and telling them what was happening.[13]

The second witness, Alisha Oyler, employed at a Speedway gas station across from Cup Foods, testified that she began recording on her cell phone when she observed police "messing with someone".

Subsequently, Darnella Frazier emotionally recounted her experience, detailing the viral video she had captured. Frazier admitted sorrowfully, "It's been nights I stayed up apologizing to George Floyd for not doing more and not physically interacting and not saving his life." She described George as "terrified" and "begging for his life", recounting how the bystanders grew increasingly upset and vocal as Floyd became increasingly unresponsive.

Genevieve Hansen, an off-duty Minneapolis firefighter and emergency medical technician, provided another perspective. She testified that she identified herself to the officers and told them Floyd needed medical attention. Despite her attempts to intervene, the officers, including Chauvin, refused to allow her close, with Chauvin even placing his hand on his Mace spray. Another witness, Kaylynn Gilbert, confirmed that Chauvin placed his hand on his Mace spray. She characterized him as "kind of scary". She heard Floyd crying out for his mother, but whenever anyone approached, Chauvin would menacingly grab his Mace spray and shake it, discouraging them from coming any closer. Gilbert described Floyd as appearing purple and limp but said that Chauvin persisted in keeping his knee on Floyd's neck until paramedics arrived and ordered him to get off.

Bystander Donald Wynn Williams vividly described Chauvin performing a "shimmy" manoeuvre while kneeling on Floyd's neck. "His eyes slowly rolled to the back of his head. You see the blood coming out of his nose. You heard him tell them before he stopped speaking, 'My stomach hurts.'"[14] After witnessing what he believed to be a murder, Williams immediately called 911. Parts of his call were played aloud for the jury. Williams could be heard saying, "He [Chauvin] just went and killed this guy. Murderers, bro . . . they just killed a man in front of the store."

The prosecution then introduced another video, this time recorded by the bodycams of the four police officers. The footage included the moment George Floyd was arrested at gunpoint after using a $20 bill to pay for cigarettes. Officer Thomas Lane confronted George in his SUV, drawing his gun and demanding, with a few expletives, that he show his hands. Floyd was visibly distressed as he pleaded with the officer, saying, "I'm sorry, I'm sorry. I got shot before. Please don't shoot me, man." As Floyd was handcuffed and escorted to the squad car, his distress grew, with him telling the officers, "I'm claustrophobic, man. Why are you doing me like this? Don't do me like this, man." At one point, an officer remarked, "I think he's passed out", and questioned whether they should "roll him onto his side", but Chauvin did not remove his knee from Floyd's neck.

Following the video presentation, Christopher Martin, the cashier at Cup Foods who accepted the $20 dollar bill, took the stand. He commented, "I thought George didn't really know that it was a fake bill. I thought I'd be doing him a favour." Initially planning to cover the amount from his own paycheck, he ultimately informed the store manager and the police were called. Martin noted that Floyd seemed to be under the influence but remained "very friendly, approachable, talkative". When asked by Prosecutor Matthew Frank about his emotions upon witnessing Floyd pinned to the ground shortly afterwards, Martin became visibly upset, confessing to feeling "disbelief and guilt".[15]

Paramedic Derek Smith testified that upon their arrival at the scene, Floyd was already deceased, with Chauvin maintaining pressure on his neck. Smith detailed how he loaded George into the ambulance, and he, along with another paramedic, Seth Bravinder, attempted to revive him using chest compressions and a defibrillator. Smith said, "He's a human being, and I was trying to give him a second chance at life." Subsequently, David Pleoger, a retired police sergeant and Chauvin's shift supervisor on the day of the incident, took the stand. Pleoger stated that when George ceased "offering up any resistance", Chauvin had the opportunity to take his knee off his neck.

The testimony then touched on Floyd's history of drug use, with his girlfriend of three years, Courtney Ross, becoming emotional as she recounted their meeting in 2017. At that time, Floyd was working as a security guard at a homeless shelter where Ross went to visit the father of one of her children. Observing her apparent sadness in the lobby, Floyd approached her and asked if he could pray with her. Ross tearfully acknowledged that she and Floyd struggled with opioid addiction, stating, "We both suffered from chronic pain. Mine was my neck, and his was his back. We got addicted and tried really hard to break that addiction, many times." She further revealed that Floyd had achieved sobriety in 2020, but in the weeks leading up to his death, he had started using pills again.[16]

After Ross concluded her testimony, Ben Crump, the Floyd family's attorney, issued a statement condemning what he deemed "defence attempts to construct the narrative that George Floyd's cause of death was the fentanyl in his system". The prosecution had used Ross's testimony under the "spark of life" doctrine, a rarity outside of Minnesota. Established in 1985, this doctrine allows prosecutors to present evidence demonstrating that a murder victim is not merely physical remains but a person with the spark of life.[17]

The next witness for the prosecution was Lieutenant Richard Zimmerman, the longest-serving officer in the Minneapolis Police Department. Zimmerman informed the court that he had thoroughly reviewed all footage relating to the incident. When questioned by Prosecutor Frank about his opinion on Chauvin's use of force, Zimmerman unequivocally responded, "Totally unnecessary." He said he was unable to comprehend why the four officers felt they were in danger and said that such a perception would be necessary to justify the level of force used. Zimmerman clarified that he had not been trained to kneel on the neck of a handcuffed individual and posed the question, "Once a person is cuffed, the level of threat goes down, all the way. They're cuffed. How can they really hurt you?"[18]

Dr Bradford Langenfeld, a senior resident at Hennepin County Medical Center, testified that upon Floyd's arrival at the hospital, his heart had already stopped. When questioned by Blackwell, he stated that, based on the available information, death by asphyxiation was "more likely than the other possibilities". Under Nelson's questioning, Dr Langenfeld acknowledged that certain drugs, including fentanyl and methamphetamine, can cause hypoxia. He also said that any amount of time a patient spends in cardiac arrest without immediate CPR diminishes their chances of survival.

His testimony was followed by that of Minneapolis Police Chief Medaria Arradondo, who said that according to official police training Chauvin should never have put his knee on George's neck. He stated, "Once Mr Floyd had stopped resisting, and certainly once he was in distress and trying to verbalize that, that should have stopped." Minneapolis Police Inspector Katie Blackwell, responsible for overseeing the department's training, provided further insight. She explained that, per their policy, a neck restraint involves the compression of one or both sides of the neck using an arm or leg. Regarding Chauvin's use of the knee, she remarked, "I don't know what kind of improvised position that is. That's not what we train." Blackwell clarified that a neck restraint should only be employed when a suspect is "actively resisting" arrest, and officers are trained to use "light to moderate" pressure unless their lives are in imminent danger.

During the video of the incident, one of the officers, Thomas Lane, could be heard asking whether Floyd was experiencing "excited delirium". In the trial's second week, Nelson questioned Nicole McKenzie, a Minneapolis police officer who instructed fellow officers in medical care, about the concept of excited delirium and whether officers were trained to recognize and respond to it. McKenzie characterized excited delirium as a combination of "psychomotor agitation, psychosis, hypothermia", and various other behaviours or symptoms that might appear bizarre. While there was no universally accepted definition, some coroners in recent decades have attributed in-custody deaths to excited delirium.[19]

Respiratory doctor Martin Tobin stated that George Floyd died "from a low level of oxygen". Tobin described how Floyd's breathing was compromised as he was "squeezed" face down on the street, handcuffed, with Chauvin and other police officers applying pressure to his neck and back. Tobin highlighted the moment Floyd's death was captured on video, telling the jury, "You can see his eyes, he's conscious, and then you see that he isn't. One second, he's alive and one second, he is no longer. That's the moment the life goes out of his body." Dismissing claims that pre-existing medical conditions or drugs contributed to Floyd's death, Tobin explained, "A healthy person subjected to what Mr Floyd was subjected to would have died."[20]

Dr Martin Tobin's conclusions were supported by Dr Andrew Baker, the chief medical examiner who conducted George's autopsy. Dr Baker attributed Floyd's heart failure to "subdual, restraint, and neck compression" but noted the presence of severe underlying heart disease and an enlarged heart that required more oxygen than normal to function. While ruling out the defence's assertion that George's death resulted from an underlying cardiac issue or a drug overdose, Dr Baker, during cross-examination, acknowledged that these factors "played a role" in his death. Cardiology expert Dr Jonathan Rich testified that Floyd "actually had an exceptionally strong heart".

On the 13th of April, after 11 days of testimony and a wealth of video evidence depicting George Floyd's final moments, the prosecution rested their case. The defence's first witness, retired Minneapolis police officer Scott Creighton, recounted an encounter with George on May 6, 2019, when Floyd was a passenger in a car.

Creighton stated that Floyd had refused to comply with orders to show his hands when he drew his gun, but the defence's attempt to suggest that Floyd had swallowed drugs was refuted by Creighton, who claimed he did not witness any such action.

During the trial, retired paramedic Michelle Moseng, who responded to the 2019 incident, testified that Floyd informed her he had been taking multiple opioids approximately every twenty minutes. She offered to take him to the hospital due to his high blood pressure, measured at 216 over 160, but Floyd resisted. However, during cross-examination by Prosecutor Erin Eldridge, Moseng admitted that Floyd's respiratory output, pulse, heart rate, EKG, and heart rhythms were normal. He was released from the hospital after two hours.

The third witness, Shawanda Hill, who was in the SUV with Floyd moments before his death, told the jury that Floyd had fallen asleep and seemed startled when he realized police were there. She described how an officer appeared at the window with a gun, prompting Floyd to grab the wheel and plead, "Please, please, don't kill me. Please don't shoot me. What did I do, just tell me what I did?"[21]

Barry Brodd, a former Santa Rosa police officer, took the stand and contradicted several authorities from the Minneapolis Police Department by asserting that Chauvin was justified. Brodd claimed Chauvin didn't use deadly force and likened the situation to one where officers use a Taser on someone engaged in a struggle, leading to the suspect falling, hitting their head, and dying, which he categorized as an "accidental death" rather than an incident of deadly force. Prosecutor Steve Schleicher used his cross-examination to revisit video footage of George Floyd pinned down, gasping, and repeating that he couldn't breathe. Schleicher argued that a reasonable officer in Chauvin's position would have known that Floyd had stopped resisting, was unconscious, and subsequently not breathing.[22]

Retired Maryland forensic pathologist Dr David Fowler contradicted several medical experts presented by the prosecution. He asserted that Floyd died from cardiac arrest induced by heart disease, illegal drug use, and other factors. Dr Fowler also suggested that potential carbon monoxide poisoning from auto exhaust might have been a contributing factor, noting the proximity of Floyd's face to the exhaust pipe of the patrol car, the motor of which was running. The defence subsequently sought Chauvin's acquittal, arguing that the prosecution had failed to prove his actions caused Floyd's death. However, Judge Cahill rejected the request.

After presenting only two days of testimony, the defence concluded its case. Chauvin chose not to testify, invoking his constitutional right against self-incrimination. Prior to closing arguments, the Floyd family attorney expressed their hope for Chauvin to be held criminally responsible, stating, "Killing unarmed Black people is unacceptable. We have to send that message to the police. Hold police officers accountable."[23]

In his closing arguments on the 19th of April, Prosecutor Steve Schleicher passionately conveyed to the jury how George Floyd, with his "very last breath", pleaded for help but received no compassion from Chauvin. He said that Floyd posed no threat and wasn't attempting to harm anyone. Schleicher contended that Chauvin deviated from training, disregarded the department's use of force rules, and neglected to perform CPR. Urging the jury to use their common sense, he implored them to convict Chauvin, stating, "What you saw, you saw. You can believe your eyes. It's exactly what you knew, it's exactly what you felt in your gut, it's what you now know in your heart."

Defence attorney Eric Nelson countered by asserting that Chauvin acted as any reasonable police officer would in a "dynamic" and "fluid" situation involving a large man struggling with four officers. The conclusion of the case prompted some Minneapolis stores to board up doors and windows fearing that the verdict, regardless of its nature, could lead to violence. The city was already tense owing to the fatal shooting of 20-year-old Daunte Wright, a Black man, by Kimberly Potter, a white police officer on the 11th of April.

The jury deliberated for ten hours before delivering the verdict to a live audience of 22.8 million viewers. They found Derek Chauvin guilty on all three charges: second-degree murder, third-degree murder, and second-degree manslaughter. The historic verdict marked the first time a white Minnesota police officer was convicted of the murder of a Black individual. Chauvin was promptly handcuffed and taken into custody to await sentencing. Described as one of the most high-profile and high-stakes court results in decades, the guilty verdict brought a sense of relief. In the aftermath, US President Joe Biden personally called the Floyd family, observing, "Nothing is going to make it all better, but at least, God, now there's some justice. We're all so relieved – not just the one verdict but all three, guilty on all three accounts."[24]

The sentencing hearing commenced on the 25th of June, featuring poignant victim impact statements from George Floyd's family, reflecting on their profound loss and enduring trauma. They appealed to the judge for the longest possible sentence – 40 years. However, Minnesota sentencing guidelines suggested a 12-and-a-half-year sentence since Chauvin was a first-time offender. Breaking his courtroom silence, Chauvin offered condolences to the family, while defence attorney Nelson remarked that Chauvin's mind was filled with "what-ifs" from that day. Judge Cahill ultimately sentenced Derek Chauvin to 22-and-a-half years in prison, telling him, "This is based on your abuse of a position of trust and authority and also the particular cruelty shown to George Floyd."

Civil rights lawyer Ben Crump described Chauvin's sentence as an "historic" step towards racial reconciliation in the United States.

Chauvin subsequently appealed, claiming a denial of a fair trial, but this was rejected. The three other officers involved in Floyd's death were convicted of violating his civil rights: Keung received a three-year prison sentence, Thao was sentenced to 42 months, and Lane was sentenced to two-and-a-half years.

On the 24th of November 2023, Chauvin survived an attack in the FCI Tucson prison by a fellow inmate named John Turscak during which Chauvin was stabbed 22 times. Turscak was charged with attempted murder, assault with intent to commit murder, assault with a dangerous weapon, and assault resulting in serious bodily injury.

------

[1] *La Crosse Tribune*, 11 June 2020 – "A Complicated Life: George Floyd, Athlete, Rapper, Family Man, Convict, Mentor"

[2] The Associated Press News Service, 29 May 2020 – "Officer Accused in Floyd's Death Opened Fire on 2 People"

[3] *The Independent*, 28 May 2020 – "Graffiti Scrawled Outside Home of White Police Officer Who Knelt on Neck of George Floyd"

[4] *The Independent*, 28 May 2020 – "George Floyd Pleaded for Young People to End Gun Violence and 'Come on Home' in Resurfaced Video"

[5] ABC – 11 WHAS, 29 May 2020 – "Derek Chauvin Charged with 3rd Degree Murder, Manslaughter in Death of George Floyd"

[6] State of Minnesota vs Derek Michael Chauvin, J. Alexander Keung, Thomas Kiernan Lane, Tou Thao

[7] The Associated Press News Service, 15 July 2020 – "Floyd Family Sues Minneapolis Officers Charged in his Death"

[8] The Associated Press News Service, 12 January 2021 – "Officer With Knee to George Floyd's Neck to be Tried Alone"

[9] The Associated Press News Service, 7 March 2021 – "Key Players in Trial of Ex-Officer Charged in Floyd's Death"

[10] AP News, 9 March 2021 – "Fiery Chants for Justice from Marchers at Chauvin Trial"

[11] Agence France-Presse, 29 March 2021 – "Opening Statements Beginning in George Floyd Murder Trial"

[12] Minnesota v. Derek Chauvin

[13] *The Independent*, 29 March 2021 – "911 Dispatcher Saus Instincts Told Her 'Something is Wrong'"

[14] *The Independent*, 29 March 2021 – "George Floyd News"

[15] Agence France-Presse, 31 March 2021 – "Graphic Bodycam Footage Played at Floyd Murder Trial"

[16] Agence France-Presse, 1 April 2021 – "Paramedic Says Floyd was 'Deceased' When He Arrived"

[17] The Associated Press News Service, 1 April 2021 – "How Floyd's 'Spark of Life' Played Out in Trial"

[18] Agence France-Presse, 2 April 2021 – "Chauvin Use of Force on Floyd 'Totally Unnecessary'"

[19] *The Independent*, 7 April 2021 – "What is Excited Delirium?"

[20] Agence France-Presse, 8 April 2021 – "George Floyd Died from Low Level of Oxygen"

[21] The Associated Press News Service, 13 April 2021 – "Defence Begins Case Against Ex-Cop in George Floyd's Death"

[22] The Associated Press News Service, 13 April 2021 – "Expert Says Cop Was Justified in Pinning Down George Floyd"

[23] Agence France-Presse, 19 April 2021 – "George Floyd Sought Help with his 'Very Last Breath'"

[24] Agence France-Presse, 20 April 2021 – "'Justice': America Reacts to Floyd Murderer's Conviction"

Picture Credits

The publisher would like to thank the following for their kind permission to reproduce their photographs:

(Key: a–above; b–below/bottom; c–centre; f–far; l–left; r–right; t–top)

Insert 1 Alamy Stock Photo: Associated Press / Charles Krupa (c); IanDagnall Computing (tl); The Picture Art Collection (bl). **Getty Images:** Bettmann (br); Bob Thomas / Popperfoto (tr). **Insert 2 Alamy Stock Photo:** ARCHIVIO GBB (tl); Sheridan Libraries / Levy / Gado (tc); Everett Collection (tr). **Getty Images:** Bettmann (b). **Insert 3 Getty Images:** Hulton Archive / General Photographic Agency / Stringer (tl); Bentley Archive / Popperfoto (bl); Hulton Archive / Topical Press Agency / Stringer (bc). **TopFoto:** (cr). **Insert 4 Alamy Stock Photo:** Chronicle (cr); Trinity Mirror / Mirrorpix (tl, bl). **Insert 5 Alamy Stock Photo:** Associated Press / Ron Barker (tl). **Getty Images:** Bettmann (b); Premium Archive / Gary Gilmore / Lawrence Schiller / Polaris Communications (cr). **Insert 6 Alamy Stock Photo:** Associated Press (clb); World History Archive (t, br). **Insert 7 Getty Images:** Robert Pearce / Fairfax Media (tl); Alan Gilbert Purcell / Fairfax Media (tr); Russell McPhedran / Fairfax Media (cra); The Asahi Shimbun (clb, br). **Insert 8 Alamy Stock Photo:** Abaca Press (tl); Evan Hurd (tr); © Branimir Kvartuc / ZUMAPRESS.com (bl). **Getty Images:** The Chronicle Collection / Robin Platzer (br). **Insert 9 Alamy Stock Photo:** AP Photo / Paul Sakuma (br); Associated Press / Ben Margot (t); Associated Press / Anonymous (bl). **Insert**